보카
VOCA BIBLE
바이블

보카 바이블

초판 2014년 1월 24일 1쇄 발행

지은이 조영재
발행인 조상현
발행처 (주)위아북스
주소 서울시 마포구 공덕동 풍림빌딩 304호
문의 02-725-9988 **팩스** 02-725-9863
등록번호 제300-2007-164호
홈페이지 www.wearebooks.co.kr

보카

VOCA BIBLE

바이블

조영재 지음

We're
위아북스

필자가 1995년부터 SAT, 토플, 텝스, 수능 외국어 등 영어 시험 과목을 지필도하면서 수많은 학생과 학부모님들에게 받는 질문이 "영어 실력을 향상하고 시험 점수도 올릴 수 있는 가장 좋은 방법이 무엇입니까?"이다. 그 답은 아주 간단하다. "단어를 많이 알수록 영어 실력은 향상하고 시험 점수도 오른다."는 것이다. 너무나 기본적이고 당연한 대답이지만, 실제로 공부를 제대로 해본 분들이라면 이 말에 공감할 것이다.

좀 더 부연하자면, 모든 수험생들이 갈망하는 비법이나 왕도는 특별히 없다. 하지만 오랫동안 다양한 학생들을 지도하면서 깨달은 것은 영어 공부에도 '빈익빈 부익부'가 존재한다는 것이다. 무슨 말이냐 하면 언어 감각이 발달되어 영어가 쉽게 느껴지는 학생이나 암기력이 뛰어난 학생은 영어 단어가 쉽게 많이 외워진다. 그래서 노력에 비해 성과가 크기 때문에 좀 더 재미를 느끼고, 더 열심히 영어 공부를 하게 된다. 반대의 경우에는 나름대로 노력해도 힘만 들고 결실이 없어 영어에 흥미를 잃게 되고, 그래서 점점 더 영어 공부가 하기 싫어지게 되는 악순환이 되는 것이다.

VOCA BIBLE

노력 대비 성과가 없어서 영어를 힘들어하는 수험생에게 한 가지 조언을 해주고 싶다. 무작정 시험 문제만 많이 풀지 말고, 어휘력을 향상하도록 노력해라. 좀 더 중요한 것은 무작정 단어를 많이 외우는 것이 아니라, '수능에 필요한 핵심 어휘'를 반복해서 공부하는 것이다. 어떤 어휘가 수능에 필요하고 어떤 어휘가 불필요한지 일일이 열거할 수도 없고, 그런 취지에 딱 맞는 책을 찾기도 쉽지 않다. 그러한 이유로 필자는 수험생들에게 꼭 필요한 어휘만 선별하여 〈보카 바이블〉을 준비하였다.

20년 가까이 오직 각종 영어 시험 과목만 전문적으로 지도한 풍부한 경험을 통해 집필한 이 책이 영어가 두렵고 버거운 수험생들에게 큰 도움이 될 것임을 자신하며, 포기하지 말고 최선을 다하길 바란다.

이 책의 구성과 특징

1st Step

Phrases with Clue

Words with Clue

타깃 어휘의 뜻을 유추할 수 있는, 동의어, 유의어, 반의어, 기타 clue가 되는 단어들이 포함된 문장을 통해 타깃 어휘의 뜻을 파악한다. clue가 있는 문장을 통해 타깃 어휘의 뜻을 유추한 후, 어휘의 정확한 의미를 여기서 확인한다. 그리고 추가적인 동의어도 같이 외워 두면 좋다.

VOCA BIBLE

2nd Step

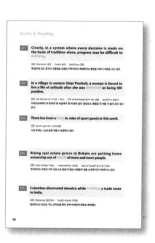

Words in Reading

타깃 어휘가 사용된 실제 수능 문장
이나 수능 수준의 문장이 제시된다.
앞에서 clue를 통해 배운 의미를 실
제 문장의 해석에 직접 활용해 본다.

3rd Step

Review Quiz

다양한 형식의 문제 풀이를 하여 앞
서 배운 어휘들을 다시 한 번 확인하
는 과정을 통해, 학습한 어휘들이 오
래 기억되도록 한다.

CONTENTS

Part I • Key Phrases for Listening, Speaking and Writing 001-200

Part II • Key Words for Reading 001-400

Voca Bible

Part I
Key Phrases for Listening, Speaking and Writing
001-200

001

A **How did you like the movie?**
그 영화 어땠니?

B **I didn't like *some parts*. But on the whole, it was OK.**
일부분은 마음에 안 들었지만 대체로 괜찮았어.

on the whole 전체적으로, 대체로

002

A **Do you have a job?**
직장이 있니?

B **I have *a part-time job*. I work on and off as a cashier.**
아르바이트를 하고 있어. 때때로 계산원으로 일해.

on and off 때때로, 불규칙적으로

003

A **I think David did that on purpose.**
David이 고의로 그렇게 했다고 생각해.

B **No, I'm sure he didn't *mean to do* it.**
아냐, 일부러 그렇게 한 게 아니라는 것은 내가 장담해.

on purpose 고의로, 일부러

004

A **I want you to make the decision on the spot.**
이 자리에서 결정해 주시기 바랍니다.

B **You mean *right now*?**
지금 당장이요?

on the spot 현장에서, 즉석에서

005

A **Did you like the story?**
그 이야기 재미있었니?

B ***Its plot was OK*, but on the other hand it was too long.**
줄거리는 괜찮았지만 반면에 너무 길었어.

on the other hand 다른 한편으로는, 반면에

006

A Henry *tried everything* he could to pass the test.
Henry는 시험에 합격하려고 할 수 있는 건 모두 해봤어.

B Yeah, he really wanted to pass it at any cost.
맞아, 정말 꼭 합격하고 싶어 했지.

at any cost　　어떻게 해서든, 꼭

007

A How did you like the picnic?
소풍 어땠니?

B It *started to rain* at the end, but at any rate I had fun.
마지막에 비가 오기 시작했지만 어쨌든 재미있었어.

at any rate　　어쨌든, 하여튼

008

A Did the teacher *spend a lot of time* on Chapter 2?
선생님이 2장에 시간을 많이 할애했니?

B Of course, he discussed it at length.
물론, 그 장을 자세히 다루셨어.

at length　　상세히

009

A If only mom changes her mind.
엄마가 마음을 바꾸시기만 한다면 좋겠는데.

B I *hope* so, too. But that will never happen.
나도 그러길 바라지만 그런 일은 절대 없을 거야.

if only　　~하기만 한다면

010

A It might rain in the afternoon.
오후에 비가 올지도 몰라.

B I'm going to the beach, *no matter what*, even if it rains.
나는 무슨 일이 있든 설사 비가 오더라도 해변에 갈 거야.

even if[though]　　비록 ~일지라도

A. Choose the right answer.

1 **A** Do you go to the gym regularly? 체육관에 정기적으로 다니세요?
   B No, I go there _____. 아뇨, 때때로 갑니다.
   (A) on purpose   (B) even if   (C) at length   (D) on and off

2 **A** Tom is very smart. Tom은 무척 똑똑해요.
   B _____, he is lazy. 반면에 게을러요.
   (A) On the spot   (B) If only   (C) On the other hand   (D) At any rate

3 **A** I can't believe Greg bought the car _____.
      Greg가 즉석에서 차를 샀다니 믿을 수가 없어.
   B He said he didn't have to think about it. 그것에 대해 생각할 필요가 없다고 말하던데.
   (A) at any rate   (B) at any cost   (C) on the spot   (D) on and off

4 **A** It was a very difficult test. 아주 어려운 시험이었어.
   B _____, we passed it. 어쨌든 우리는 합격했어.
   (A) At any cost   (B) On the whole   (C) Even if   (D) At any rate

B. Fill in the blanks.

| on the whole   on and off   on purpose   on the spot   on the other hand |
| at any cost   at any rate   at length   if only   even if |

1 We need to discuss the issue _____. 우리는 그 문제를 상세히 논의할 필요가 있어요.

2 I won't be angry _____ you lied to me.
   네가 나한테 거짓말을 했더라도 나는 화내지 않을 거야.

3 _____ it was a good day. 대체로 좋은 하루였어.

4 The player wanted to win the game _____. 그 선수는 꼭 경기에서 이기고 싶어 했어.

5 She could have passed the test _____ she had got one more point.
   그녀가 1점만 더 받았더라면 시험에 합격할 수 있었을 텐데.

Answers **A** 1. D 2. C 3. C 4. D
   B 1. at length 2. even if 3. On the whole 4. at any cost 5. if only

C. Complete the conversations using the sentences given.

1 **A** It looks like it's going to snow. 눈이 올 것 같은데.

   B _____

2 **A** James hit me intentionally. James가 의도적으로 나를 때렸어요.

   B _____

3 **A** Did you spend a lot of time reviewing for the test? 시험 공부는 많이 했니?

   B _____

4 **A** How did the students do on the test in general? 학생들이 대체로 시험을 어떻게 봤나요?

   B _____

> (A) On the whole, they did well.
> (B) No, I don't think he hit you on purpose.
> (C) Yes, I studied it at length.
> (D) Even if it snows, I'm going to the movie.

D. Speak or write.

1 Your friend did his best, but he lost the game. What do you say to comfort him? 당신의 친구가 최선을 다했지만 경기에서 졌다. 무슨 말로 위로할까?

2 You wish that you had more time to finish the homework. What do you have to say? 당신은 숙제를 마칠 시간이 더 있었으면 하고 바란다. 뭐라고 말해야 할까?

3 You don't golf often. How do you say it? 당신은 골프를 자주 치지 않는다. 뭐라고 말할까?

4 You want to buy the house regardless of the price. What would you have to say? 당신은 가격에 상관없이 집을 사고 싶어 한다. 뭐라고 말해야 할까?

> (A) I want to buy the house at any cost.
> (B) I play golf on and off.
> (C) If only I had more time to finish the homework.
> (D) At any rate, you did your best.

c 1. D 2. B 3. C 4. A
D 1. D 2. C 3. B 4. A

011

A **What is your *purpose* of visit?**
방문하신 목적이 무엇입니까?

B **I came in order to attend the meeting.**
회의에 참석하기 위해 왔어요.

in order to   ~하기 위하여

012

A **Can you *move* a little?**
좀 비켜 줄래?

B **Sorry, I didn't know that I was in the way.**
미안해, 방해가 되는 줄 몰랐어.

in the way   방해가 되어

013

A **Are you coming back *soon*?**
금방 돌아올 거야?

B **Of course, I'll be here in no time.**
그럼, 곧 올 거야.

in no time   즉시, 곧

014

A **Can you say *a few words* about the meeting?**
그 회의에 대해서 몇 마디 해 주시겠습니까?

B **In short, it went great.**
한마디로 말해 대성공이었습니다.

in short   한마디로 말해, 요컨대

015

A **Did you realize that you were hurt *after* the game?**
경기가 끝난 후에 다친 걸 알았니?

B **No, I knew it in the course of the game.**
아니, 경기 도중에 알았어.

in (the) course of   ~ 중에

016

A **In a sense**, Victor is right.
어떤 의미에서는 Victor가 맞아.

B I guess that's *one way of looking at it*.
그것을 그렇게 볼 수도 있겠지.

in a sense[way]   어떤 의미에서, 얼마간

017

A *Why* did you choose this one?
왜 이것을 고르셨나요?

B I like this one in that it is cheaper.
이게 더 싸니까 좋아요.

in that   ~라는 점에서, ~이므로

018

A You need to exercise in addition to a change in diet.
식단 변경 이외에도 운동을 하셔야 합니다.

B So do I need to work out *and* watch what I eat?
그러면 운동도 하고 먹는 것을 조심하기도 해야 하나요?

in addition to   ~에 더하여, ~뿐 아니라

019

A Has David *always been* a hard worker?
David는 항상 열심히 일해 왔니?

B Yeah, he is like that by nature.
그래, 그는 본래 그런 것 같아.

by nature   본래, 선천적으로

020

A *Are you sure* you want to do this?
정말 이걸 하고 싶니?

B By all means, I'm ready.
좋고말고, 준비됐어.

by all means   반드시, 좋고말고

A. Choose the right answer.

1 **A** Is Doug always this quiet? Doug는 항상 이렇게 조용하니?

   B Yes, he is shy _____. 그래, 그는 원래 수줍어해.

  (A) by all means   (B) in short   (C) by nature   (D) in the way

2 **A** You don't look sad about not getting the job. 그 일자리를 얻지 못한 것이 슬퍼 보이지 않는구나.

   B _____, I'm glad that I didn't get it. 어느 정도는 그 일자리를 얻지 못한 것이 기뻐.

  (A) In no time   (B) In the course of (C) In a sense   (D) In addition to

3 **A** Can I have another cookie? 쿠키 하나 더 먹어도 돼요?

   B _____, you can have one more. 좋고말고, 하나 더 먹어도 돼.

  (A) By all means (B) By nature   (C) In order to   (D) In a sense

4 **A** Can you move your book bag? 네 책가방 좀 치워 줄래?

   B I didn't realize that it was _____. 그게 방해가 되는 줄 몰랐어.

  (A) by all means   (B) in the way   (C) in that   (D) in the course of

B. Fill in the blanks.

| in order to | in the way | in no time | in short | in the course of |
| in a sense | in that | in addition to | by nature | by all means |

1 I had to read the article again · _____ understand it.
  나는 그 기사를 이해하기 위해 다시 읽어야 했다.

2 Don't worry. You'll finish the report _____. 걱정하지 마. 리포트를 곧 끝낼 수 있을 거야.

3 Please don't talk _____ the movie. 영화 상영 중에는 이야기하지 말아 주세요.

4 Mindy got the job _____ she could speak English.
  Mindy는 영어를 할 수 있었기 때문에 그 일자리를 얻었다.

5 You need to read chapter 3 _____ chapter 2. 2장 이외에 3장도 읽어야 해.

C. Complete the conversations using the sentences given.

1 **A** _____

   B Me, too. 나도 그래.

2 **A** Do you ever get nervous? 혹시 떨리니?

   B _____

3 **A** Can I take this chair? 이 의자를 가져가도 될까요?

   B _____

4 **A** Why are you studying all the time? 너는 왜 항상 공부를 하고 있니?

   B _____

> (A) I'm studying in order to get all A's.
> (B) In a sense, I'm happy you are here.
> (C) No, I'm very calm by nature.
> (D) By all means, you can take it.

D. Speak or write.

1 Jason's car is blocking your car. What do you have to say to Jason?
Jason의 차가 당신 차를 가로막고 있다. Jason에게 뭐라고 말해야 할까?

2 You don't like to study math because it is hard. How would you express your feeling? 당신은 수학이 힘들어 공부하기 싫다. 당신의 기분을 어떻게 표현하겠는가?

3 Bob needs to clean his room and the bathroom. What do you have to say to Bob? Bob이 자기 방과 화장실을 청소해야 한다. Bob에게 어떻게 말해야 할까?

4 You think Sandy will get better soon. How would you say it to Sandy?
당신은 Sandy가 곧 괜찮아질 것으로 생각한다. Sandy에게 그 말을 어떻게 하겠는가?

> (A) You will get better in no time.
> (B) You have to clean your room in addition to the bathroom.
> (C) I don't like to study math in that it is hard.
> (D) Your car is in the way.

C 1. B 2. C 3. D 4. A
D 1. D 2. C 3. B 4. A

021　　A **Did you really live here *for thirty years*?**
　　　　정말 여기서 30년 동안 사셨나요?

　　　B **Yeah, I lived here for ages.**
　　　　네, 여기서 오랫동안 살았지요.

　　　for ages　　오랫동안

022　　A **How often do you get to see your brother?**
　　　　남동생을 얼마나 자주 보니?

　　　B ***Not much*, I only see him from time to time.**
　　　　별로 많이 못 봐, 가끔 볼 뿐이야.

　　　from time to time　　가끔, 때때로

023　　A **According to David, everything will be OK.**
　　　　David에 따르면 모두 잘될 거래.

　　　B **Well, I don't really believe *what he says*.**
　　　　글쎄, 난 그가 하는 말은 정말 못 믿겠어.

　　　according to　　~에 의하면, ~에 따라

024　　A **Did Mr. Smith mention *about* my plan?**
　　　　Smith 씨가 제 계획에 대해 언급했나요?

　　　B **He said nothing as to your plan.**
　　　　당신의 계획에 대해서는 아무 말도 하지 않았어요.

　　　as to　　~에 관하여

025　　A **My favorite season is winter. How *about you*?**
　　　　내가 제일 좋아하는 계절은 겨울이야. 너는 어때?

　　　B **As for me, I like summer.**
　　　　나로서는 여름이 좋아.

　　　as for　　~에 관해 말하자면

026

A **Adam acts *like* a pig.**
Adam이 돼지처럼 행동해.

B **So, let's treat him as such.**
그렇다면 그를 그렇게 대우해 주자.

as such   그렇게, 그런 식으로

027

A ***How far* did you travel?**
어디까지 여행하셨나요?

B **I went as far as Seattle.**
Seattle까지 갔어요.

as far as   ~까지, ~하는 한

028

A ***How long* can you stay here?**
여기에 얼마나 있을 수 있어?

B **I'll stay here as long as you want.**
네가 원하는 만큼 오래 있을게.

as long as   ~하는 동안은, ~하는 한은

029

A **Mom *is going to* kill you.**
엄마가 너를 죽이려고 할 거야.

B **I know! I'm as good as dead.**
알아! 나는 죽은 거나 마찬가지야.

as good as   ~와 다름없는, 마찬가지인

030

A **Do you accept late homework?**
늦게 내는 숙제를 받아 주시나요?

B **As a rule, I don't, *but* I do make *exceptions*.**
원칙적으로 안 받지만, 예외로 해 주지.

as a rule   원칙적으로, 일반적으로

A. Choose the right answer.

1   **A** It seems like you always study. 너는 항상 공부하는 것 같아.

    B I do a lot, but I also have fun ＿＿＿＿＿＿. 많이 하지만 가끔 놀기도 해.

    (A) as a rule   (B) from time to time   (C) for ages   (D) as long as

2   **A** Do you have any idea ＿＿＿＿＿＿ what I should do?

      내가 뭘 해야 할지에 대해 무슨 아이디어가 있니?

    B Yes, you should tell the truth. 그래. 사실대로 말해야 해.

    (A) as such   (B) as far as   (C) according to   (D) as to

3   **A** I haven't seen Rob ＿＿＿＿＿＿. Rob을 못 본 지 오래됐어.

    B He didn't visit us for a long time. 그는 오랫동안 우리 집에 안 왔어.

    (A) as far as   (B) as long as   (C) from time to time   (D) for ages

4   **A** I'm going to the party. How about you? 나 파티에 갈 건데. 너는?

    B ＿＿＿＿＿＿ me, I'm not really sure. 나로서는 확실히 잘 모르겠어.

    (A) As long as   (B) According to   (C) As far as   (D) As for

B. Fill in the blanks.

| for ages | from time to time | according to | as to | as for |
| as such | as far as | as long as | as good as | as a rule |

1   Wow, your car looks ＿＿＿＿＿＿ new! 와, 네 차는 새 차와 다름없어 보여!

2   ＿＿＿＿＿＿, repairing the car will be difficult. 그 상태로는 그 차를 수리하기는 어려울 거야.

3   ＿＿＿＿＿＿ I know, Vince will attend the meeting.

    내가 아는 한, Vince는 그 모임에 참석할 거야.

4   Mark should be here by now ＿＿＿＿＿＿ the train schedule.

    열차 시간표에 의하면 Mark는 지금쯤 여기에 와 있어야 해.

5   You can stay here ＿＿＿＿＿＿ you want. 여기에 네가 원하는 만큼 오래 있어도 돼.

Answers   **A**   1. B   2. D   3. D   4. D

          B   1. as good as   2. As such   3. As far as   4. according to   5. as long as

C. Complete the conversations using the sentences given.

1 **A** _____

  B I guess you have a few more days to work on it. 며칠 정도 할 시간이 더 있을 거야.

2 **A** I don't think this is the right answer. 이게 정답이 아닌 것 같은데.

  B _____

3 **A** Where did you guys go? 너희들 어디 갔었니?

  B _____

4 **A** How long are you going to work on the problem? 그 문제 푸는 데 얼마나 걸리겠니?

  B _____

> (A) We walked as far as the lake.
> (B) My science project as such is not ready.
> (C) I work on it as long as it takes.
> (D) According to the teacher, it is.

D. Speak or write.

1 You hayen't seen a movie for a long time. How do you say this?
당신은 오랫동안 영화를 보지 않았다. 이것을 어떻게 말할까?

2 You think Peter's idea is equal to Eric's. How do you say this?
당신은 Peter의 생각이 Eric과 같다고 생각한다. 이것을 어떻게 말할까?

3 You normally call your mother on Sundays. How do you say this?
당신은 보통 일요일마다 어머니께 전화를 한다. 이것을 어떻게 말할까?

4 You occasionally go shopping. How do you say this?
당신은 때때로 쇼핑하러 간다. 이것을 어떻게 말할까?

> (A) I think Peter's idea is as good as Eric's.
> (B) I go shopping from time to time.
> (C) I haven't seen a movie for ages.
> (D) As a rule, I call my mother on Sundays.

C 1. B 2. D 3. A 4. C
D 1. C 2. A 3. D 4. B

031

A **I may as well study for the test.**
시험 공부를 하는 게 낫겠다.

B **Yeah, there is *no reason not to*.**
그럼, 안 할 이유가 없지.

may as well ～하는 게 낫다

032

A **Mom, can I watch TV all night?**
엄마, 밤새도록 TV 봐도 되나요?

B **Jimmy, *don't be silly*. That's out of the question.**
Jimmy, 바보 같은 소리 하지 마. 그건 말도 안 돼.

out of the question 전혀 불가능한, 말도 안 되는

033

A **Were there *many students* at the library?**
도서관에는 학생들이 많았니?

B **Yeah, quite a few people were still there.**
그래, 여전히 꽤 많은 사람들이 있었어.

quite a few 꽤 많은

034

A **How often do you go to the movies?**
영화관에는 얼마나 자주 가니?

B ***Not too often*, I only see a movie once in a while.**
별로 자주는 아니고 가끔 영화 한 편 볼 뿐이야.

(every) once in a while 가끔, 종종

035

A ***How long* have you been playing baseball?**
야구를 한 지는 얼마나 됐니?

B **Ever since I was ten.**
10살 때 이후로 지금까지.

ever since ～ 이후로 줄곧

24

036

A **Did anything go wrong during the trip, *except* the plane delay?**
비행기 지연을 제외하고 여행 중에 무슨 문제가 있었나요?

B **Apart from the delay, it was just fine.**
비행 지연 이외에는 괜찮았어요.

apart from   ~을 제외하고, ~ 이외에도

037

A **Is the book fun to read?**
그 책 읽어 보니 재미있니?

B ***No*, it is anything but fun.**
아니, 이 책은 재미라고는 전혀 없어.

anything but   ~이 결코 아닌, ~ 외에는 다

038

A **We need to move for the sake of our children.**
우리 아이들을 위해 이사해야 돼요.

B **Yes, we should do that for their future.**
그래요, 아이들의 장래를 위해 그렇게 해야 돼요.

for the sake of   ~을 위하여

039

A **Do you *take* the bus to work?**
버스 타고 출근하니?

B **Yes, I get there by means of bus.**
그래, 버스로 출근해.

by means of   ~에 의해, ~의 도움으로

040

A **Did you stop because you guys *didn't have* money?**
너희들은 돈이 없어서 그만둔 거니?

B **Yeah, we gave it up for lack of money.**
그래, 돈이 부족해서 포기했어.

for lack of   ~이 부족해서, ~이 없기 때문에

A. Choose the right answer.

1　**A** What kind of vegetable do you like? 어떤 종류의 채소를 좋아하세요?

　B I like ＿＿＿＿＿＿＿＿ carrot. 당근 빼고는 다 좋아해요.

(A) anything but　(B) apart from　(C) once in a while　(D) quite a few

2　**A** Did I get every question right? 내가 문제들을 모두 맞혔니?

　B ＿＿＿＿＿＿＿＿ this one, everything else is correct. 이 문제 이외에 다른 것은 모두 맞았어.

(A) For lack of　(B) Ever since　(C) For the sake of　(D) Apart from

3　**A** Can I have another piece of cake? 케이크 한 조각 더 먹어도 되나요?

　B You already ate two pieces. It's ＿＿＿＿＿＿＿＿. 넌 벌써 두 조각이나 먹었어. 절대 안 돼.

(A) quite a few　(B) out of the question　(C) anything but　(D) once in a while

4　**A** Did you catch a lot of fish? 물고기 많이 잡으셨어요?

　B Yes, I caught ＿＿＿＿＿＿＿＿. 네, 꽤 많이 잡았어요.

(A) once in a while　(B) out of the question　(C) quite a few　(D) may as well

B. Fill in the blanks.

| may as well　out of the question　quite a few　once in a while　ever since |
| apart from　anything but　for the sake of　by means of　for lack of |

1　Greg is so busy that he only visits his parents ＿＿＿＿＿＿＿＿.

　Greg는 아주 바빠서 부모님을 가끔 방문할 뿐이다.

2　Most people get to work ＿＿＿＿＿＿＿＿ mass transportation.

　대부분의 사람들은 대중교통 수단으로 출퇴근한다.

3　I have known him ＿＿＿＿＿＿＿＿ I was in the fifth grade.

　나는 5학년 때부터 그를 알고 지낸다.

4　Harry didn't pass the exam, but not ＿＿＿＿＿＿＿＿ trying.

　Harry가 시험에 합격하지 못했지만 노력이 부족했기 때문은 아니었다.

5　I'm only doing this ＿＿＿＿＿＿＿＿ our friendship.

　나는 우리의 우정을 위해 이것을 하고 있을 뿐이다.

C. Complete the conversations using the sentences given.

1 **A** Oh, no! It's too late to see the movie. 아, 이런! 너무 늦어서 영화를 볼 수 없겠는데.

   B _____

2 **A** How long did you have this pain? 이런 통증이 얼마나 오래되었죠?

   B _____

3 **A** How did your brother become so successful? 네 형은 어떻게 해서 그렇게 성공했니?

   B _____

4 **A** Why was the teacher yelling? 왜 선생님이 고함치셨니?

   B _____

> (A) Ever since the accident, my back has been hurting.
> (B) He was criticizing his students for lack of effort.
> (C) We may as well stay home.
> (D) He became successful by means of hard work.

D. Speak or write.

1 The dinner tasted terrible. How do you say this?
   저녁 식사가 정말 맛없었다. 이것을 어떻게 말할까?

2 You made many mistakes on the report. How do you say this?
   당신은 리포트에 실수를 많이 했다. 이것을 어떻게 말할까?

3 Everyone came on time except Tom. How do you say this?
   Tom을 제외하고는 모두가 제시간에 왔다. 이것을 어떻게 말할까?

4 It's impossible that you skip school. How do you say this?
   당신이 학교 수업을 빼먹는 일은 불가능하다. 이것을 어떻게 말할까?

> (A) Everyone came on time apart from Tom.
> (B) It's out of the question that I skip school.
> (C) The dinner was anything but delicious.
> (D) I made quite a few mistakes on the report.

041　A **Mr. Jefferson worked at the expense of his health.**
Jefferson 씨는 건강을 해쳐 가며 일했어.

　　B **I know. He shouldn't have *sacrificed* his health for the company.** 알아. 그는 회사를 위해 건강을 희생하지 말았어야 했어.

at the expense of 　～을 희생하며

042　A **I heard Bob made *a lot of* money.**
Bob이 돈을 많이 벌었다고 들었어요.

　　B **Yeah, he has earned a good deal of money.**
네, 그는 많은 돈을 벌었지요.

a good deal of 　많은, 다량의

043　A **You *don't care about* the cost?**
너는 비용은 신경 안 쓰니?

　　B **Yeah, I'm going to buy it regardless of the price.**
그래, 나는 가격에 상관없이 그걸 살 거야.

regardless of 　～에 상관없이

044　A **Do you *like* the plan?**
그 계획이 마음에 드니?

　　B **Yeah, I'm in favor of it.**
그래, 나는 그 계획에 찬성이야.

in favor of 　～에 찬성하여, ～에 호의적인

045　A **What should I do *if something happens*?**
무슨 일이 생기면 어떻게 해야 하지?

　　B **In case of emergency, you should call me.**
비상 사태가 발생하면 나한테 전화해.

in case of 　～이 발생할 시에는

046

A **I thought John would be careless *with* money.**
나는 John이 돈을 함부로 쓸 거라고 생각했어.

B **No, he is very careful in terms of money.**
아니야, 그는 돈에 관해서는 아주 조심한다고.

in terms of　~면에서는, ~에 관해서는

047

A **Who is in charge of the store?**
가게의 책임자가 누구죠?

B **I'm the *manager*.**
제가 매니저인데요.

in charge of　~을 맡고 있는, 담당하는

048

A **In spite of rain, many people attended the party.**
비가 오는데도 불구하고, 많은 사람들이 파티에 참석했군요.

B **Yes, the weather *didn't stop* them from coming.**
네, 날씨가 사람들이 오는 것을 막지 못했어요.

in spite of　~에도 불구하고

049

A **We gave up a run *because of* Jack's error.**
Jack의 실수 때문에 우리가 한 점을 내줬어.

B **Yeah, we lost the game on account of him.**
그래, 우리는 Jack 때문에 경기에서 졌어.

on account of　~ 때문에

050

A **Does Tom have *many* friends?**
Tom은 친구가 많니?

B **Yes, he has plenty of friends.**
그래, 그는 친구가 많아.

plenty of　많은, 넉넉한

A. Choose the right answer.

1　A　I didn't get the promotion. 나 승진 못했어.

　　B　Don't worry. There will be _____ chances for you.
　　　　걱정하지 마. 너한테 기회는 많아.

　(A) in charge of　(B) plenty of　(C) on the account of　(D) in spite of

2　A　Connie thinks you should not take the job.
　　　　Connie는 네가 그 일자리를 얻지 말아야 한다고 생각해.

　　B　Well, I'm going to take the job _____ of her opinion.
　　　　글쎄, Connie의 의견과는 상관없이 나는 그 일자리를 얻을 거야.

　(A) plenty of　(B) regardless of　(C) a good deal of　(D) on account of

3　A　Are you _____ the group? 당신이 이 그룹을 맡고 있나요?

　　B　Yes, I'm the leader. 네, 제가 리더입니다.

　(A) in charge of　(B) in terms of　(C) in favor of　(D) in case of

4　A　Did you find anything for your report from the article?
　　　　그 기사에서 리포트에 쓸 만한 것 좀 찾았니?

　　B　Yes, there was _____ useful information. 그래, 유용한 정보가 아주 많았어.

　(A) on account of　(B) at the expense of　(C) in charge of　(D) a good deal of

B. Fill in the blanks.

| at the expense of　a good deal of　regardless of　in favor of　in case of |
| in terms of　in charge of　in spite of　on account of　plenty of |

1　You should not drive _____ snow. 눈이 올 경우에는 운전하면 안 돼.

2　This city is ranked last in the world _____ pollution.
　　공해 면에서 이 도시는 세계 최하위이다.

3　The wealthy is getting richer _____ the poor.
　　부자들은 가난한 사람들을 희생시키며 점점 더 부유해지고 있다.

4　The voters are _____ lowering the income tax.
　　유권자들은 소득세를 낮추는 데 찬성한다.

5　He cancelled the trip _____ his poor health. 그는 건강 악화 때문에 여행을 취소했다.

C. Complete the conversations using the sentences given.

1 **A** Is the picnic still on? 소풍은 그래도 가는 건가요?
   B _____

2 **A** I heard Rob got hurt during the match. Rob이 시합 중에 다쳤다고 들었는데.
   B _____

3 **A** It's going to be very expensive to build a new bridge.
       새 다리를 건설하려면 비용이 무척 많이 들 겁니다.
   B _____

4 **A** Is there enough of food for everybody? 모두 먹을 만큼 음식은 충분히 있나요?
   B _____

(A) It also will be built at the expense of the taxpayers.
(B) Yeah, there is plenty of food.
(C) Yes, we will have one regardless of the weather.
(D) In spite of his injury, he won the match.

D. Speak or write.

1 You want to know who is responsible for planning the party. How do you ask? 당신은 파티 계획을 책임지고 있는 사람이 누구인지 알고 싶다. 어떻게 물어볼까?

2 Taylor made a lot of money in stocks. How can you say this?
   Taylor는 주식으로 많은 돈을 벌었다. 이것을 어떻게 말할 수 있을까?

3 Adam should call you if there is an emergency. How do you say it to Adam? Adam은 긴급 상황이 생기면 당신에게 전화해야 한다. Adam에게 그것을 어떻게 말할까?

4 The teacher is very strict regarding late homework. How do you say it?
   그 선생님은 숙제를 늦게 내는 것에 아주 엄격하다. 그것을 어떻게 말할까?

(A) He made a good deal of money in stocks.
(B) Who is in charge of planning the party?
(C) The teacher is very strict in terms of late homework.
(D) You should call me in case of an emergency.

C 1. C   2. D   3. A   4. B
D 1. B   2. A   3. D   4. C

051 A **It snowed *so much*!**
눈이 무척 많이 왔어!

  B **Yeah, I can see nothing but snow.**
그래, 보이는 것이라곤 눈밖에 없어.

nothing but   오직, ~뿐인

052 A **Your birthday is around the corner, right?**
네 생일이 곧 다가오지, 그렇지?

  B **Yeah, it's *next week*.**
그래, 다음 주야.

around the corner   아주 가까운, 멀지 않은

053 A **I think we need to *meet*.**
우리 만나야겠다.

  B **You're right! We should talk face to face.**
맞아! 얼굴을 마주보고 이야기해야 돼.

face to face   마주 대하여

054 A **It's *clear* that Sandy is the best candidate.**
Sandy가 최고의 후보인 게 분명해.

  B **It goes without saying that she is the best.**
그녀가 최고인 것은 말할 필요도 없지.

it goes without saying that   ~은 말할 필요도 없다, 물론이다

055 A **Did you *really* receive an 'A' on the test?**
시험에서 정말 A 받았니?

  B **To tell the truth, I only got a 'B.'**
사실대로 말하자면 B밖에 못 받았어.

to tell the truth   사실은, 사실대로 말하자면

056

A **So who won the match?**
그래서 시합에서 누가 이겼니?

B **Neither Jake nor Eric won. It was a *tie*.**
Jake도 Eric도 이기지 못했어. 무승부였어.

neither A nor B   A와 B 둘 다 아닌

057

A **I like pizza as well as hamburger.**
나는 햄버거는 물론 피자도 좋아해.

B **Me too. They are *both* delicious.**
나도 그래. 둘 다 맛있어.

A as well as B   B는 물론 A도

058

A **Why did you choose not the red tie but the blue one?**
왜 빨간색 넥타이가 아니라 파란색 넥타이를 골랐니?

B **I *like* the blue tie *better*.**
파란색 넥타이가 더 좋아.

not A but B   A가 아니고 B인

059

A **Tom certainly *looks like* his father.**
Tom은 확실히 아버지를 닮았어.

B **Yeah, he sure reminds me of his father.**
그래, 그는 그의 아버지를 생각나게 해.

remind A of B   A에게 B를 생각나게 하다

060

A **Who informed Jill of the news?**
누가 Jill에게 그 소식을 알려 주었나요?

B **It was Jack who *told* her that she was fired.**
그녀에게 해고되었다고 이야기해 준 사람은 Jack이었어요.

inform A of B   A에게 B를 알려 주다

A. Choose the right answer.

1   **A** It's December already. 벌써 12월이야.

   B Yeah, and that means Christmas is _____.

   그래, 그 말은 머지않아 크리스마스라는 거야.

(A) nothing but   (B) to tell the truth   (C) around the corner   (D) face to face

2   **A** I heard Victor gave you a present. Victor가 너한테 선물을 주었다면서.

   B No, it was _____ Victor _____ Eric who gave me a gift.

   아니, 나한테 선물을 준 사람은 Victor가 아니고 Eric이야.

(A) remind, of   (B) neither, nor   (C) not, but   (D) inform, of

3   **A** We need to discuss the problem in person. 우리가 개인적으로 그 문제를 의논할 필요가 있어.

   B You're right. We should talk _____. 맞아. 우리 얼굴을 마주보고 이야기해야 돼.

(A) to tell the truth   (B) around the corner   (C) nothing but   (D) face to face

4   **A** Did you hear that Frank got the job? Frank가 취직했다는 소식 들었니?

   B Yes, Doug _____ me _____ the news.

   그래, Doug가 나한테 그 소식을 알려 줬어.

(A) informed, of   (B) not, but   (C) reminded, of   (D) neither, nor

B. Fill in the blanks.

| nothing but   around the corner   face to face   it goes without saying |
| to tell the truth   neither, nor   as well as   not, but   remind, of   inform, of |

1   _____ Sam _____ Nancy is going to the meeting.

Sam도 Nancy도 그 모임에 가지 않을 거야.

2   I want to get the red coat _____ the blue sweater.

파란색 스웨터뿐 아니라 빨간색 코트도 갖고 싶어요.

3   _____ that Mark should be the class president.

Mark가 반장이 되어야 하는 것은 말할 필요도 없지.

4   _____, it was Bob who broke the plate. 사실대로 말하자면, 그 접시를 깬 사람은 Bob이야.

5   These pictures _____ me _____ the vacation we took.

이 사진들은 우리가 갔던 휴가를 생각나게 해.

Answers   **A** 1. C   2. C   3. D   4. A

   B 1. Neither, nor   2. as well as   3. It goes without saying   4. To tell the truth
   5. remind, of

C. Complete the conversations using the sentences given.

1 **A** _____

   B I can't believe they both missed school. 둘 다 학교에 오지 않았다니 믿을 수가 없네.

2 **A** Who told you that the meeting was cancelled? 누가 모임이 취소됐다고 이야기해 주었니?

   B _____

3 **A** Why do you like Pam so much? 너는 Pam을 왜 그렇게 좋아하니?

   B _____

4 **A** You wanted your jeans to be washed, right? 청바지 세탁해 주기를 원했지?

   B _____

> (A) Roger informed me of the cancellation.
> (B) No, I wanted not my jeans but my shirt to be washed.
> (C) Neither Cindy nor Ellen came to school.
> (D) She reminds me of my younger sister.

D. Speak or write.

1 You like both pizza and hamburger. How do you say it?
   당신은 피자와 햄버거 둘 다 좋아한다. 그것을 어떻게 말할까?

2 You want to talk to Nancy in person. How do you say it?
   당신은 개인적으로 Nancy와 대화하고 싶다. 그것을 어떻게 말할까?

3 Your father's birthday is coming soon. How do you say it?
   아버지의 생일이 곧 다가온다. 그것을 어떻게 말할까?

4 Molly only eats salad for lunch. How do you say it?
   Molly는 점심으로 샐러드만 먹는다. 그것을 어떻게 말할까?

> (A) I want to talk to Nancy face to face.
> (B) My father's birthday is around the corner.
> (C) She eats nothing but salad for lunch.
> (D) I like hamburger as well as pizza.

C 1. C 2. A 3. D 4. B
D 1. D 2. A 3. B 4. C

061
   A **Which do you *like more* a white or a black shirt?**
      흰색 셔츠와 검은색 셔츠 중에서 어느 것이 더 좋니?

   B **I prefer the black one to the white one.**
      나는 흰색 셔츠보다는 검은색이 더 좋아.

prefer A to B   B보다 A를 더 좋아하다

062
   A **Sam *thinks* you took his laptop.**
      Sam은 네가 자기 노트북을 가져갔다고 생각해.

   B **Oh, that's why he looked on me as a thief.**
      아, 그래서 그가 나를 도둑으로 여겼구나.

look on A as B   A를 B라고 여기다

063
   A **It *would be better* for you come with us to the movie.**
      우리와 함께 영화 보러 가는 편이 나을 거야.

   B **Yeah, I might as well have some fun as stay home.**
      그래, 집에 있느니 재미있게 노는 편이 낫겠지.

might as well A as B   B할 바엔 차라리 A하는 편이 낫다

064
   A **Let me relieve you of these bags.**
      이 가방들을 좀 들어 드릴게요.

   B **Thank you very much for *carrying* them *for* me.**
      가방을 들어 주셔서 감사합니다.

relieve A of B   A의 B를 덜어 주다

065
   A **Who should I *turn for* help?**
      누구한테 도움을 청하지?

   B **You should look to John for help.**
      John에게 도움을 기대해야 해.

look to A for B   A에 B를 기대하다

066

A Joseph and John *look a lot alike.*
Joseph과 John은 많이 닮았어.

B Yeah, I can't tell Joseph from John, either.
그래, 나도 Joseph과 John을 구별하지 못하겠어.

tell A from B   A와 B를 구별하다

067

A I'm sorry you *didn't* pass the test.
시험에 합격하지 못했다니 안됐다.

B One mistake deprived me of the chance to pass the test.
실수 하나 때문에 시험에 합격할 기회를 놓쳤어.

deprive A of B   A에게서 B를 빼앗다

068

A Did Kevin's help *allow* you to complete the assignment?
Kevin이 도와주어서 과제를 끝낼 수 있었니?

B Yeah, he enabled me to finish the work on time.
그래, 그가 제시간에 일을 끝낼 수 있게 해 줬어.

enable A to B   A가 B할 수 있게 하다

069

A You didn't *make* Ellen have an accident.
너 때문에 Ellen이 사고를 당한 건 아니야.

B I know, but I feel like my call caused her to lose focus.
알아. 하지만 내 전화 때문에 그녀가 집중력을 잃었던 것 같아.

cause A to B   A가 B하게 하다

070

A I took the stranger for our new teacher.
나는 그 낯선 사람을 새로 온 우리 선생님인 줄 잘못 알았어.

B That was a *mistake.*
실수한 거야.

take A for B   A를 B라고 잘못 생각하다

A. Choose the right answer.

1 A Is your flight delayed? 항공편이 지연됐니?

   B Yeah, the storm _____ my flight _____ be delayed.
그래, 폭풍우 때문에 항공편이 지연됐어.

(A) caused, to (B) look to, for (C) preferred, to (D) enable, to

2 A You have the same type of book bag as John's.
John의 것과 같은 타입의 책가방을 갖고 있구나.

   B Yeah, but I can still _____ mine _____ his.
그래, 하지만 나는 그래도 내 것과 그의 것을 구별할 수 있어.

(A) prefer, to (B) relieve, of (C) deprive, of (D) tell, from

3 A Why do you look upset? 왜 화난 표정이니?

   B Amy _____ me _____ a liar. Amy가 나를 거짓말쟁이로 여겨.

(A) looks to, for (B) tells, from (C) looks on, as (D) enables, to

4 A I'm so bored. 너무 지루해.

   B You _____ study _____ do nothing.
아무것도 안 하느니 차라리 공부하는 편이 나을 텐데.

(A) cause, to (B) prefer, to (C) enable, to (D) might as well, as

B. Fill in the blanks.

prefer, to	look on, as	might as well, as	relieve, of	look to, for
tell, from	deprive, of	enable, to	cause, to	take, for

1 You should _____ your family _____ help.
가족들에게 도움을 구해야 해요.

2 William's error _____ his team _____ a victory.
William의 실수 때문에 그의 팀이 승리하지 못했어.

3 Peter's help _____ me _____ finish the project.
Peter의 도움으로 내가 그 프로젝트를 끝낼 수 있었어.

4 I _____ reading _____ watching TV.
나는 TV 시청보다 책 읽기를 더 좋아한다.

5 Watching a movie should _____ you _____ your stress.
영화를 보면 스트레스가 풀릴 거야.

C. Complete the conversations using the sentences given.

1   **A** It was a great speech. 훌륭한 연설이었어.

   B _____

2   **A** Did you hear the bad news? 그 안 좋은 소식 들었나요?

   B _____

3   **A** The doctor looks very tired. 의사 선생님이 무척 피곤해 보여.

   B _____

4   **A** You know who to talk to if you can't decide, right?
      네가 결정하지 못한다면 누구한테 말할지 알지?

   B _____

(A) Someone should relieve him of his duty.
(B) Yeah, I should look to you for an advice.
(C) Yes, it deprived me of enjoying the weekend.
(D) Yeah, it enabled me to have hope for the future.

D. Speak or write.

1   You think it is better to tell the truth than lie. How do you say it?
당신은 거짓말하는 것보다 사실대로 말하는 것이 낫다고 생각한다. 그것을 어떻게 말할까?

2   James thought the stranger was his uncle. How do you say it?
James는 그 낯선 사람이 자기 삼촌이라고 생각했다. 그것을 어떻게 말할까?

3   You consider Sean is a hard worker. How do you say it to Sean?
당신은 Sean이 열심히 일한다고 생각한다. Sean에게 그것을 어떻게 말할까?

4   You still can't distinguish Greg and his brother. How do you tell Greg about it? 당신은 아직도 Greg와 그의 형을 구분하지 못한다. Greg에게 그것을 어떻게 이야기할까?

(A) He took the stranger for his uncle.
(B) I might as well tell the truth as lie.
(C) I still can't tell you from your brother.
(D) I look on you as a hard worker.

c 1. D   2. C   3. A   4. B
D 1. B   2. A   3. D   4. C

071 A **Are you *comfortable*?**
편안하세요?

B **Yes, I made myself at home.**
예, 편안합니다.

make oneself at home   (자기 집에 있는 것처럼) 편안히 쉬다

072 A **Can Sunhee make herself understood in English?**
선희는 영어로 의사소통이 가능합니까?

B **Yeah, she *speaks* the language *very well*.**
그럼요, 그녀는 영어를 아주 잘해요.

make oneself understood   자기 의사를 전달하다

073 A **Have you decided on which car to buy?**
어느 차를 살지 결정하셨나요?

B **No, I haven't made up my mind.**
아뇨, 아직 결정하지 못했어요.

make up one's mind   결심하다

074 A **Oh, I made a mistake because I was *in a hurry*.**
아, 서두르는 바람에 실수를 했어요.

B **That's why you should take your time doing your homework.** 그러니까 숙제 할 때는 천천히 해야 돼.

take one's time   천천히 하다

075 A **Can I have another one?**
하나 더 먹어도 돼요?

B **Sure, help yourself to another sandwich.**
그럼, 샌드위치 하나 더 먹어.

help oneself to   마음껏 먹다

076

A **Victor *doesn't listen to anyone*.**
Victor는 누구 말도 안 들어.

B **Yeah, he has his own way in everything.**
그래, 그는 만사에 제멋대로야.

have one's (own) way   제멋대로 하다

077

A **Tom *works very hard*.**
Tom은 아주 열심히 일해.

B **Yeah, he applies himself to everything.**
그래, 그는 모든 일에 최선을 다하지.

apply oneself to   ～에 전념[몰두]하다

078

A **Jane *said good things about* you.**
Jane이 너에 대해 좋게 말하던데.

B **I'm glad that she spoke well of me.**
그녀가 나를 칭찬하다니 기분 좋은데.

speak well of   ～에 대해 좋게 말하다, 칭찬하다

079

A **We *don't have much* fuel, right?**
연료가 별로 없지, 그렇지?

B **Yeah, we're running short of fuel.**
그래, 연료가 떨어져 가고 있어.

run short of   ～이 동이 나다, 다 떨어지다

080

A **I'm sorry I'm late again. I didn't *know* what time it was.**
또 늦어서 죄송해요. 몇 시인지 몰랐어요.

B **You should keep track of time.**
시간 관념이 있어야 해요.

keep track of   ～에 대해 계속 알고 있다

A. Choose the right answer.

1   **A** Can I _____ one more piece of pie? 파이 한 조각 더 먹어도 돼요?
   B Of course, you can eat as much as you want. 그럼. 원하는 만큼 먹어.

   (A) help myself to   (B) keep track of
   (C) apply myself to   (D) have my own way

2   **A** Hi, my name is Pam. 안녕. 내 이름은 Pam이야.
   B It's so nice to meet you. Sandra _____ you.
   만나서 정말 반가워. Sandra가 네 칭찬 많이 했어.

   (A) kept track of (B) ran short of (C) helped herself to (D) spoke well of

3   **A** Ben, we're _____ sugar. Ben. 설탕이 거의 다 떨어졌어.
   B I'll buy some later. 나중에 사올게.

   (A) keeping track of   (B) speaking well of
   (C) running short of   (D) helping ourselves to

4   **A** Harry always gets what he wants. Harry는 원하는 것은 항상 얻지.
   B That's because he cries until he _____. 제 뜻대로 될 때까지 울기 때문에 그래.

   (A) takes his time   (B) has his way
   (C) makes up his mind   (D) make himself understood

B. Fill in the blanks.

> make oneself at home   make oneself understood   make up one's mind
> take one's time   help oneself to   have one's own way   apply oneself to
> speak well of   run short of   keep track of

1   Roger became successful because he _____ his work.
   Roger는 자기 일에 전념했기 때문에 성공하게 되었다.

2   I can't seem to _____ about the vacation. 휴가에 대해 결정하지 못할 것 같아.

3   John _____ and fell asleep on my sofa. John은 편안히 쉬다가 내 소파에서 잠들었다.

4   _____. We still have 30 minutes. 천천히 해. 아직도 30분 남았어.

5   You need to _____ time if you don't want to be late.
   늦고 싶지 않으면 시간을 계속 확인해야 돼.

C. Complete the conversations using the sentences given.

1 A _____

    B This is the third time that you're late this week.
       당신이 이번 주 들어 지각한 게 이번이 3번째예요.

2 A You're doing it too fast. 너무 빨리 하고 있어.

    B _____

3 A Are you comfortable yet? 이제 좀 편안하세요?

    B _____

4 A I don't know when I'm going to finish my report.
       언제 리포트를 끝낼지 알 수가 없어.

    B _____

> (A) OK, I'll take my time.
> (B) You'll finish it soon if you apply yourself to it.
> (C) I'm sorry I didn't keep track of time.
> (D) Yes, I am. I made myself at home.

D. Speak or write.

1 Danny complains until he gets what he wants. How do you say this about Danny? Danny는 자신이 원하는 것을 얻을 때까지 불평한다. Danny에 대해 이것을 어떻게 말할까?

2 You want to drink a cup of coffee. How do you ask?
당신은 커피를 한잔 마시고 싶다. 어떻게 부탁할까?

3 Tom wants others to know how he feels. How do you say this about Tom?
Tom은 다른 사람들이 자신의 감정을 알기를 바란다. Tom에 대해 이것을 어떻게 말할까?

4 You don't have much money left. How do you say it?
당신은 남은 돈이 별로 없다. 그것을 어떻게 말할까?

> (A) Can I help myself to a cup of coffee?
> (B) He wants to make himself understood.
> (C) I'm running short of money.
> (D) He complains until he has his own way.

C 1. C 2. A 3. D 4. B
D 1. D 2. A 3. B 4. C

081

A People try to *use* John because he is such a generous person. John이 워낙 너그러운 사람이라서 사람들이 그를 이용하려고 해.

B That's really bad. They shouldn't try to take advantage of his generosity. 그건 정말 나쁘지. 그들이 그의 너그러움을 이용하려고 해서는 안 돼.

take advantage of 이용하다

082

A You need *to do* your *best* no matter what.
어쨌든 너는 최선을 다해야 해.

B Yes, I need to make the most of the opportunity.
네, 기회를 최대한 활용해야죠.

make the most of 최대한 활용하다

083

A Can I ask a favor of you?
부탁 하나 해도 될까요?

B Sure, *what do you want me to do?*
물론, 내가 뭘 해 줄까?

ask a favor of ~에게 부탁하다, 청하다

084

A Mr. Thomson is retiring. I don't know who is going to *replace* him. Thomson 씨가 은퇴해요. 누가 그의 후임자가 될지 모르겠어요.

B I don't think no one can take the place of him.
아무도 그를 대신할 수 없을 거예요.

take the place of ~을 대신하다

085

A Tom sure *likes to* talk.
Tom은 정말 말하기를 좋아해.

B Yeah, he has a tendency to do just that.
그래, 그렇게 하는 경향이 있지.

have a tendency to ~하는 경향이 있다 (= tend to)

086

A **Do you think Susan *can change* Robert's *mind*?**
Susan이 Robert의 마음을 바꿀 수 있다고 생각하니?

B **Of course, she has a great influence on him.**
물론, 그녀는 그에게 큰 영향력이 있어.

have an influence on   ~에 영향력이 있다, 영향을 주다

087

A **I'm sure Nancy *can tell* which painting is better.**
Nancy는 어느 그림이 나은지 분간할 수 있을 거야.

B **Yeah, she certainly has an eye for art.**
그래, 그녀는 확실히 미술에 안목이 있지.

have an eye for   ~을 보는 눈이 있다

088

A **What's so *important* about arriving early?**
일찍 도착하는 게 뭐가 그리 중요해?

B **Believe me. It does make a difference.**
나를 믿어. 확실히 차이가 있어.

make a difference   차이가 나다, 중요하다

089

A **Do you think Tom *would do* what he said?**
Tom이 자기가 말한 대로 할 거라고 생각해?

B **Don't worry. He will make good on his promise.**
걱정하지 마. 그는 약속을 꼭 지킬 거야.

make good   성공하다, 실행하다

090

A **How did you guys drive *nonstop* for 36 hours?**
너희들은 어떻게 36시간 연속으로 운전을 했니?

B **We took turns driving.**
우리는 교대로 운전을 했어.

take turns   교대로 하다

A. Choose the right answer.

1 A Can I _____ you? 부탁 하나 해도 될까?

   B Sure, what do you want me to do? 물론, 뭘 해 줄까?

   (A) ask a favor of   (B) have a tendency to

   (C) make the most of   (D) take the place of

2 A What was your secret to your success? 성공하신 비결이 무엇입니까?

   B I just _____ what I had. 그냥 제가 가진 것을 최대한 활용했죠.

   (A) took the place of   (B) made the most of

   (C) asked a favor of   (D) had a tendency to

3 A I think Ron is selfish. Ron은 이기적인 것 같아.

   B Yeah, he _____ people whenever he can.
      그래, 그는 할 수만 있다면 언제든지 사람들을 이용해.

   (A) makes the mot of   (B) takes the place of

   (C) have an influence on   (D) takes advantage of

4 A Ben always dresses nicely. Ben은 항상 옷을 잘 입어.

   B He _____ fashion. 그는 패션에 대한 안목이 있어.

   (A) has an eye for   (B) has an influence on

   (C) has a tendency to   (D) takes an advantage of

B. Fill in the blanks.

take advantage of   make the most of   ask a favor of   take the place of
have a tendency to   have an influence on   have an eye for
make a difference   make good   take turns

1 It will be difficult to _____ Professor Robinson.
   Robinson 교수를 대신하기는 어려울 거야.

2 The parents _____ watching their sick baby. 부모들은 아픈 아기를 번갈아 돌보았다.

3 I don't trust John because he _____ lie.
   나는 John이 거짓말하는 경향이 있기 때문에 그를 신뢰하지 않아.

4 My father _____ on his word. 우리 아버지는 자신이 한 말을 잘 지킨다.

5 Your donation will _____ to these poor children.
   당신의 기부는 이 불쌍한 아이들을 바꾸어 놓을 것입니다.

C. Complete the conversations using the sentences given.

1 **A** _____

   B Of course, we wouldn't have won the game without him.
   물론, 그가 없었다면 우리는 경기에서 이길 수 없었을 거야.

2 **A** Jason is going to miss the next game. Jason은 다음 경기에 빠질 거야.

   B _____

3 **A** Nancy says she'll study harder next year. Nancy가 내년에는 더 열심히 공부할 거래.

   B _____

4 **A** _____

   B Yeah, that's a good idea. 그래, 그거 좋은 생각이다.

(A) I hope she makes good on her plan.
(B) Do you think Ron made a difference?
(C) Let's take turns doing the dishes.
(D) Oh, no! I don't know who will take the place of him.

D. Speak or write.

1 You want Peter to do something for you. How do you ask Peter?
   당신은 Peter가 무엇을 해 주기를 원한다. Peter에게 어떻게 부탁할까?

2 Bob does what his brother tells him to do. How do you say this about
   Bob's brother? Bob은 형이 하라고 말하는 대로 한다. Bob의 형에 대해 이것을 어떻게 말할까?

3 Mark should use his experience to the greatest advantage. How do you
   say that to Mark? Mark는 자신의 경험을 최대한 활용해야 한다. Mark에게 그것을 어떻게 말할까?

4 The coach always chooses good players. How do you say this about the
   coach? 그 코치는 항상 좋은 선수들을 선택한다. 그 코치에 대해 이것을 어떻게 말할까?

(A) The coach has an eye for good players.
(B) You should make the most of your experience.
(C) Can I ask a favor of you?
(D) His brother has an influence on him.

C 1. B 2. D 3. A 4. C
D 1. C 2. D 3. B 4. A

091　A　**Did you *memorize* all the lines?**
　　대사를 모두 외웠니?

　　B　**Yes, I learned them by heart.**
　　네, 대사를 외웠어요.

learn ~ by heart　　외우다

092　A　**Do you want *more* pizza?**
　　피자 더 먹을래?

　　B　**Yeah, I cannot eat too much today.**
　　그래, 오늘은 아무리 먹어도 더 먹을 수 있겠어.

cannot ~ too　　아무리 ~해도 지나치지 않다

093　A　**The news certainly *shocked* Sean.**
　　Sean이 그 소식에 틀림없이 충격을 받았을 거야.

　　B　**It certainly took him by surprise.**
　　확실히 놀랐겠지.

take ~ by surprise　　기습하다, 깜짝 놀라게 하다

094　A　**I can't believe my brother left for college. I *thought* he would *always* be here.**
　　오빠가 대학 때문에 가 버린 것이 믿어지지 않아. 항상 여기 있을 줄 알았어.

　　B　**I guess you took him for granted.**
　　오빠를 당연하게 생각했던 것 같구나.

take ~ for granted　　당연하게 생각하다

095　A　**Please *remember* to call Dad.**
　　아빠한테 전화하는 것 기억해.

　　B　**I'll bear it in mind.**
　　명심할게요.

bear ~ in mind　　명심하다(= keep in mind)

A **Sam is likely to get the job.**
Sam이 직장을 구할 것 같아.

B **I'm glad that he *might* work again.**
그가 다시 일할 수도 있다니 기쁘다.

be likely to ~할 것 같다

A **How did you get so sick?** 어쩌다 그렇게 아팠니?

B **I shouldn't have been *out* too long. I was exposed to too much cold air.**
바깥에 너무 오래 있지 말았어야 했어. 찬 바람을 너무 많이 쐬였어.

be exposed to ~에 노출되다

A **Tom is supposed to be here, right?**
Tom이 여기로 오기로 했지, 그렇지?

B **Yeah, he *should be* arriving at anytime now.**
그래, 이제 곧 올 거야.

be supposed to ~하기로 되어 있다

A **Do I *have to* pay extra to change my flight?**
항공편 예약을 바꾸려면 추가 요금을 내야 하나요?

B **Yes, the schedule change is subject to a fee.**
네, 일정 변경은 수수료가 부과됩니다.

be subject to ~의 대상이 되다, 지배를 받다

A **How come you answered the phone *so quickly*?**
어떻게 전화를 그렇게 빨리 받았니?

B **I was about to call you, then the phone rang.**
너한테 막 전화하려던 참인데 전화가 울렸어.

be about to 막 ~하려고 하다

Review Quiz

A. Choose the right answer.

1. A Which team do you think would win? 어느 팀이 이길 것 같아?
   B I think the Lions will _____ win. 라이언스 팀이 이길 것 같아.
   (A) be likely to (B) be supposed to (C) be subject to (D) be about to

2. A I didn't expect it to be sunny today. 오늘 해가 날 것이라고 예상하지 못했어.
   B Yeah, it _____ rain all day. 그래, 하루 종일 비가 오기로 되어 있었지.
   (A) was about to (B) was likely to (C) was supposed to (D) was exposed to

3. A When is the play going to start? 경기가 언제 시작되니?
   B It _____ begin. 막 시작되려는 참이야.
   (A) is about to (B) is exposed to (C) is likely to (D) is subject to

4. A Please remember to call us once you arrive. 일단 도착하면 우리한테 전화하는 거 기억해.
   B OK, I'll _____ that _____. 알았어, 명심할게.
   (A) cannot, too (B) bear, in mind (C) learn, by heart (D) take, by surprise

B. Fill in the blanks.

> learn, by heart   cannot, too   take, by surprise   take, for granted
> bear, in mind   be likely to   be exposed to
> be supposed to   be subject to   be about to

1. It is good to _____ different cultures. 다양한 문화들에 노출되는 것이 좋다.

2. Eric should not _____ this great opportunity _____.
   Eric은 이렇게 멋진 기회를 당연하게 여겨서는 안 된다.

3. The sudden announcement _____ all of us _____.
   갑작스런 발표에 우리 모두는 깜짝 놀랐다.

4. You'll _____ penalty if you return the book late.
   책을 늦게 반납하면 벌금을 물게 됩니다.

5. You should always double-check the answers because you _____
   be _____ careful. 아무리 주의해도 지나치지 않으니까 정답을 항상 재확인해야 해.

Answers A 1.A 2.C 3.A 4.B
B 1. be exposed to 2. take, for granted 3. took, by surprise 4. be subject to
5. cannot, too

50

C. Complete the conversations using the sentences given.

1 A _____

   B I guess they didn't call to let you know about the visit.
      방문하신다고 전화로 알려 주지 않으셨구나.

2 A How can you make this plant grow faster? 이 화초를 어떻게 더 빨리 자라게 만들 수 있나요?

   B _____

3 A Why are you moving so slowly? 왜 그렇게 천천히 움직여?

   B _____

4 A Did you start cleaning the house? 집을 청소하기 시작한 거야?

   B _____

(A) You cannot be too careful when you're walking on ice.
(B) My parents took me by surprise.
(C) I was about to do just that.
(D) Let it be exposed to sunlight at least two hours a day.

D. Speak or write.

1 Molly memorized everything about her favorite singer. How would you say about Molly? Molly는 좋아하는 가수에 관한 모든 것을 암기했다. Molly에 대해 어떻게 말할까?

2 There is a great chance that Peter would get the job. How would you say this to Peter? Peter에게 직장을 구할 좋은 기회가 생겼다. Peter에게 그것을 어떻게 말할까?

3 You expected William to come home early. How would you say this to William? 당신은 William이 집에 일찍 올 것으로 예상했다. William에게 이것을 어떻게 말할까?

4 The weather can change unexpectedly. How would you say this?
날씨가 예기치 않게 바뀔 수 있다. 이것을 어떻게 말할까?

(A) The weather is subject to unexpected change.
(B) She learned everything about her favorite singer by heart.
(C) You'll be likely to get the job.
(D) You were supposed to come home early.

C 1. B 2. D 3. A 4. C
D 1. B 2. C 3. D 4. A

101 A **Do you *know* that Erica got into an accident?**
   Erica가 사고 당한 것 알고 있니?

B **Yeah, I am aware of it.**
   그래, 알고 있어.

be aware of   ~을 알고 있다

102 A **The new novel is *very popular*.**
   새 소설이 인기가 아주 많아.

B **Yes, it is much sought after.**
   그래, 수요가 많아.

be (much) sought after   수요인기가가 많다

103 A **I am through with helping Cindy.**
   Cindy를 도와주는 일 그만할래.

B **Yeah, you should *be tired of* it.**
   그래, 너도 지쳤을 거야.

be through with   끝내다, 그만두다

104 A **Do you think Greg *could do* it?**
   Greg가 그것을 할 수 있을 것 같아?

B **Yes, he is capable of doing his homework.**
   그럼, 그는 숙제를 할 능력이 있어.

be capable of   ~할 수 있다, 능력이 있다

105 A **Is Emily on good terms with Susan?**
   Emily는 Susan과 사이가 좋니?

B **No, they hate each other.**
   아니, 서로 싫어해.

be on good terms with   ~와 사이가 좋다

106

A Our team *finally* won a game.
우리 팀이 드디어 경기에서 이겼어.

B It was bound to happen. The team can't lose forever.
그럴 줄 알았어. 늘 지기만 하란 법은 없거든.

be bound to 반드시 ~하다, ~하게 마련이다

107

A Should I get the DVD?
그 DVD를 사야 할까?

B Yeah, it is worth buying.
그래, 살 만한 가치가 있지.

be worth -ing ~할 만한 가치가 있다

108

A Do you really wake up at 5 a.m. every day?
정말 매일 아침 5시에 깨어나니?

B Yeah, I am used to waking up early.
그래, 나는 일찍 깨어나는 데 익숙해.

be used to -ing ~하는 데 익숙하다

109

A I *couldn't* sleep last night.
어젯밤에 잠을 못 잤어.

B Me, too. I had a hard time sleeping.
나도 그랬어. 잠자느라 애를 먹었어.

have a hard time -ing ~하느라 애를 먹다

110

A Our boss made a point of working hard.
우리 사장님은 열심히 일할 것을 강조했어.

B I knew that he would *stress* that.
그분이 그 점을 강조하곤 하는 것을 알고 있었어.

make a point of -ing ~할 것을 강조하다

A. Choose the right answer.

1   **A** Bob received the highest award. Bob이 최고상을 받았어.

   B He _____ get it because he tried so hard.
   그렇게 열심히 노력했으니까 받을 줄 알았어..

   (A) was bound to   (B) was through with
   (C) was aware of   (D) was capable of

2   **A** This singer _____ these days. 이 가수는 요즘 인기가 많아.

   B I know. All of his concerts are sold out. 알아. 그의 모든 콘서트가 전부 매진이야.

   (A) is capable of   (B) is bound to   (C) is sought after   (D) is through with

3   **A** Do you think I should buy the stock? 그 주식을 사야 할까?

   B Yeah, it _____ investing. 그럼. 투자할 만한 가치가 있지.

   (A) has a hard time   (B) makes a point of   (C) is worth   (D) is used to

4   **A** I can't stand the noise. 저 시끄러운 소리를 견딜 수가 없어.

   B Me, too. I _____ concentrating. 나도 그래. 집중하기가 힘들어.

   (A) am worth   (B) am used to   (C) make a point of   (D) have a hard time

B. Fill in the blanks.

| be aware of   be sought after   be through with   be capable of |
| be on good terms with   be bound to   be worth |
| be used to   have a hard time   make a point of |

1   The talented artist _____ making great things.
   그 재능 있는 예술가는 위대한 것들을 만들어 낼 수 있다.

2   I _____ walking because I don't have a car.
   나는 차가 없기 때문에 걸어 다니는 데 익숙하다.

3   Our teacher always _____ studying hard.
   우리 선생님은 항상 열심히 공부할 것을 강조하셨다.

4   Mike is late again. I _____ waiting for him.
   Mike가 또 늦는다. 나는 그를 기다리는 걸 그만두겠다.

5   I'm happy that I _____ my family. 나는 가족과 사이가 좋아서 행복하다.

C. Complete the conversations using the sentences given.

1 **A** Are you getting along with your roommate? 룸메이트와는 잘 지내니?

    B _____

2 **A** Isn't it difficult to stand all day long? 하루 종일 서 있기가 어렵지 않나요?

    B _____

3 **A** What did your father say? 아버지가 뭐라고 하셨니?

    B _____

4 **A** Are you finished with your homework? 숙제 끝냈니?

    B _____

> (A) Yes, I am finally through with it.
> (B) Yeah, I'm on good terms with him.
> (C) Not really, I'm used to standing.
> (D) He made a point of telling the truth.

D. Speak or write.

1 You already know that Rob lied to you. How do you say this to Rob?
당신은 Rob이 당신에게 거짓말한 것을 이미 알고 있다. Rob에게 이것을 어떻게 말할까?

2 You are sure that Frank is going to get the job. How do you say this to Frank? 당신은 Frank가 취직할 것이라고 확신한다. Frank에게 이것을 어떻게 말할까?

3 The newly designed Sonata is very much in demand. How do you say this? 새 디자인의 소나타는 수요가 아주 많다. 이것을 어떻게 말할까?

4 You have difficulty walking because you hurt your ankle. How do you say this? 당신은 발목을 다쳐서 걷기가 어렵다. 이것을 어떻게 말할까?

> (A) The newly designed Sonata is much sought after.
> (B) I have a hard time walking because I hurt my ankle.
> (C) I am aware of your lie.
> (D) You are bound to get the job.

C 1. B 2. C 3. D 4. A
D 1. C 2. D 3. A 4. B

111　A　**Should I *always* have breakfast before I leave to work?**
항상 출근하기 전에 아침을 먹어야 할까?

　　B　**Of course, you should never start a day without eating something.**　물론이지, 하루를 시작하려면 반드시 뭘 먹어야 해.

never A without -ing　　A하면 반드시 ~하다

112　A　**The noise is really *bothering* me.**
저 시끄러운 소리가 정말 거슬린다.

　　B　**Me, too. It keeps me from studying.**
나도 그래. 저 소리 때문에 공부를 할 수가 없어.

keep A from -ing　　A가 ~하지 못하게 하다

113　A　**Are you done with your project?**
프로젝트 다 끝냈니?

　　B　***Not even close.* I'm far from finishing it.**
어림없어. 끝내려면 멀었어.

far from -ing　　전혀 ~ 아닌

114　A　**Are you *still* thinking about the game?**
아직도 그 경기에 대해 생각하고 있니?

　　B　**Yeah, I cannot help thinking about it.**
그래, 생각하지 않을 수가 없어.

cannot help -ing　　~하지 않을 수 없다

115　A　**Frankly speaking, I don't like it.**
솔직히 말해 나는 그게 싫어.

　　B　**I'm glad you're being *honest*.**
나는 네가 정직해서 기뻐.

frankly speaking　　솔직히 말해서

116
A **Who *caused* the accident?**
누가 사고를 낸 거야?

B **Susan is responsible for it.**
그건 Susan의 책임이야.

be responsible for   ~에 책임이 있다

117
A **Where did you find your keys?**
열쇠는 어디에서 찾았니?

B **I came across them under the table.**
탁자 밑에서 우연히 찾았어.

come across   우연히 만나다, 발견하다

118
A **Are you *close with* your roommate?**
룸메이트와 친하니?

B **Yeah, we get along great.**
그래, 우리는 아주 잘 지내.

get along (with)   (~와) 사이좋게 지내다

119
A **You *resemble* your father a lot.**
너는 아버지를 많이 닮았어.

B **Yeah, everyone says that I took after him.**
그래, 모두 내가 아버지를 닮았다고 말해.

take after   ~을 닮다

120
A **How did you *save* so much money?**
어떻게 그렇게 많은 돈을 모으셨나요?

B **I put aside extra cash whenever I could.**
가능할 때마다 남는 현금을 챙겨 두었어요.

put aside   제쳐 놓다, 따로 떼어 두다 (= lay aside)

A. Choose the right answer.

1 **A** How did you find this wonderful apartment? 이렇게 멋진 아파트를 어떻게 구했니?
   B I _____ it by accident. 우연히 발견했어.

   (A) got along   (B) came across   (C) took after   (D) put aside

2 **A** Did you solve the problem? 그 문제를 풀었니?
   B No, I _____ getting the answer. 아니, 정답을 구하려면 멀었어.

   (A) am far from   (B) put aside   (C) cannot help   (D) take after

3 **A** Who _____ cleaning up the room? 방 청소 하는 게 누구 책임이었니?
   B Jane should have done it. Jane이 했어야 해요.

   (A) came across   (B) took after   (C) put aside   (D) was responsible for

4 **A** Who did you _____? 너는 누구를 닮았니?
   B People tell me I look a lot like my mother. 사람들 말로는 내가 엄마를 많이 닮았대요.

   (A) get along with   (B) come across   (C) take after   (D) are responsible for

B. Fill in the blanks.

> never, without   keep, from   far from   cannot help   frankly speaking
> be responsible for   come across   get along with   take after   put aside

1 _____, you're wrong. 솔직히 말해 네가 잘못한 거야.

2 My parents _____ money for an emergency.
   우리 부모님은 비상시에 대비해 돈을 저축하신다.

3 I _____ leave _____ checking the door.
   나는 외출할 때는 반드시 문을 점검한다.

4 Ron didn't _____ his sister. Ron은 누이와 사이가 좋지 않았다.

5 The music _____ me _____ sleeping. 음악 때문에 잠을 잘 수가 없다.

C. Complete the conversations using the sentences given.

1 **A** _____

  B Of course, we're best friends. 물론, 우리는 가장 친한 친구들이야.

2 **A** Do you check your e-mail regularly? 이메일을 정기적으로 확인하니?

  B _____

3 **A** How come you have radio on? 왜 라디오를 켜 놓았니?

  B _____

4 **A** _____

  B Thank you for your honesty. 정직하게 말해 줘서 고마워.

(A) Frankly speaking, I think the dress is too tight for you.
(B) It keeps me from falling asleep.
(C) I never go to bed without checking my e-mail.
(D) You seem to get along with Vince very well.

D. Speak or write.

1 You're not close to completing your homework. How would you say this?
당신이 숙제를 마치려면 아직 멀었다. 이것을 어떻게 말할까?

2 Sean cannot stop playing video games. How would you say this about Sean? Sean은 비디오 게임을 그만둘 수가 없다. Sean에 대해 이것을 어떻게 말할까?

3 You met your old friend the other day. How would you say this?
당신은 며칠 전에 옛 친구를 만났다. 이것을 어떻게 말할까?

4 John made his team lose the game. How would you say this about John?
John 때문에 그의 팀이 경기에 졌다. John에 대해 이것을 어떻게 말할까?

(A) He cannot help playing video games.
(B) I'm far from completing my homework.
(C) He is responsible for his team losing the game.
(D) I came across my old friend the other day.

---

c 1. D   2. C   3. B   4. A
D 1. B   2. A   3. D   4. C

121   A   **You didn't *throw away* that old sofa.**
그 낡은 소파를 버리지 않았구나.

      B   **Yeah, I can't seem to do away with it.**
그래, 없애지를 못할 것 같아.

do away with   ~을 없애다

122   A   **Did the police *catch* all the suspects?**
경찰이 용의자들을 모두 잡았니?

      B   **No, two of them got away.**
아니, 그들 중의 두 명은 도주했어.

get away   달아나다, 떠나다

123   A   **Why did you *leave* the hammer *outside*?**
망치를 왜 바깥에 두었니?

      B   **I wanted to keep it away from my sons.**
그것을 아들들한테서 멀리 떨어뜨려 놓으려고 한 거야.

keep away from   가까이하지 않다, 멀리하다

124   A   **Parking spaces are hard to come by around here.**
이 주변에서는 주차 공간을 찾기가 힘들어.

      B   **Yeah, I had a hard time *finding* one.**
그래, 나도 찾기 힘들었어.

come by   얻다, 방문하다

125   A   **The ending was so sad that I *nearly* cry.**
결말이 무척 슬퍼서 울 뻔했어.

      B   **I came close to crying myself.**
나도 하마터면 울 뻔했어.

come close to   하마터면 ~할 뻔하다

126

A **I can't seem to *finish* the report.**
리포트를 끝내지 못할 것 같아.

B **Try harder and have done with it.**
더 열심히 노력해서 끝내.

have done with   끝내다, 마무리하다

127

A **How come you *don't like* Peter?**
Peter를 왜 좋아하지 않니?

B **Well, I look down upon lazy people.**
글쎄, 나는 게으른 사람들을 경멸해.

look down upon[on]   ~을 업신여기다, 얕보다

128

A **Helen *rejected* the job offer.**
Helen이 그 취업 제안을 거절했어.

B **I can't believe she turned it down.**
그녀가 그것을 거절했다니 믿을 수가 없어.

turn down   거절하다, (음량 · 온도를) 낮추다

129

A **You need to *explain* what happened.**
무슨 일이 있었는지 설명해 봐.

B **I'm sorry, but I can't account for the accident.**
미안하지만 나는 그 사고를 설명할 수 없어.

account for   ~을 설명[해명]하다, (비율을) 차지하다

130

A **I'm *responsible for* the mistake.**
그 실수는 제 책임입니다.

B **It's good that you answered for your action.**
당신이 자신의 행동에 책임진다니 좋습니다.

answer for   ~에 대해 책임지다, 보증하다

A. Choose the right answer.

1 **A** Why don't you _____ tomorrow? 내일 들르지 않을래?
   B Sure, what time should I be there? 좋아, 몇 시에 그곳에 갈까?

   (A) answer for   (B) come close to (C) come by   (D) do away with

2 **A** Sam, the radio is too loud. Sam, 라디오 소리가 너무 커.
   B I'll _____ the volume. 소리를 줄일게.

   (A) get away   (B) turn down   (C) look down on (D) account for

3 **A** _____ cleaning the room quickly. 방 청소를 빨리 끝내.
   B OK, I'll try to finish it as soon as possible. 알았어요, 가능한 한 빨리 끝내도록 할게요.

   (A) Come by   (B) Answer for   (C) Account for   (D) Have done with

4 **A** Can you explain why $10 is missing? 10달러가 빠진 이유를 설명할 수 있니?
   B I'm sorry, but I can't _____ it. 죄송하지만 설명할 수 없어요.

   (A) look down on (B) account for   (C) get away   (D) keep away from

B. Fill in the blanks.

do away with	get away	keep away from	come by	come close to
have done with	look down on	turn down	account for	answer for

1 Peter really _____ winning the race. Peter는 정말 경주에서 이길 뻔했다.

2 It is not nice to _____ poor people. 가난한 사람들을 업신여기는 것은 좋지 않다.

3 Dangerous chemicals need to be _____ children.
   위험한 화학 약품들은 아이들의 손이 닿지 않는 곳에 두어야 한다.

4 I would love to _____ to somewhere warm. 어디론가 따뜻한 곳으로 떠나고 싶다.

5 It was good of you to _____ your mistake. 자신의 실수에 책임지다니 좋은 분이군요.

C. Complete the conversations using the sentences given.

1 **A** _____

   B Yeah, we almost had a terrible accident. 그래, 우리는 끔찍한 사고를 당할 뻔했어.

2 **A** I admit that what I did was illegal. 내가 했던 게 불법이었다고 인정해요.

   B _____

3 **A** I'm going to win my tennis match easily. 테니스 시합을 쉽게 이길 거야.

   B _____

4 **A** I'm going outside to play, mom. 엄마, 바깥에 나가서 놀게요.

   B _____

> (A) You shouldn't look down upon your opponent.
> (B) Keep away from trouble, John.
> (C) I came close to hitting the tree.
> (D) I'm glad that you answered for your crime.

D. Speak or write.

1 People want to get rid of different types of taxes. How do you say this?
   사람들은 여러 종류의 세금을 없애기를 원한다. 이것을 어떻게 말할까?

2 It is very difficult to get a good job. How would you say this?
   좋은 직장을 구하기는 매우 어렵다. 이것을 어떻게 말할까?

3 Ellen rejected Jack's invitation to his party. How would say this about
   Ellen? Ellen은 Jack의 파티 초대를 거절했다. Ellen에 대해 이것을 어떻게 말할까?

4 You needed to give a reason for your absence. How do you say this?
   당신은 결석한 것에 대한 이유를 말해야 했다. 이것을 어떻게 말할까?

> (A) A good job is hard to come by.
> (B) People want to do away with different types of taxes.
> (C) I had to account for my absence.
> (D) She turned down Jack's invitation to his party.

131

A **Care for some tea?**
차 좀 드시겠어요?

B **Oh, yes. I *like to* have it.**
아, 그래요. 한잔 주세요.

care for   ~을 돌보다, 좋아하다

132

A **Can you *bring* James here?**
James를 여기로 데려올 수 있니?

B **I already asked Susan to send for him.**
이미 Susan한테 그를 불러오라고 부탁했어.

send for   ~을 데리러 보내다, 불러오다

133

A **Are you *excited* about the picnic?**
피크닉 가니까 흥분되니?

B **Yes, I'm really looking forward to it.**
그럼, 정말 고대하고 있어.

look forward to   ~을 손꼽아 기다리다, 고대하다

134

A **Thanks for *taking* my *side*.**
내 편 들어 줘서 고마워.

B **Not a problem, I'll always stand up for my friends.**
별말을. 나야 언제나 내 친구 편이지.

stand up for   ~의 편을 들다, 옹호하다

135

A **Eric is studying *really hard*.**
Eric이 정말 열심히 공부하고 있어.

B **He is trying to make up for lost time.**
낭비한 시간을 보충하려고 노력하는 거야.

make up for   ~을 보충하다, 보상하다

136

A **You should *stop*.**
그만 먹지.

B **It's hard to refrain from eating this delicious cake.**
이렇게 맛있는 케이크를 먹는 것은 그만두기 힘들어.

refrain from   그만두다, 삼가다

137

A **Is Dongsoo *sick*?**
동수가 아파?

B **Yeah, he suffers from flu.**
그래, 감기에 걸려 있어.

suffer from   고통을 겪다, 병에 걸리다

138

A **Did someone visit you?**
누가 찾아왔었니?

B **Sam dropped in for an hour.**
Sam이 들러서 한 시간 동안 있었어.

drop in   ~에 잠깐 들르다(= drop by)

139

A **Who *loses* when you guys have an argument?**
두 사람이 싸우면 누가 져?

B **I usually give in to my wife.**
보통 내가 아내한테 지지.

give in   항복하다, 굴복하다

140

A **Did you hand in your report yet?**
리포트 벌써 냈니?

B **No, I'm going to *give* it to the teacher later.**
아니, 나중에 선생님한테 낼 거야.

hand in   제출하다

A. Choose the right answer.

1 **A** Why are you going back to the classroom? 왜 교실에 돌아가는 거야?

   B I forgot to _____ my homework. 숙제 내는 것을 잊어버렸어.

   (A) make up for   (B) give in   (C) hand in   (D) send for

2 **A** Please _____ talking in the library. 도서관 안에서는 대화를 삼가 주세요.

   B OK, I'll be quiet. 네, 조용히 할게요.

   (A) suffer from   (B) stand up for   (C) look forward to   (D) refrain from

3 **A** I thought your parents didn't want you to go to the party.

   너희 부모님이 네가 파티에 가는 걸 원하지 않으실 줄 알았는데.

   B They _____ and agreed to let me go. 부모님이 양보하시고 가도 좋다고 하셨어.

   (A) gave in   (B) dropped in   (C) refrained from   (D) made up for

4 **A** Why are you working on Saturday? 왜 토요일에 일하나요?

   B I missed work on Tuesday, and I have to _____ it.

   화요일에 일을 안 해서 보충해야 돼요.

   (A) stand up for   (B) make up for   (C) care for   (D) send for

B. Fill in the blanks.

| care for | send for | look forward to | stand up for | make up for |
| refrain from | suffer from | drop in | give in | hand in |

1 I need to stay home and _____ my little sister. 집에 있으면서 여동생을 돌봐야 돼.

2 The workers _____ their rights and went on a strike.

   노동자들은 자신의 권리를 옹호하며 파업에 들어갔다.

3 My grandfather felt sick, so we had to _____ a doctor.

   할아버지가 아프셔서 우리는 의사 선생님을 불러와야 했다.

4 It was nice of you to _____ and see my sick mother.

   아프신 어머니를 뵈러 찾아와 주시니 감사합니다.

5 Unfortunately, Mr. Adams _____ a rare disease.

   불행히도, Adams 씨는 희귀병을 앓고 있습니다.

Answers   **A** 1. C   2. D   3. A   4. B

            B 1. care for   2. stood up for   3. send for   4. drop in   5. suffers from

C. Complete the conversations using the sentences given.

1 **A** Are you guys still arguing? 너희들은 아직도 다투고 있니?

   B _____

2 **A** Why are you guys protesting? 당신들은 왜 항의하는 겁니까?

   B _____

3 **A** Why did Mike buy a present for Tanya? Mike는 왜 Tanya에게 선물을 사 줬니?

   B _____

4 **A** _____

   B OK, I'll turn it off before I go into the meeting. 네, 회의에 들어가기 전에 끄겠습니다.

   > (A) Please refrain from using your cell phone during the meeting.
   > (B) Yeah, I'm not going to give in to Tom's demand.
   > (C) He wanted to make up for forgetting her birthday.
   > (D) We are standing up for what is right.

D. Speak or write.

1 You can't wait to see your family. How do you say your feeling?
   당신은 가족을 얼른 만나고 싶어 한다. 당신의 느낌을 어떻게 말할까?

2 You told Frank to bring his brother. How would you say this?
   당신은 Frank에게 형을 데려오라고 말했다. 이것을 어떻게 말할까?

3 Many people get motion sickness on a moving boat. How do you say this?
   많은 사람들이 움직이는 배 위에서 멀미를 한다. 이것을 어떻게 말할까?

4 You want Peter to visit you sometime. How would you say this to Peter?
   당신은 Peter가 언제 한 번 찾아와 주기를 바란다. Peter에게 이것을 어떻게 말할까?

   > (A) I told him to send for his brother.
   > (B) Why don't you drop in sometime?
   > (C) I'm looking forward to seeing my family.
   > (D) Many people suffer from motion sickness on a moving boat.

C 1. B 2. D 3. C 4. A
D 1. C 2. A 3. D 4. B

141

A **Peter persists in going to the park.**
Peter가 공원에 가겠다고 고집을 부리고 있어.

B **If he *wants* to, he *will not change* his mind.**
그가 가고 싶다면 생각을 바꾸지 않을 거야.

persist in   고집하다, 우기다

142

A **Do you *still talk to* your high school friends?**
고등학교 친구들하고 여전히 연락하니?

B **Yeah, I keep in touch with them.**
그래, 그들과 계속 연락하고 지내.

keep in touch with   ~와 연락을 계속하다

143

A **I saw you *start* talking to Peter.**
네가 Peter랑 대화하기 시작하는 것을 봤어.

B **Yes, I entered into a long conversation with him.**
그래, 그와 한참 대화를 나누게 되었어.

enter into   시작하다, ~에 들어가다, 빠져들다

144

A **Did you *consider* his age?**
그의 나이를 고려한 거야?

B **Yes, I did take into account that he is only 20 years old.**
그럼, 그가 겨우 20세라는 것을 분명히 감안했어.

take into account   고려하다, 감안하다

145

A ***How many* people are *in* your study group?**
너희 스터디 그룹에는 몇 사람이 있니?

B **It consists of two boys and three girls.**
남자 둘과 여자 셋으로 이루어져 있어.

consist of   ~으로 이루어지다

146

A **The concert has been *cancelled*.**
콘서트가 취소되었어.

B **I can't believe that it was called off.**
취소되었다는 걸 믿을 수가 없어.

call off 취소하다, 중지하다

147

A **I *hate* it when people *walk on* my lawn.**
사람들이 내 잔디밭을 밟고 다니는 게 정말 싫어.

B **You should put up a sign to keep off the grass.**
잔디밭에 들어가지 말라는 표지판을 세워야 해.

keep off 멀리하다, 피하다, 막다

148

A **The meeting has been put off until next week.**
모임이 다음 주로 연기되었어.

B **Again! It has been *postponed* twice already.**
또! 벌써 두 차례나 연기되었는데.

put off 연기하다, 미루다

149

A **Did your brother *leave for* a vacation?**
오빠는 휴가 떠났니?

B **Yeah, he set off for Los Angeles yesterday.**
그래, 어제 LA로 떠났어.

set off 출발하다, (폭탄을) 터뜨리다, (경보를) 울리다

150

A **Steve *boasted* about how rich he is.**
Steve가 자기가 얼마나 부자인지 뽐내더라.

B **Yeah, he likes to show off his wealth.**
그래, 그는 돈 자랑하기 좋아해.

show off 과시하다, 자랑하다

A. Choose the right answer.

1 **A** When was the party cancelled? 파티가 언제 취소됐니?
   B It was _____ last night. 어젯밤에 취소됐어.
   (A) persisted in   (B) put off   (C) called off   (D) kept off

2 **A** Be sure to _____ us! 꼭 우리랑 연락하고 지내!
   B Don't worry. I'll call you guys often. 걱정하지 마. 자주 전화할게.
   (A) call off   (B) keep in touch with   (C) enter into   (D) take into account

3 **A** Greg likes to _____ his car. Greg는 자기 차를 자랑하기를 좋아해.
   B Well, I would do it too if I have a new car. 음, 나도 새 차가 있으면 그렇게 할 거야.
   (A) consist of   (B) enter into   (C) show off   (D) set off

4 **A** Tom, don't _____ your homework. Tom, 숙제를 미루지 마라.
   B OK, I'll do it right now. 네, 지금 당장 할게요.
   (A) keep off   (B) set off   (C) call off   (D) put off

B. Fill in the blanks.

| persist in | keep in touch with | enter into | take into account | consist of |
| call off | keep off | put off | set off | show off |

1 Sandy _____ paying for the dinner. Sandy는 저녁을 사겠다고 고집했다.

2 By signing the document, you'll _____ a contract.
   이 서류에 서명하시면 계약이 시작됩니다.

3 My teacher _____ that I was sick for a few days.
   우리 선생님은 내가 며칠 동안 아팠던 것을 감안해 주셨다.

4 The movie _____ three central characters.
   그 영화는 중심 인물이 3명으로 이루어져 있다.

5 Bobby _____ for his house an hour ago. Bobby는 1시간 전에 자신의 집으로 출발했다.

Answers A 1. C 2. B 3. C 4. D
B 1. persisted in 2. enter into 3. took into account 4. consists of 5. set off

C. Complete the conversations using the sentences given.

1 **A** _____

   B Yes, I did take into consideration. 네, 분명히 고려했습니다.

2 **A** What's in the dish? 이 요리에는 뭐가 들어가 있니?

   B _____

3 **A** I heard a bomb went off. 폭탄이 터지는 소리를 들었어.

   B _____

4 **A** How did the meeting go? 회의는 어떻게 됐나요?

   B _____

(A) We finally entered into an agreement.
(B) Yeah, it was set off by an accident.
(C) It consists of meat and vegetables.
(D) Did you take into account that this is Harry's first job?

D. Speak or write.

1 Your aunt insisted that she buy you dinner. How would you say it?
   이모가 당신에게 저녁을 사 주겠다고 고집하셨다. 그것을 어떻게 말할까?

2 You closed the window to prevent the rain from coming in. How would you say it? 당신은 비가 들어오지 못하게 하려고 창문을 닫았다. 그것을 어떻게 말할까?

3 You want Molly not to delay cleaning her room. How do you say it to Molly? 당신은 Molly가 자기 방 청소를 미루지 않기를 원한다. Molly에게 그것을 어떻게 말할까?

4 Tom wants to communicate with Eric. How do you say this?
   Tom은 Eric과 연락을 주고받기를 원한다. 이것을 어떻게 말할까?

(A) You should not put off cleaning your room.
(B) She persisted in buying me dinner.
(C) He wants to keep in touch with Eric.
(D) I closed the window to keep off the rain.

---

c 1. D 2. C 3. B 4. A
D 1. B 2. D 3. A 4. C

151
A **When will your plane take off?**
네가 탈 비행기가 언제 출발하니?

B **It is supposed to *depart* in three hours.**
3시간 후에 출발할 예정이야.

take off   벗다, 이륙하다, 떠나다

152
A **Did everyone *continue* to work on the project?**
모든 사람이 그 프로젝트에 계속 참여했니?

B **No, only Nancy carried on until it was completed.**
아니, Nancy 혼자만 프로젝트가 완료될 때까지 계속했어.

carry on   계속하다

153
A **Can you *trust* Mike?**
Mike를 신뢰할 수 있니?

B **I can count on him for anything.**
그는 무슨 일이 있어도 믿을 수 있어.

count on   믿다, 기대하다 (= rely on)

154
A **Why is the train arriving late?**
열차가 왜 늦게 도착하는 거지?

B **It's due to the fog.**
안개 때문이야.

due to   ~ 때문에

155
A **Why did you *keep* wearing that shirt?**
왜 그 셔츠를 계속 입었던 거니?

B **I had to because my mother insisted on it.**
엄마가 그 옷을 강요해서 입을 수밖에 없었어.

insist on[upon]   강요하다, 고집하다

156

A **Are you going to *keep* your old computer?**
쓰던 컴퓨터는 계속 갖고 있을 거니?

B **Yeah, I think I'll hold onto it.**
그래, 계속 갖고 있을 생각이야.

hold onto 쥐고 있다, 계속 유지하다

157

A **Do you want us to *continue*?**
우리가 계속하길 원하시나요?

B **Please go on with your work.**
하던 일을 계속해 줘요.

go on with 계속하다

158

A **I hope that your business is *getting better*.**
하시는 일이 더 잘되길 바랍니다.

B **Yes, things are looking up.**
네, 상황이 나아지고 있어요.

look up (사전에서) 찾다, (상황이) 나아지다

159

A **Do you think Tom *could do* it?**
Tom이 그 일을 할 수 있을 것 같아?

B **Yes, he could carry out the task.**
그래, Tom은 그 과제를 해낼 수 있을 거야.

carry out 실행하다, 완수하다

160

A **Did you *solve* the problem?**
그 문제를 풀었니?

B **Yeah, I finally figured it out.**
그래, 드디어 알아냈어.

figure out 이해하다, 계산하다

A. Choose the right answer.

1   **A** I can't _____ this. 이걸 계속할 수 없어.
   B Let's rest a little before we continue. 잠깐 쉬었다가 계속하자.
   (A) take off   (B) hold on to   (C) insist on   (D) go on with

2   **A** Did Mark finish the race? Mark가 경주를 끝까지 했나요?
   B Yes, he _____ despite his pain. 네, 통증에도 불구하고 계속했어요.
   (A) carried out   (B) looked up   (C) carried on   (D) took off

3   **A** I can't seem to solve this question. 이 문제는 못 풀 것 같은데.
   B Jason could help you _____ the answer.
      Jason이 답을 알아내는 걸 도와줄 수 있을 거야.
   (A) look up   (B) insist on   (C) hold onto   (D) figure out

4   **A** It's so hot in here. 이 안은 무척 덥다.
   B You should _____ your jacket. 재킷을 벗어야 해.
   (A) take off   (B) carry on   (C) figure out   (D) hold on to

B. Fill in the blanks.

take off	carry on	count on	due to	insist on
hold onto	go on with	look up	carry out	figure out

1   The team _____ its early lead and won the game.
   그 팀은 일찌감치 계속 앞서 나가다가 경기에서 승리했다.

2   Bart can't ski _____ his ankle injury. Bart는 발목 부상 때문에 스키를 탈 수 없다.

3   My grandmother _____ paying for my bus ticket.
   할머니가 내 버스 요금을 내 주시겠다고 고집하셨다.

4   I had to _____ the dictionary several times. 나는 사전을 몇 번 찾아보아야 했다.

5   The players _____ the game plan perfectly. 선수들은 작전을 완벽하게 실행했다.

Answers   **A** 1. D   2. C   3. D   4. A
        B 1. held onto   2. due to   3. insisted on   4. look up   5. carried out

C. Complete the conversations using the sentences given.

1 **A** _____

    B I hope snow would stop tomorrow. 내일은 눈이 그치면 좋겠어요.

2 **A** Why are you wearing that coat? 왜 그 코트를 입고 있니?

    B _____

3 **A** Martha won't be coming today. Martha는 오늘 오지 않을 거야.

    B _____

4 **A** Did Will say goodbye to you? Will이 네게 작별 인사는 했니?

    B _____

> (A) No, he took off without saying a word.
> (B) Today's class is cancelled due to the snowstorm.
> (C) I guess we should carry on without her.
> (D) My mother insisted on it.

D. Speak or write.

1 You want Cindy to keep her old computer. How do you say it to her?
당신은 Cindy가 옛날 컴퓨터를 계속 갖고 있기를 원한다. 그녀에게 그것을 어떻게 말할까?

2 Your grandfather's conditions are improving. How would you say this?
당신의 할아버지의 상태가 호전되고 있다. 이것을 어떻게 말할까?

3 You expect Mike to score a goal. How do you say this?
당신은 Mike가 한 골을 넣을 것이라고 기대한다. 이것을 어떻게 말할까?

4 Tim can't continue to maintain a negative attitude. How do you say this to Tim? Tim이 부정적인 태도를 계속 유지할 수는 없다. Tim에게 이것을 어떻게 말할까?

> (A) I count on him to score a goal.
> (B) You can't go on with a negative attitude.
> (C) His conditions are looking up.
> (D) You should hold onto your old computer.

C 1. B   2. D   3. C   4. A
D 1. D   2. C   3. A   4. B

161 A **Did you leave out anything?**
     뭔가 빠뜨리지 않았니?

     B **No, I *packed* everything we need.**
     아니, 우리한테 필요한 것은 모두 챙겼어.

leave out   빼다, 생략하다

162 A **Did you *understand* today's class?**
     오늘 수업 내용 모두 이해했니?

     B **No, I couldn't make out what the teacher said.**
     아니, 선생님이 말씀하신 게 이해가 안 돼.

make out   이해하다

163 A **What did Mr. Angelo *mention*?**
     Angelo 씨가 뭐라고 말했니?

     B **He pointed out a couple of mistakes.**
     두 가지 실수를 지적했어.

point out   지시하다, 지적하다

164 A ***How did* the meeting *go*?**
     회의는 어떻게 됐니?

     B **Everything turned out to be just fine.**
     모두가 잘 진행됐어.

turn out   되어 가다, ~으로 밝혀지다

165 A **Did you *take care of* the problem?**
     네가 그 문제를 처리했니?

     B **Yeah, it worked out.**
     그래, 잘 해결됐어.

work out   잘 풀리다, 운동하다

166　A　**Did you look over David's proposal?**
David가 낸 제안서 검토해 보셨나요?

　　B　**Yes, I *read* it this morning.**
네, 오늘 아침에 읽었어요.

look over　훑어보다, 검토하다

167　A　**Who is going to *run* the store after Mr. Dobson retires?**
Dobson 씨가 은퇴하면 누가 가게를 운영하는 거야?

　　B　**I heard his son is going to take over the store.**
그의 아들이 가게를 물려받을 거래.

take over　인수하다

168　A　**Martin is *considering* quitting his job.**
Martin이 직장을 그만둘 것을 고려하고 있어.

　　B　**He should carefully think over what is best for him.**
그는 자신에게 무엇이 최선인지 신중하게 생각해야 해.

think over　심사숙고하다, 충분히 생각하다

169　A　**Who would you *turn to* if you lose your job?**
직장을 잃으면 누구에게 의지할 거야?

　　B　**No one. I have enough savings to fall back on.**
아무도 없어. 의지할 만큼 충분히 저축해 뒀어.

fall back on[upon]　～에 기대다, 의지하다

170　A　**Can you *tell* me *briefly* about the speech?**
그 연설에 대해 간단히 이야기해 줄 수 있니?

　　B　**OK, I'll try to sum up what the speaker said.**
알았어, 연사가 한 말을 요약해 볼게.

sum up　요약하다

A. Choose the right answer.

1 **A** I think I'm gaining weight. 체중이 늘고 있는 것 같아.
   B You should _____ three times a week. 일주일에 세 번은 운동해야 돼.

   (A) turn out   (B) leave out   (C) point out   (D) work out

2 **A** What does that sign say? 저 표지판에 뭐라고 적혀 있니?
   B I don't know. I can't _____ what it says. 몰라. 뭐라고 적혀 있는지 알 수가 없네.

   (A) leave out   (B) make out   (C) take over   (D) point out

3 **A** Did you tell everything to your father? 아버지께 모든 것을 말씀드렸니?
   B Yes, I didn't _____ anything. 그래. 아무것도 빠뜨리지 않았어.

   (A) think over   (B) work out   (C) leave out   (D) look over

4 **A** Was Nick's injury serious? Nick의 부상이 심각했니?
   B No, it _____ to be minor. 아니. 가벼운 부상이었어.

   (A) took over   (B) summed up   (C) turned out   (D) fell back on

B. Fill in the blanks.

> leave out   make out   point out   turn out   work out
> look over   take over   think over   fall back on   sum up

1 Who is going to _____ Mr. Johnson's position?
   누가 Johnson 씨의 자리를 물려받는 거야?

2 The coach _____ what the players should improve on.
   코치는 선수들이 개선해야 할 사항을 지적했다.

3 You need to _____ the contract before you sign it.
   계약서에 서명하기 전에 검토해야 한다.

4 David did a good job of _____ the story. David는 그 이야기를 잘 요약했다.

5 Poor Mrs. Harris didn't have anyone to _____ .
   가엾은 Harris 씨는 의지할 사람이 아무도 없었다.

C. Complete the conversations using the sentences given.

1 **A** Who is going to help you with your tuition? 네 수업료 마련을 누가 도와줄 거니?

    B _____

2 **A** Greg is going to quit the play. Greg는 그 연극에 불참할 거야.

    B _____

3 **A** Can you tell about the show? 그 쇼가 어땠는지 이야기해 줄래?

    B _____

4 **A** What did you think about my essay? 내 에세이 어땠니?

    B _____

> (A) I'm sorry, but I didn't have a chance to look it over.
> (B) I have my parents to fall back on.
> (C) Who is going to take over his role?
> (D) OK, I'll sum it up quickly.

D. Speak or write.

1 Ron should answer every question on the test. How would you say this to Ron? Ron은 시험지에 있는 모든 문제에 답해야 한다. Ron에게 이것을 어떻게 말할까?

2 You can't recognize who is coming toward you. How do you say this?
당신은 다가오는 사람이 누군지 분간할 수 없다. 이것을 어떻게 말할까?

3 You need time to consider your options. How do you say this?
당신은 선택 방안을 고려할 시간이 필요하다. 이것을 어떻게 말할까?

4 You hope that everything will be all right. How do you say this?
당신은 모든 일이 잘되기를 바란다. 이것을 어떻게 말할까?

> (A) I need time to think over my options.
> (B) I hope that everything will work out all right.
> (C) You should not leave out any question on the test.
> (D) I can't make out who is coming toward me.

c 1. B   2. C   3. D   4. A
D 1. C   2. D   3. A   4. B

171　A　**Do you think copying homework is *like* cheating?**
숙제를 베끼는 것이 부정행위 같은 거라고 생각하니?

　　B　**Yes, that amounts to cheating.**
그럼, 그건 부정행위나 마찬가지야.

amount to　　(합계가) ~에 이르다, ~와 마찬가지이다

172　A　**Sally knows a lot *about* cooking.**
Sally는 요리에 대해 아는 게 많아.

　　B　**Yeah, when it comes to cooking, she is the best.**
그래, 요리에 관한 한 그녀가 최고지.

when it comes to　　~에 관한 한, ~에 대해서라면

173　A　**I heard Tom *agreed to* drive Susan to the train station.**
Tom이 Susan을 기차역까지 데려다 주는 데 동의했대.

　　B　**Yeah, he gave way to her demand.**
그래, 그가 Susan의 요구에 굴복했어.

give way to　　~에게 지다, 양보하다

174　A　**What *caused* Bob to get fired?**
무엇 때문에 Bob이 해고당했니?

　　B　**His bad attitude led to it.**
그의 나쁜 태도가 그런 결과를 낳았어.

lead to　　~으로 이어지다, 유발하다

175　A　**Mary's father *wanted* her *to be* a doctor.**
Mary의 아버지는 그녀가 의사가 되기를 바라셨어.

　　B　**She certainly lived up to his expectation.**
그녀는 확실히 아버지의 기대에 부응했지.

live up to　　~에 맞게 살다, (기대·명성에) 부응하다

176

A Do you *respect* Mr. Adams?

Adams 씨를 존경하니?

B Of course, everyone looks up to him.

그럼, 모두가 그를 존경해.

look up to   우러러보다, 존경하다 (= respect)

177

A Sam is *against* going to the picnic.

Sam은 소풍 가는 것에 반대해.

B I didn't know he would object to it.

그가 소풍에 반대할 줄 몰랐어.

object to   ~에 반대하다

178

A Did you *think* about quitting?

그만두는 것에 대해 생각했니?

B No, it never occurred to me.

아니, 그런 생각은 한 번도 안 났어.

occur to   (생각이) ~에게 떠오르다

179

A Should I pay attention to the chart?

차트에 주목해야 할까요?

B Yes. It is important to *focus* on it.

그래요. 그것에 주목하는 것이 중요해요.

pay attention to   ~에 주목하다, 유의하다

180

A Do you exercise regularly?

규칙적으로 운동하니?

B I used to, but I don't these days.

예전에는 그렇게 했는데 요즘은 안 해.

used to   ~하곤 했다

A. Choose the right answer.

1 **A** Who do you respect? 너는 누구를 존경하니?
B I really _____ my parents. 우리 부모님을 정말 존경해.
(A) live up to   (B) look up to   (C) object to   (D) pay attention to

2 **A** Is everyone in favor of the plan? 모두가 그 계획에 찬성하니?
B No, Thomas _____ it. 아니, Thomas는 반대하고 있어.
(A) looks up to   (B) gives way to   (C) objects to   (D) does well to

3 **A** Danny has a lot of ideas about the project. Danny는 그 프로젝트에 관한 아이디어가 많아.
B Yeah, but his ideas don't _____ anything.
그래, 하지만 그의 아이디어는 아무것도 아니야.
(A) occur to   (B) amount to   (C) look up to   (D) live up to

4 **A** You need to _____ the teacher's instruction. 선생님의 지시에 주목해야 해.
B OK, I'll listen carefully. 알았어요, 주의해 들을게요.
(A) lead to   (B) live up to   (C) pay attention to   (D) give way to

B. Fill in the blanks.

| amount to | when it comes to | give way to | lead to | live up to |
| look up to | object to | occur to | pay attention to | used to |

1 I'll be glad to _____ someone who is better than I.
나보다 나은 사람에게 양보하면 기쁘겠어요.

2 It never _____ me that I should call my parents.
부모님께 전화해야겠다는 생각이 전혀 나지 않는다.

3 Mickey's mistake _____ an accident. Mickey의 실수는 사고로 이어졌다.

4 Nick _____ practice piano every day. Nick은 매일 피아노를 연습하곤 했다.

5 The concert _____ my expectation. 그 콘서트는 내 기대에 부응했다.

C. Complete the conversations using the sentences given.

1　**A** _____

　　B Joshua kicked me. Joshua가 나를 찼어.

2　**A** Do you think people will still buy this model? 사람들이 아직도 이 모델을 살 것 같니?

　　B _____

3　**A** Do you play any instrument? 악기 연주할 줄 아니?

　　B _____

4　**A** Was there anything important on the news? 뉴스에 중요한 게 있었니?

　　B _____

(A) No, it will give way to the new model soon.
(B) I used to play the piano, but not anymore.
(C) No, I wasn't paying attention to it.
(D) What led to the fight?

D. Speak or write.

1　Not saying the truth is equal to lying. How would you say this?
　　진실을 말하지 않는 것은 거짓말하는 것과 같다. 이것을 어떻게 말할까?

2　Anthony admires his older brother. How do you say this about Anthony?
　　Anthony는 형을 높이 평가한다. Anthony에 대해 이것을 어떻게 말할까?

3　Your parents are very strict concerning grades. How would you say this about your parents? 당신의 부모님은 성적에 대해 매우 엄격하다. 부모님에 대해 이것을 어떻게 말할까?

4　Your test scores met your expectation. How do you say this?
　　당신의 시험 점수가 당신의 기대를 만족시켰다. 이것을 어떻게 말할까?

(A) My test scores lived up to my expectation.
(B) Not saying the truth amounts to lying.
(C) He looks up to his older brother.
(D) When it comes to grades, my parents are very strict.

C 1. D　2. A　3. B　4. C
D 1. B　2. C　3. D　4. A

181   A   **I can't *stand* Tom.**
나는 Tom을 견딜 수가 없어.

B   **Well, you need to put up with him for a few more days.**
글쎄, 며칠은 더 참아야 해.

put up with   참다, 견디다

182   A   **David studies really hard not to *fall behind*.**
David는 뒤처지지 않기 위해 정말 열심히 공부해.

B   **Yeah, he does try his best to keep up with the course work.** 그래, 그는 수업 내용을 따라가기 위해 정말 최선을 다하지.

keep up with   ~에 뒤떨어지지 않다

183   A   **Is Tom's visit *connected to* your problem?**
Tom이 찾아온 게 네 문제와 관련 있는 거야?

B   **No, it has nothing to do with my trouble.**
아뇨, 내 문제와는 아무런 관계가 없어요.

have nothing to do with   ~와 아무런 관계가 없다

184   A   **Are you doing well at work?**
직장에서 잘하고 있니?

B   **Yeah, I just got *promoted*.**
그래, 얼마 전에 승진했어.

do well   잘하다, 건강하다

185   A   **Are you *finished* with your work?**
일은 다 마쳤니?

B   **I just got through with it.**
방금 끝냈어.

get through   끝내다, 통과하다, 이해시키다

186

A **We need to run fast to** catch up **with Peter.**
우리가 Peter를 따라잡으려면 빨리 뛰어야 해.

B **Forget it. He is too far ahead to** *get closer to*.
잊어버려. 그는 너무 멀리 앞서가서 더 가까이 갈 수 없어.

catch up   따라잡다, 만회하다

187

A **I didn't know that you** *stopped* **playing golf.**
골프를 중단하신 줄은 몰랐어요.

B **I** gave **it** up **last year.**
작년에 그만두었어요.

give up   그만두다, 포기하다

188

A **John finally** *decided* **to move.**
John이 드디어 이사하기로 결정했어.

B **He took a long time to** make up **his mind.**
결심하는 데 시간이 오래 걸렸어.

make up   날조하다, 화해하다, 결정하다

189

A **Who** *founded* **the company?**
누가 그 회사를 설립했니?

B **It was** set up **by my grandfather.**
우리 할아버지가 세우셨어.

set up   설립하다, 세우다, 배치하다

190

A **Where did you** *find* **your wallet?**
네 지갑을 어디에서 찾았니?

B **You never guess where it** turned up.
그게 어디에서 나왔는지 너는 절대 모를 거야.

turn up   나타나다, (음량 · 온도를) 높이다

A. Choose the right answer.

1 **A** Is Bob involved in the accident? Bob이 그 사고에 관련되어 있니?

　　B No, he _____ it. 아니. 그는 아무런 관련이 없어.

　　(A) keeps up with (B) puts up with (C) catches up (D) has nothing to do with

2 **A** Are you still mad at Rob? 아직도 Rob한테 화나 있니?

　　B No, we _____. 아니. 우리는 화해했어.

　　(A) gave up　　(B) set up　　(C) made up　　(D) turned up

3 **A** Jimmy is having a hard time _____ his schoolwork.
　　　Jimmy가 학교 공부를 따라가기 힘들어해.

　　B He should get help if he is having trouble. 그가 문제를 겪고 있다면 도움을 받아야지.

　　(A) doing well (B) keeping up with (C) turning up (D) putting up with

4 **A** How do you _____ this noise? 이 시끄러운 소리를 어떻게 견디니?

　　B I just got used to it. 그냥 익숙해졌어.

　　(A) set up　　(B) get through　　(C) put up with　　(D) keep up with

B. Fill in the blanks.

put up with	keep up with	have nothing to do with	do well	get through
	catch up	give up	make up	set up	turn up	

1 You go ahead. I'll _____ with you later. 먼저 가. 나중에 따라갈게.

2 We need to _____ the tent quickly. 우리가 빨리 텐트를 쳐야 해.

3 You are almost there. You can't _____ now. 거의 다 왔어. 지금 포기할 수는 없어.

4 Greg had many friends who helped him to _____ difficult times.
　　Greg는 어려운 시기를 통과하도록 도와준 친구들이 많았다.

5 Chris, can you _____ the volume? Chris. 소리 좀 크게 해 줄래?

C. Complete the conversations using the sentences given.

1 **A** _____

    B Thanks for your encouragement. 격려해 줘서 고마워.

2 **A** Were you able to change Henry's mind? Henry의 마음을 바꿀 수 있었니?

    B _____

3 **A** _____

    B Thanks, I'll try my best. 고마워, 최선을 다할게.

4 **A** Everyone thinks Sean is a liar. 모두가 Sean이 거짓말쟁이라고 생각해.

    B _____

> (A) Yes, I was able to get through to him.
> (B) I hope that you do well on the test.
> (C) That is because he makes up stories.
> (D) You should not give up hope.

D. Speak or write.

1 The teacher is not going to tolerate Mark's laziness anymore. How would you say this about the teacher?
선생님은 Mark의 게으름을 더 이상 묵인하지 않을 것이다. 선생님에 대해 이것을 어떻게 말할까?

2 You are not involved in Jenny's injury. How would you say this?
당신은 Jenny의 부상에 관련되어 있지 않다. 이것을 어떻게 말할까?

3 Mr. Thomson is recovering nicely. How would you say this about Mr. Thomson? Thomson 씨는 잘 회복되고 있다. Thomson 씨에 대해 이것을 어떻게 말할까?

4 Omar reads a newspaper to follow current events. How do you say this about Omar? Omar는 시사 문제를 쫓아가려고 신문을 읽는다. Omar에 대해 이것을 어떻게 말할까?

> (A) He is doing well.
> (B) The teacher is not going to put up with his laziness anymore.
> (C) He reads a newspaper to keep up with current events.
> (D) I have nothing to do with her injury.

C 1. D 2. A 3. B 4. C
D 1. B 2. D 3. A 4. C

191

A **Tom said he** used up **his money.**

Tom이 돈을 다 썼대.

B **I can't believe he *spent* it all.**

그걸 전부 썼다니 믿을 수가 없어.

use up   다 써 버리다

192

A **Thank you for** taking part in **the survey.**

설문 조사에 참여해 주셔서 감사합니다.

B **It was my pleasure to *participate* in it.**

참가해서 저도 즐거웠어요.

take part in   ~에 참가하다

193

A How come **he's late?**

어째서 그가 늦었니?

B **I don't know *why*, either.**

왜 늦었는지 나도 몰라.

how come   어째서, 왜

194

A **Let's not talk about him while he's *not around*.**

그가 여기에 없을 때 그에 대해 이야기하지 말자.

B **Right. We shouldn't talk** behind his back.

맞아. 그가 없는 데서 이야기하지 말아야지.

behind one's back   ~의 등 뒤에서, ~가 없을 때

195

A **I'm really worried about Tom. He'll be in prison if he doesn't change.** Tom이 정말 걱정이야. 그가 변하지 않는다면 감옥에 가게 될 거야.

B **Me, too. I'm afraid he'll** end up **in jail.**

나도 그래. 그가 결국 감옥에 갈 것 같아.

end up   결국 ~하게 되다

196

A **It's so hard to *do everything by myself*.**
혼자서 모든 걸 하기는 무척 힘들어.

B **That's why you need to learn to depend on others.**
그래서 다른 사람에게 의지해야 하는 거야.

depend on　~에 의지하다, 믿다, ~에 달려 있다

197

A **Bob looks really depressed.**
Bob이 정말 우울해 보여.

B **He just went through a difficult *experience*.**
얼마 전에 힘든 경험을 해서 그래.

go through　경험하다, 통과하다, 살펴보다

198

A **Children are *quiet*.**
아이들이 조용해.

B **They settled down after their mother punished them.**
어머니가 벌준 후에 아이들이 얌전해졌어.

settle down　자리 잡다, 진정되다

199

A **I have heard you *met* John yesterday.**
어제 John을 만났다면서.

B **Yeah, I ran into him at the mall.**
그래, 몰에서 우연히 마주쳤어.

run into　우연히 만나다, ~에 부딪치다

200

A **The job calls for a professional help.**
그 일은 전문가의 도움이 필요해.

B **Do you really think we *need* a plumber?**
정말 배관공이 필요하다고 생각해?

call for　필요로 하다, 요구하다

A. Choose the right answer.

1 **A** Did your brother help you when you are growing up? 네가 자랄 때 형이 도와주었니?

   B Yeah, I _____ him a lot. 그래, 나는 형한테 많이 의지했어.

(A) depended on (B) ran into   (C) went through (D) ended up

2 **A** Where did Tom decide to live? Tom은 어디에서 살기로 결정했니?

   B He _____ in Texas. 그는 텍사스에 정착했어.

(A) used up   (B) settled down (C) ran into   (D) depended on

3 **A** How was the review session? 복습 시간은 어땠니?

   B We _____ the chapters very quickly. 우리는 여러 장을 아주 빨리 살펴봤어.

(A) ended up   (B) called for   (C) used up   (D) went through

4 **A** Do we have any more paper left? 종이 더 남은 것 있니?

   B No, we _____ all the paper. 아니, 우리는 종이를 다 써 버렸어.

(A) called for   (B) depended on (C) settled down (D) used up

B. Fill in the blanks.

| use up take part in how come behind, back end up |
| depend on go through settle down run into call for |

1 _____ Jenny didn't come to the party? 어째서 Jenny가 파티에 오지 않았니?

2 I will be glad to _____ the after-school activity. 기꺼이 방과 후 활동에 참여할 거야.

3 We _____ James the other day. 며칠 전에 우연히 James를 만났어.

4 Jane called Sam _____ her mother's _____.
Jane이 엄마가 안 계실 때 Sam에게 전화했대.

5 Sally worked hard not to _____ like her sister.
Sally는 언니처럼 되지 않으려고 열심히 일했다.

C. Complete the conversations using the sentences given.

1   **A** _____

  B I took a wrong train. 기차를 잘못 탔어.

2   **A** _____

  B OK, I'll do it. It sounds like fun. 좋아, 참가할게. 재미있겠다.

3   **A** Why is Peter angry at Sarah? 왜 Peter가 Sarah한테 화나 있니?

  B _____

4   **A** You look very tired. 너 무척 피곤해 보인다.

  B _____

(A) Why don't you take part in the festival?
(B) I used up all my energy to get here.
(C) How did you end up in Seattle?
(D) She lied about him behind his back.

D. Speak or write.   .

1   Jenny didn't come to the party. How do you ask Jenny about it?
Jenny가 파티에 오지 않았다. Jenny에게 그것에 대해 어떻게 물어볼까?

2   You want Mike to relax. How do you say it to Mike?
당신은 Mike가 긴장을 풀기를 원한다. Mike에게 그것을 어떻게 말할까?

3   The team wants to celebrate the victory. How do you say this?
그 팀은 승리를 축하하고 싶어 한다. 이것을 어떻게 말할까?

4   Mr. Sanders experienced a lot of things. How would you say this about
Mr. Sanders? Sanders 씨는 많은 일을 경험했다. Sanders 씨에 대해 이것을 어떻게 말할까?

(A) You need to settle down.
(B) How come you didn't come to the party?
(C) He went through a lot of things.
(D) The victory calls for a celebration.

Voca Bible

Part II
Key Words for Reading
001-400

001

Melinda worked hard to *reach* her goal and achieve success.
Melinda는 자신의 목표를 달성하고 성공을 이루기 위해 열심히 일했다.

achieve
[ətʃíːv]
(통) 이루다, 성취하다 accomplish, attain, realize

002

He hopes to detect who is lying and *find* the one who stole his wallet.
그는 누가 거짓말하고 있는지 알아내 자기 지갑을 훔친 사람을 찾아내고 싶어 한다.

detect
[ditékt]
(통) 발견하다, 알아내다 find, discover, recognize
간파하다 uncover, reveal

003

He can leap higher than any other *jumper* in his school.
그는 자기 학교에서 다른 모든 높이뛰기 선수들보다 더 높이 뛰어오를 수 있다.

leap
[liːp]
(통) 뛰어오르다, 도약하다 hop, jump
급상승하다 soar, hike
(명) 뛰어오름, 도약, 급증 jump, soaring, rise

004

I wanted to *get in touch with* Greg, but I couldn't reach him.
나는 Greg한테 연락하려고 했지만 그와 연락이 되지 않았다.

reach
[riːtʃ]
(통) 도달하다, 실현하다 arrive, realize
연락하다 communicate, contact
(명) 범위 range, scope

005

Henry sought a position at the company but never *got* one.
Henry는 그 회사에서 일자리를 찾아보았지만 도저히 구할 수 없었다.

seek
[siːk]
(통) 찾다, 찾으러 가다 search, look for
추구하다, 노력하다 strive for
요구하다 request

006

Cooper vanished so quickly that *no one knew where he went*. Cooper가 워낙 빨리 사라져 그가 어디로 갔는지 아무도 알지 못했다.

vanish
[vǽniʃ]

(동) 사라지다, 없어지다 disappear, dissipate, evaporate

007

I revere him as a writer, but I don't *respect* as a person. 나는 그를 작가로서 존경하지만 인간으로서는 존경하지 않는다.

revere
[rivíər]

(동) 존경하다 respect, admire, venerate
- reverence (명) 존경 respect

008

His debts mounted as he *increased* his spending. 그의 씀씀이가 늘어날수록 그의 빚도 증가했다.

mount
[maunt]

(동) 오르다 climb
증가하다 increase, rise
(공격을) 개시하다 attack
(명) 산, 언덕

009

The dentist needs to extract Ron's tooth, but he is afraid of having it *pull out*. 치과 의사는 Ron의 이를 빼야 하지만 그는 이 빼는 것을 무서워한다.

extract
[ékstrækt]

(동) 뽑아내다 get, derive
추출하다 remove, take out
(명) 발췌 excerpt
추출물

010

The film depicts the reality by *showing* how people are in pain. 그 영화는 사람들이 얼마나 고통스러워하는지를 보여 줌으로써 현실을 묘사한다.

depict
[dipíkt]

(동) 묘사하다 describe, portray, illustrate
그리다 paint, sketch

001 Clearly, in a system where every decision is made on the basis of tradition alone, progress may be difficult to achieve.

(어휘) decision 결정　basis 토대　tradition 전통
확실하게, 모든 결정이 전통만을 토대로 이루어지는 체제에서는 발전을 이루기 어려울 수도 있다.

002 In a village in eastern Uttar Pradesh, a woman is forced to live a life of solitude after she was detected as being HIV positive.

(어휘) be forced to 억지로 ~하다　life of solitude 혼자 사는 생활　positive 양성의
우타르프라데시 주 동부의 한 마을에서 한 여성이 HIV 양성으로 판명된 후 어쩔 수 없이 혼자 살고 있다.

003 There has been a leap in sales of sport goods in this week.

(어휘) sport goods 스포츠용품
이번 주에는 스포츠용품 매출이 급증하고 있다.

004 Rising real estate prices in Britain are putting home ownership out of reach of more and more people.

(어휘) real estate 부동산　ownership 소유권　out of reach 손이 닿지 않는
영국에서는 부동산 가격 상승으로 점점 더 많은 사람들이 집을 소유하기가 어려워지고 있다.

005 Columbus discovered America while seeking a trade route to India.

(어휘) discover 발견하다　trade route 교역로
콜럼버스는 인도로 가는 교역로를 찾던 중에 아메리카 대륙을 발견했다.

006

The researchers discovered that the new drug could also make depression vanish almost right away.

어휘 depression 우울증   vanish 사라지다
연구자들은 새 약물이 우울증을 거의 즉시 사라지게 할 수도 있음을 발견했다.

007

They are Native Americans who live in the forest and revere nature.

어휘 native 원주민(의)   nature 자연
그들은 숲에 살면서 자연을 숭배하는 아메리카 원주민들이다.

008

Mounting evidence indicates that acid rain is damaging historic sites in Boston and Philadelphia.

어휘 indicate 나타내다, 가리키다   historic 역사적인   site 장소, 위치
늘어나는 증거들은 산성비가 보스턴과 필라델피아에 있는 역사적인 장소들을 훼손하고 있음을 보여준다.

009

Extracted from flaxseed, linseed oil is the principal source of drying oil for paint and varnish.

어휘 principal 주요한, 주된   paint 그림 물감   varnish 니스, 겉치레
아마인에서 추출되는 아마인유는 페인트와 니스에 사용되는 건성유의 주원료이다.

010

Embroidery depicting scenic views became popular in the United States toward the end of the eighteenth century.

어휘 embroidery 자수(법)   scenic 풍경의, 경치 좋은   toward ~경, 무렵
풍경을 표현하는 자수법은 18세기 말경에 미국에서 대중화되었다.

A. Choose the right answer for the underlined word.

1 Duke Ellington achieved fame in the late 1920s.

Duke Ellington은 1920년대 말에 명성을 얻었다.

(A) removed   (B) registered   (C) communicated   (D) attained

2 I called but couldn't reach you.

네게 전화했지만 통화할 수 없었다.

(A) find   (B) feel   (C) realize   (D) contact

3 The pain vanished after he took an aspirin.

그가 아스피린 한 알을 먹은 후 통증이 사라졌다.

(A) realized   (B) attacked   (C) disappeared   (D) painted

4 Security officials say that computer crime is easy to accomplish and hard to detect. 보안 당국은 컴퓨터를 이용한 범죄는 저지르기 쉽고 색출하기 어렵다고 말한다.

(A) dissipate   (B) climb   (C) rise   (D) discover

5 Speculation mounts over Nobel Prize.

노벨상에 대한 추측이 무성해지고 있다.

(A) arrives   (B) increases   (C) jumps   (D) accomplishes

6 You need to seek permission from your supervisor before taking a sick leave. 병가를 떠나기 전에 상사에게 허락을 요청해야 한다.

(A) describe   (B) attack   (C) request   (D) evaporate

7 The grasshopper is an insect that can leap about twenty times the length of its own body. 메뚜기는 자기 몸길이의 20배 정도를 도약할 수 있는 곤충이다.

(A) portray   (B) search   (C) strive   (D) hop

8 The first thing John does in the morning is to extract juice from oranges.

John이 아침에 가장 먼저 하는 일은 오렌지에서 즙을 짜내는 것이다.

(A) uncover   (B) hike   (C) venerate   (D) derive

Answers   **A**   1. D   2. D   3. C   4. D   5. B   6. C   7. D   8. D

B. Fill in the blanks.

achieve	detect	leap	reach	seek
vanish	revere	mount	extract	depict

1 I _____ over a pool of water.
나는 물웅덩이를 건너뛰었다.

2 The two nations _____ peace after many years of war.
두 나라는 여러 해 동안 전쟁을 치른 후 평화를 이루었다.

3 We finally _____ the decision after three hours of discussion.
우리는 3시간의 토론을 거친 후에 마침내 결론에 도달했다.

4 Many people went to the West to _____ their fortune.
많은 사람들이 부를 찾아 서부로 갔다.

5 This painting _____ the peacefulness of rural life.
이 그림은 시골 생활의 평화로움을 묘사하고 있다.

C. Choose the right answer.

1 The magician had _____ from sight and everyone was wondering where he went. 그 마술사가 눈앞에서 사라지자 모두들 그가 어디로 갔는지 의아해했다.

(A) mounted　　(B) extracted　　(C) vanished　　(D) achieved

2 My mother checked the stove after _____ the smell of gas.
어머니는 가스 냄새를 맡고 나서 스토브를 확인했다.

(A) detecting　　(B) achieving　　(C) leaping　　(D) reaching

3 The cow is _____ as a god in some cultures.
소는 일부 문화권에서는 신으로 숭배되고 있다.

(A) vanished　　(B) revered　　(C) extracted　　(D) sought

4 The army will _____ an attack in the morning.
군대는 아침에 공격을 개시할 것이다.

(A) mount　　(B) reach　　(C) vanish　　(D) seek

B　1. leaped　2. achieved　3. reached　4. seek　5. depicts
C　1. C　2. A　3. B　4. A

011

The idea is so plain and *simple* that even a child can understand it. 그 아이디어는 매우 평이하고 간단해서 아이라도 이해할 수 있다.

plain
[plein]

> (형) 분명한, 알기 쉬운 clear, obvious
> 소박한, 평범한 homely, humble
> (명) 평야 grassland, prairie

012

This compact camera is *small* enough to fit your pocket. 이 소형 카메라는 호주머니에 들어갈 정도로 작다.

compact
[kəmpǽkt]
[kámpækt](명)

> (형) 꽉 들어찬, 빽빽한 dense
> 소형의 small
> 간결한 concise, succinct
> (동) 압축하다 compress, pack
> (명) 협정, 조약 agreement, treaty

013

It was a rough week, but it will *get better* next week. 고된 한 주였지만 다음 주는 나아질 것이다.

rough
[rʌf]

> (형) 거친 coarse, crude
> 가공되지 않은 unprocessed, unrefined
> 힘든, 고된 uncomfortable
> 대강의, 대략적인 vague, approximate
> - roughly (부) 거칠게, 꾸밈없이; 대충, 대략

014

The program is for gifted and *highly able* students. 그 프로그램은 재능 있고 능력이 뛰어난 학생들을 위한 것이다.

gifted
[gíftid]

> (형) 천부적인, 타고난 재능이 있는 talented, able, skilled

015

The most significant event in his life was *to win the gold medal*. 그의 생애에서 가장 중요한 사건은 금메달을 딴 것이었다.

significant
[signífikənt]

> (형) 중요한, 중대한 important, vital, essential
> 상당한 considerable, substantial

016

The sickness left him feeble and *weak*.
병으로 인해 그는 허약하고 힘없는 상태가 되었다.

feeble   형 약한   weak
[fíːbl]   허약한, 미미한   ailing, frail, fragile
                 불충분한, 부적당한   insufficient, inadequate

017

This keen knife can *cut through anything*.
이 예리한 칼은 무엇이든 자를 수 있다.

keen   형 예리한, 예민한   sharp, edged
[kiːn]   영리한, 이해가 빠른   acute, clever, quick
                열망하는   eager
          - keenly 부 날카롭게, 예민하게, 빈틈없이

018

A prudent man is always *careful* about his decisions.
현명한 사람은 항상 신중하게 결정한다.

prudent   형 신중한   careful, cautious, discreet
[prúːdənt]   현명한   wise

019

It was a formidable task, and everyone *had a hard time completing it*. 그것은 매우 힘든 일이어서 모두가 끝내느라고 애를 먹었다.

formidable   형 엄청난, 매우 뛰어난   great
[fɔ́ːrmidəbl]   무서운, 가공할   dreadful, fearful

020

Math is a compulsory subject, so everyone *has to* study in school. 수학은 필수 과목이라서 모든 사람이 학교에서 배워야 한다.

compulsory   형 의무적인   obligatory, mandatory, binding
[kəmpʌ́lsəri]   필수의   required

011 **The water funneled through the gorge and out onto the plain.**

어휘 funnel 좁은 통로를 지나다　gorge 협곡
물은 협곡을 지나 평야로 흘러 나갔다.

012 **The proposed economic compact between Germany and France made both sides happy.**

어휘 economic 경제의
독일과 프랑스 간에 제안된 경제 조약은 양측 모두를 만족시켰다.

013 **A cup of whole milk provides roughly one hundred sixty-six calories of energy.**

어휘 whole milk (지방을 빼지 않은) 전유(全乳)
일반 우유 한 잔은 대략 166칼로리의 에너지를 제공한다.

014 **Charles Wilson Peale is generally considered the most gifted of the Philadelphia colonial artists.**

어휘 generally 일반적으로　consider 고려하다　colonial 식민지의
Charles Wilson Peale은 일반적으로 필라델피아 식민지 예술가 중에 가장 재능이 많다고 여겨진다.

015 **The most significant gain, however, is the potential to reshape India's global image.**

어휘 potential 가능성　reshape 다시 만들다
그러나 가장 중요한 소득은 인도의 세계적인 이미지를 바꿀 가능성이다.

016 By feeble contractions, the jelly fish propels itself along, buoyed up by the surrounding water.

(어휘) contraction 수축, 축소   propel 나아가게 하다   buoy 뜨게 하다
해파리는 주변의 물에 의해 떠 있는 상태로 약하게 수축하여 앞으로 나아간다.

017 Many young people are keenly aware of the advantages of a college education in today's world.

(어휘) aware 알고 있는   advantage 유리한 점, 우위
많은 젊은이들이 오늘의 세상에서 대학 교육의 이점을 깊이 인식하고 있다.

018 I decided that going home and waiting for William to visit me were the most prudent course.

(어휘) course 방침, 방법
나는 집에 가서 William이 찾아오기를 기다리는 것이 가장 현명한 방법이라고 결정했다.

019 She was one of the most formidable intellects of her time.

(어휘) intellect 지적 능력이 뛰어난 사람
그녀는 당대에 가장 막강한 지성인들 중의 한 사람이었다.

020 After 1850, various states in the United States began to pass compulsory school attendance laws.

(어휘) pass 통과시키다   attendance 출석, 참석
1850년 이후 미국의 여러 주에서 의무 교육 법안을 통과시키기 시작했다.

A. Choose the right answer for the underlined word.

1 Doug is such a <u>formidable</u> boxer that no one's to fight him.

Doug는 어느 누구도 싸우고 싶어 하지 않는 아주 막강한 권투 선수다.

(A) succinct   (B) crude   (C) fragile   (D) fearful

2 He is a <u>gifted</u> writer who is respected by many readers.

그는 많은 독자들에게 존경받는 재능 있는 작가이다.

(A) cautious   (B) vague   (C) able   (D) inadequate

3 Mr. Carter never had an accident because he is <u>prudent</u> and cautious.

Carter 씨는 신중하고 조심스러운 사람이라서 한 번도 사고를 낸 적이 없다.

(A) careful   (B) skilled   (C) essential   (D) quick

4 The mechanic gave me a <u>rough</u> estimate.

정비사는 내게 대략적인 견적을 제시했다.

(A) compress   (B) ailing   (C) approximate   (D) clear

5 The <u>plain</u> truth is that the nation's capital is in the firm grip of lobbyists.

명백한 진실은 그 국가의 자본을 로비스트들이 완전히 장악하고 있다는 사실이다.

(A) vital   (B) obvious   (C) acute   (D) coarse

6 A <u>significant</u> number of people came to see the show.

상당히 많은 수의 사람들이 그 쇼를 보러 왔다.

(A) discreet   (B) required   (C) dreadful   (D) considerable

7 She is really <u>keen</u> on going swimming.

그녀는 수영하러 가는 것을 정말 좋아한다.

(A) substantial   (B) eager   (C) wise   (D) great

8 Even though he is only 30 years old, he walks like a <u>feeble</u> old man.

그는 30세밖에 안 되었는데도 힘없는 노인처럼 걸어 다닌다.

(A) humble   (B) dense   (C) unrefined   (D) frail

Answers   A   1. D   2. C   3. A   4. C   5. B   6. D   7. B   8. D

B. Fill in the blanks.

| plain | compact | rough | gifted | significant |
| feeble | keen | prudent | formidable | compulsory |

1 I'm very tired because I had a _____ day at work.

나는 오늘 직장에서 힘들었기 때문에 아주 피곤하다.

2 People prepared for _____ weather.

사람들은 험악한 날씨에 대비했다.

3 He is a _____ but lazy musician.

그는 재능은 있지만 노력은 하지 않는 음악가다.

4 Bloodhounds have a _____ sense of smell.

블러드하운드는 예민한 후각을 갖고 있다.

5 The new policy is _____ and sensible.

새로운 정책은 신중하고 적절하다.

C. Choose the right answer.

1 The movie was _____ bad.

그 영화는 정말 형편없었다.

(A) plainly　　　(B) keenly　　　(C) formidably　　　(D) prudently

2 He was so weak that he spoke in a _____ voice.

그는 너무 허약해서 아주 힘없는 목소리로 말했다.

(A) keen　　　(B) compact　　　(C) compulsory　　　(D) feeble

3 Everyone in the class had to take the test because it was _____.

의무 사항이어서 반 학생 전부가 시험을 치러야 했다.

(A) rough　　　(B) compulsory　　　(C) significant　　　(D) plain

4 There was no _____ difference between two plans.

두 계획 사이에 큰 차이는 없었다.

(A) feeble　　　(B) keen　　　(C) significant　　　(D) compulsory

021

I gained a lot of experience in business after *getting* this job. 이 직장을 구한 후 나는 많은 업무 경험을 얻었다.

gain
[gein]

동 얻다, 획득하다 earn, attain, win
증가하다, 늘리다 put on
명 이익, 이득 profit, benefit

022

He wanted to compensate Linda for her trouble, but she didn't want to *get paid*.
그는 Linda가 해 준 수고에 보답하고 싶었지만 그녀는 돈을 받으려고 하지 않았다.

compensate
[kámpənsèit]

동 보상하다 pay, reimburse
상쇄하다 offset, counterbalance

023

He tried to preserve and *protect* as many wild animals as possible. 그는 가능한 한 많은 야생 동물들을 보존하고 보호하려고 노력했다.

preserve
[prizə́ːrv]

동 보존하다 maintain, sustain
보호하다 protect, shield
명 자연 보호 구역 preservation

024

The program will lessen demand for imported water and *reduce* wastewater flows.
그 프로그램은 수입되는 물에 대한 수요를 줄이고 폐수 방류를 줄여 줄 것이다.

lessen
[lésən]

동 줄이다, 감하다 diminish, abate, ease, reduce

025

He tried very hard to locate his lost dog but couldn't *find* it.
그는 잃어버린 개를 찾으려고 아주 열심히 노력했지만 찾지 못했다.

locate
[lóukeit]

동 찾아내다 find, discover, detect
~의 장소를 정하다, 설치하다 place, establish

026 **Despite the salesman's claim that bullet can't penetrate the vest, it *went through*.**
총알이 그 조끼를 관통할 수 없다는 영업사원의 주장에도 불구하고 총알은 뚫고 지나갔다.

penetrate   ⑧ 꿰뚫다, 관통하다 break through, puncture, pierce
[pénitrèit]   통과하다 pass through
                 침투하다 invade

027 ***Listening to loud music* impaired Mark's hearing.**
시끄러운 음악을 들어서 Mark의 청각이 손상되었다.

impair   ⑧ 손상시키다 damage, harm, ruin
[impέər]

028 **It was time *to leave*, but it was hard to detach himself from his friends.** 떠날 시간이 되었지만 그는 친구들과 헤어지기가 힘들었다.

detach   ⑧ 떼어놓다, 분리하다 separate, remove, disengage
[ditǽtʃ]

029 **The manager *asked* and then urged him to take the job.**
매니저는 그에게 그 일을 맡도록 간청했다.

urge   ⑧ 재촉하다, 자극하다 stimulate, propel
[ə́ːrdʒ]   간청하다 ask, plead
            강요하다 force
          ⑲ 추진력, 본능적인 충동 drive, yearning, impulse

030 **The research team was able to devise and *develop* a new system.** 연구팀은 새 시스템을 고안하고 개발할 수 있었다.

devise   ⑧ 고안하다, 계획하다 form, plan
[diváiz]   창안하다, 발명하다 invent, create, establish, fashion

021 Almost all economists agree that nations gain by trading with one another.

(어휘) economist 경제학자 trade 무역하다
거의 모든 경제학자들은 국가들이 서로 간의 무역으로 이익을 얻는다는 것에 동의한다.

022 This poses no serious problems at airports where long runways help to compensate for thrust loss and provide the pilot with an adequate distance for takeoff.

(어휘) serious 심각한 runway 활주로 thrust 추진력 adequate 적당한
긴 활주로가 추진력 손실을 보상하고 조종사에게 이륙에 적당한 거리를 제공하는 데 도움이 되는 공항에서는 이것이 아무런 심각한 문제를 야기하지 않는다.

023 They feared that construction would harm the natural habitats of the creatures that populate the 9,155-acre preserve.

(어휘) construction 건설 habitat 서식지 creature 생물 populate ~에 살다
그들은 건설 공사가 9,155에이커의 자연 보호 구역에 사는 생물들의 자연 서식지에 해를 끼치게 될 것을 우려했다.

024 The company is urging consumers to conserve energy as much as possible, but they are also taking steps to lessen the blow of the higher costs this winter.

(어휘) urge 촉구하다 consumer 소비자 conserve 절약하다
그 회사는 소비자들에게 가능한 한 많은 에너지를 절약해 달라고 촉구하고 있지만 그들은 또한 이번 겨울에 닥칠 고유가의 충격을 줄이기 위한 조치들을 취하고 있다.

025 The spleen is a small organ located beneath the left side of the rib cage.

(어휘) spleen 지라 rib cage 흉곽
지라는 흉곽 왼쪽 밑에 위치한 작은 기관이다.

026 Automobile experts have shown that halogen headlights penetrate thick fog more effectively than traditional incandescent headlights and thus help to reduce accidents.

[어휘] thick 짙은, 빽빽한   fog 안개   reduce 줄이다
자동차 전문가들은 할로겐 전조등이 전통적인 백열등 전조등보다 더 효과적으로 짙은 안개를 투과함으로써 사고를 줄이는 데 도움이 된다는 것을 보여 주고 있다.

027 Research has already been severely impaired at the Lowell Observatory in Flagstaff, Arizona, by the lights of the encircling city of 30,000.

[어휘] observatory 관측소, 천문대   encircle 에워싸다
애리조나 주의 Flagstaff에 있는 Lowell 천문대에서의 연구는 3만 명이 사는 주변 도시의 불빛들에 의해 이미 심각한 피해를 보고 있다.

028 The author presented highly emotional ideas in a coolly detached tone.

[어휘] highly 매우   emotional 감정적인   coolly 냉정하게
그 작가는 아주 감정적인 생각들을 차분하고 냉정한 어조로 제시했다.

029 Marcus Garvey, who urged the Back to Africa movement, attempted to establish colonies of Black Americans in Africa.

[어휘] attempt 시도하다   establish 설립하다   colony 집단 거주지
'아프리카로 돌아가기' 운동을 촉구했던 Marcus Garvey는 아프리카에 미국 흑인들의 집단 거주지를 세우려고 시도했다.

030 Astronauts are subject to the most rigorous training that has ever been devised for human beings.

[어휘] astronaut 우주비행사   be subject to ~의 대상이 되다   rigorous 혹독한
우주비행사는 인간을 위해 여태껏 고안된 것 중에서 가장 혹독한 훈련을 받는다.

A. Choose the right answer for the underlined word.

1 Bell literally spent the rest of his life trying to <u>devise</u> other useful things.

Bell은 글자 그대로 남은 생애를 다른 유용한 물건들을 발명하려고 노력하며 보냈다.

(A) protect   (B) earn   (C) diminish   (D) invent

2 Our company will begin to <u>compensate</u> workers for education starting next year. 우리 회사는 내년부터 근로자들의 교육에 보상을 시작할 것이다.

(A) stimulate   (B) reimburse   (C) shield   (D) establish

3 Mr. Smith wants to <u>lessen</u> his hours at work.

Smith 씨는 근무 시간을 줄이기를 원한다.

(A) ask   (B) ruin   (C) reduce   (D) pierce

4 The company's new products are <u>gaining</u> ground in suburban areas.

그 회사의 신제품이 교외 지역에서 입지를 넓혀 가고 있다.

(A) winning   (B) passing through   (C) removing   (D) easing

5 He <u>detached</u> the damaged part and fixed it.

그는 손상된 부분을 떼어내어 고쳤다.

(A) formed   (B) separated   (C) paid   (D) attained

6 It is obvious that drinking <u>impairs</u> one's judgment.

음주가 판단력을 흐리게 하는 것이 분명하다.

(A) damages   (B) detects   (C) sustains   (D) disengages

7 The president <u>urged</u> international companies to invest in the country.

대통령은 국제 기업들에게 그 나라에 투자해 달라고 촉구했다.

(A) fashioned   (B) offset   (C) pleaded   (D) created

8 The committee still hasn't made the decision where to <u>locate</u> the new community center. 위원회는 새 커뮤니티 센터를 어디에 세울지 아직 결정하지 못했다.

(A) force   (B) abate   (C) establish   (D) invade

Answers   A   1. D   2. B   3. C   4. A   5. B   6. A   7. C   8. C

B. Fill in the blanks.

| gain | compensate | preserve | lessen | locate |
| penetrate | impair· | detach | urge | devise |

1 Traveling was _____ by recent snowstorms.
여행이 최근의 폭설로 지장을 받았다.

2 We tried very hard to _____ a plan to make money.
우리는 돈을 벌 계획을 세우려고 매우 열심히 노력했다.

3 He'll vote for any measures to protect or _____ the environment.
그는 환경을 보호하고 보존하기 위한 어떤 조치에도 찬성할 것이다.

4 Dr. King _____ Blacks to use nonviolent sit-ins.
King 박사는 흑인들에게 비폭력 연좌 농성을 할 것을 촉구했다.

5 It is important to _____ yourself from the problem.
네 자신을 그 문제에서 떨어뜨려 놓는 것이 중요하다.

C. Choose the right answer.

1 The smell was so strong that it _____ the entire building.
그 냄새가 너무 강해서 건물 전체에 스며들었다.

(A) penetrated (B) gained (C) impaired (D) urged

2 Mrs. Parker thinks she is not being _____ fairly for her work.
Parker 씨는 자신의 일에 대해 정당한 보상을 받지 못하고 있다고 생각한다.

(A) preserved (B) located (C) compensated (D) devised

3 I should stop eating late dinners because I have _____ ten pounds since last year. 저녁을 늦게 먹는 것을 그만두어야겠다. 왜냐하면 작년 이후로 10파운드가 늘었기 때문이다.

(A) located (B) detached (C) lessened (D) gained

4 The best part about living here is that everything is so conveniently _____ nearby. 여기에서 사는 것의 가장 좋은 점은 모든 것이 가까이에 아주 편리하게 위치해 있다는 것이다.

(A) located (B) impaired (C) detached (D) lessened

B 1. impaired 2. devise 3. preserve 4. urged 5. detach
C 1. A 2. C 3. D 4. A

031

Out of his many *hobbies*, skiing is Tom's favorite activity.
여러 취미 중에서 스키는 Tom이 제일 좋아하는 여가 활동이다.

activity   몡 활동 action, motion, movement
[æktívəti]   여가 활동 pursuit, diversion

032

His *laziness* is the source of his problem.
게으름이 그의 문제의 근원이다.

source   몡 근원, 원천 origin, root
[sɔːrs]   정보원 informant
               자료 material

033

Successful factories meant that bankers and investors were making profits. 성공적인 공장은 은행가와 투자자가 수익을 내는 것을 의미했다.

profit   몡 수익, 이익 return, revenue
[práfit]   소득 earnings, yield
             몽 도움이 되다, 이익을 얻다 gain, benefit

034

Bad weather will *limit* the machine's sensitivity and range.
악천후는 기계의 감도와 사정 거리를 제한할 수도 있다.

range   몡 범위 scope, extend, limit, scale
[reindʒ]   사정거리 distance
            몽 변동하다 vary, fluctuate
               뻗다, 퍼지다 extend

035

The business leaders *met* in the conference and *discussed* many things. 기업 총수들은 그 회의에서 만나 많은 것들을 논의했다.

conference   몡 회의, 회담, 총회 meeting, convention, symposium, seminar
[kánfərəns]   협의회, 연맹 league, association

036

Trying to teach our children through punishment is a hopeless endeavor.

우리 아이들을 처벌을 통해 가르치려고 하는 것은 가망 없는 시도이다.

endeavor   명 노력 effort
[endévər]   시도 attempt, undertaking
       동 노력하다 attempt, try, undertake

037

The editor *got rid of a lot of details* for the sake of brevity.

편집자는 간결함을 위해 세부 사항을 많이 삭제했다.

brevity   명 (시간 · 기간의) 짧음 shortness
[brévəti]   간결함 briefness, conciseness, succinctness

038

He didn't understand why Ellen *became angry* without any provocation or reason.

그는 Ellen이 아무런 자극이나 이유도 없이 화가 난 이유를 이해하지 못했다.

provocation   명 자극, 도발 instigation, incitemen
[pràvəkéiʃən]   도전 challenge
     - provoke 동 자극하다

039

The company is still under scrutiny after three months of *investigations.* 그 회사는 3개월에 걸친 조사 이후에도 여전히 정밀 조사를 받고 있다.

scrutiny   명 정밀 조사 study, inspection, examination
[skrú:təni]

040

We will sure to have *rain* tomorrow since the chance of precipitation is 100 percent.

내일은 강수 확률이 100%이므로 확실히 비가 올 것입니다.

precipitation   명 강수(량), 강우(량) rain, rainfall
[prisìpitéiʃən]   촉진 acceleration
     허둥대기, 경솔함 haste
     - precipitate 동 재촉하다, 서두르게 하다

031 **There was not much activity in the stock market today.**

어휘 activity 활동　stock market 주식 시장
오늘 주식 시장은 활발하게 움직이지 않았다.

032 **It is the primary responsibility of journalist to protect the identity of his or her source.**

어휘 primary 일차적인　responsibility 책임, 의무　protect 보호하다
자신에게 정보를 제공한 사람의 신원을 보호하는 것이 언론인의 가장 중요한 책임이다.

033 **Ford believed that his plan would actually increase his profits by increasing productivity and efficiency.**

어휘 efficiency 효율성
Ford는 자신의 계획이 생산성과 효율성을 증대시켜 실제로 수익을 높여 줄 것이라고 믿었다.

034 **The polar bears of the Hudson Bay are a distinct population thriving at the southern end of their range.**

어휘 distinct 녹특한, 별개의　thrive 번성하다
Hudson 만에 있는 북극곰은 그들의 영역의 남쪽 끝에서 번성하고 있는 별개의 개체군이다.

035 **It was inconceivable to him to go to the Paris Peace Conference only to risk a break with his former allies by taking the side of the defeated powers.**

어휘 inconceivable 생각할 수 없는　ally 동맹국, 우방
그가 단지 패전국들의 편을 들어 이전 동맹국들과의 관계 단절을 감수하게 될 뿐인 파리 평화 회담에 가는 것은 생각할 수 없는 일이었다.

036

After many years of unsuccessfully endeavoring to form his own orchestra, Glenn Miller finally achieved world fame in 1939 as a big band leader.

어휘 fame 명성

여러 해 동안 자신의 오케스트라를 구성하려고 노력했으나 실패한 후에 Glenn Miller는 1939년에 마침내 빅밴드의 리더로서 세계적인 명성을 얻었다.

037

Epigrams are sayings characterized by wit and brevity.

어휘 epigram 경구, (짧은) 풍자시　characterize ~의 특징을 이루다　wit 재치

경구는 재치와 간결함이 특징인 말이다.

038

Wild pigs are fierce and courageous fighters and may charge with little or no provocation.

어휘 fierce 사나운　courageous 용감한　charge ~에 돌격하다

야생 돼지들은 사납고 용감한 싸움꾼이며 거의 또는 전혀 자극 없이도 돌격할 수 있다.

039

In particular, the southern border is under scrutiny over lack of enforcement and physical barriers.

어휘 enforcement (법률의) 시행, 집행　barrier 방벽, 장애물

특히 남쪽 국경은 법 집행과 물리적인 장벽의 부족함이 있는지에 대해 정밀 조사를 받고 있다.

040

He smiled at himself as he walked away with a quick step, for, an instant before, he had been internally blaming his own precipitation.

어휘 internally 속으로　blame 비난하다

그는 미소를 띠며 빠른 걸음으로 사라져 갔다. 조금 전에 속으로 자신의 경솔함을 탓하고 있었기 때문이다.

A. Choose the right answer for the underlined word.

1 As we grow older, the range of sounds that we can hear becomes smaller.
우리는 늙어감에 따라 들을 수 있는 소리의 범위가 점점 작아진다.

(A) root   (B) yield   (C) scale   (D) briefness

2 The aim of the conference is to promote international friendship.
그 회담의 목적은 국제적인 우의를 증진하는 것이다.

(A) symposium   (B) instigation   (C) undertaking   (D) informant

3 The company works on a small margin of profit.
그 회사는 작은 수익 마진으로 운영된다.

(A) effort   (B) scope   (C) association   (D) return

4 One very important and interesting feature of Japanese is an emphasis on brevity. 일본인들의 매우 중요하고 흥미로운 한 가지 특징은 간결함을 강조하는 것이다.

(A) action   (B) rainfall   (C) succinctness   (D) material

5 The source of the Mississippi River is located more than two thousand miles from its mouth. 미시시피 강의 발원지는 강의 입구로부터 2천 마일 이상 떨어진 곳에 위치해 있다.

(A) motion   (B) origin   (C) challenge   (D) extend

6 Two countries would start a war at the slightest provocation.
아주 사소한 도발에도 두 나라는 전쟁을 시작할 것이다.

(A) shortness   (B) incitement   (C) limit   (D) earning

7 The precipitation should stop by morning, and the sun will break through the clouds in the afternoon. 비는 오전에 그칠 것이며, 오후에는 해가 구름 사이로 빠져나올 것입니다.

(A) study   (B) movement   (C) rain   (D) league

8 Many people question the practicality of undertaking such an endeavor.
많은 사람들이 그러한 시도를 감행하는 것의 실용성에 의문을 제기한다.

(A) conciseness   (B) attempt   (C) meeting   (D) haste

Answers   **A**   1. C   2. A   3. D   4. C   5. B   6. B   7. C   8. B

B. Fill in the blanks.

activity	source	profit	range	conference
endeavor	brevity	provocation	scrutiny	precipitation

1   I have a parent-teacher _____ with my son's teacher.
나는 아들 선생님과 학부모-교사 회의를 한다.

2   Marvin feels bad about acting with _____.
Marvin은 경솔하게 행동한 것에 대해 후회한다.

3   He made a lot of _____ from selling his house.
그는 집을 팔아서 큰 이익을 남겼다.

4   The best way to lose weight is to increase your physical _____.
체중을 줄이는 가장 좋은 방법은 신체 활동을 늘리는 것이다.

5   Experts believe the possibility exists for a sudden _____ by the
terrorist group. 전문가들은 그 테러 집단이 갑자기 도발할 가능성이 있다고 믿는다.

C. Choose the right answer.

1   Which foods are _____ of calcium?
어느 음식들이 칼슘의 공급원이지?

(A) endeavors   (B) precipitations (C) provocation   (D) sources

2   Flexibility or stretching exercises increase a person's _____ of motion.
유연성 또는 스트레칭 운동은 개인의 동작 범위를 넓혀 준다.

(A) conference   (B) brevity   (C) range   (D) activity

3   Researchers know that their work will be open to general _____.
연구자들은 자신들의 연구가 전면적인 정밀 조사를 받아야 한다는 것을 알고 있다.

(A) source   (B) provocation   (C) scrutiny   (D) endeavor

4   In spite of the _____ of the speech, people fell asleep well before it
was finished. 연설 시간이 짧았음에도 불구하고 사람들은 연설이 끝나기 한참 전에 잠들었다.

(A) brevity   (B) profit   (C) scrutiny   (D) source

B 1. conference   2. precipitation   3. profits   4. activity   5. provocation
C 1. D   2. C   3. C   4. A

041 **His reading skills have *improved*, but his writing has not advanced.** 그의 독해력은 향상되고 있지만 작문은 진보하지 않고 있다.

advance
[ədvǽns]
동 진보하다 improve, evolve, develop, progress
제시하다 propose
승진하다 promote
선불하다, 가불하다

042 **He declared an end to the war, and his *announcement* made the people happy.** 그가 종전을 선언했을 때 그의 발표는 사람들을 행복하게 만들었다.

declare
[diklέər]
동 선언하다, 공표하다, 분명히 말하다 announce, proclaim, disclose
(소득액 · 과세품을) 신고하다 report, disclose
주장하다, 단언하다 claim, maintain, assert

043 **Singing can lift one's mood and *raise* one's spirits.**
노래는 사람의 기분을 좋게 하고 기운을 북돋워 준다.

lift
[lift]
동 들어올리다, 북돋우다 raise, elevate, boost
해제하다 cancel, end, repeal

044 **Mike said he would treat me to dinner, but I ended up *paying for* it.** Mike가 저녁을 사 주겠다고 말했지만 결국 내가 밥값을 냈다.

treat
[tri:t]
동 논하다 address, discuss / 다루다 handle, deal with
대접하다, 한턱내다 provide, buy, entertain
치료하다 attend
명 대접 entertainment, gift
큰 기쁨, 즐길 거리 delight, pleasure

045 **We need to remain calm and *stay* seated.**
우리는 계속 조용히 자리에 앉아 있어야 한다.

remain
[riméin]
동 남다, 계속 ~이다 stay, linger, last, persist, prevail
명 나머지, 남은 것 remainder, remnant
유해 corpse
유물 artifact

046

The town's population mushroomed, and no one expected this *rapid growth*.

그 도시의 인구는 급증했는데, 아무도 이렇게 빠른 성장을 예상하지 못했다.

mushroom   동 급속히 성장하다 grow quickly, boom, snowball, swell
[mʌ́ʃru(ː)m]   명 버섯

047

We grumble and sometimes *complain* loudly, but we do support our team.

우리는 투덜거리고 때로는 큰 소리로 불평하지만 우리 팀을 정말 지지한다.

grumble   동 불평하다, 투덜대다 complain, murmur, gripe
[grʌ́mbl]   으르렁거리다 growl

048

We can terminate our working relationship, but shouldn't *end* our personal one.

우리가 업무 관계는 종료할 수 있지만 인간관계를 끝내서는 안 된다.

terminate   동 끝내다, 종료하다 finish, stop, end
[tə́ːrmənèit]   해고하다 fire, dismiss

049

I derive happiness from reading and also *get* many new ideas from books.

나는 독서에서 행복을 얻고 또한 책에서 많은 새로운 아이디어를 얻는다.

derive   동 얻다, 끌어내다 obtain, gain
[diráiv]   유래하다, 파생하다 originate, stem

050

The son lamented and *cried* over his father's death.

아들은 아버지의 죽음을 슬퍼하며 울었다.

lament   동 한탄하다, 슬퍼하다 mourn, grieve, bemoan
[ləmént]   후회하다 regret
           명 비탄, 애도 grief, mourning

Words in Reading

041
The tools needed to advance our knowledge in this way are the disciplines of mathematics and physics applied to solve meteorological problems.

어휘 tool 도구　discipline 학과, 분야　apply 적용하다　meteorological 기상의
이러한 방식으로 우리의 지식을 향상시키는 데 필요한 도구들은 기상 문제를 해결하는 데 적용되는 수학과 물리학 분야이다.

042
Joseph Jefferson III also declared that he was a pioneer in the movement.

어휘 pioneer 개척자, 선구자
Joseph Jefferson 3세 역시 자신이 그 운동의 개척자라고 선언했다.

043
If the original material is large and bulky, like a book, you can lift the cover of the machine and place the material on top of the glass plate.

어휘 bulky 부피가 큰　plate 판, 접시
원래 자료가 책처럼 부피가 크다면 기계의 덮개를 들어올려 자료를 유리판 위에 놓으십시오.

044
Television and junk food are banned and the children have to earn their treats, she told a magazine interviewer.

어휘 junk food 정크푸드(인스턴트 음식이나 패스트푸드)　ban 금지하다
TV와 정크푸드가 금지되어 있어 어린이들은 즐길 거리를 스스로 찾아야 한다고 그녀는 잡지 인터뷰 담당자에게 말했다.

045
Building at the site was halted after human remains were unearthed earlier this month.

어휘 site 장소　halt 중지하다　unearth 발굴하다
이달 초, 사람의 유해가 발굴된 후 그 장소에 건물을 짓는 일이 중단되었다.

046

In the 1820s cities in the United States mushroomed as a result of the Industrial Revolution.

어휘 Industrial Revolution 산업 혁명

1820년대에 미국의 도시들은 산업 혁명의 결과로 급속히 성장했다.

047

Many have grumbled about the potential costs related to hosting another Summer Olympic Games.

어휘 host 주최하다

많은 사람들이 또 한 번의 하계 올림픽 대회를 주최하는 데 관련된 잠재 비용에 대해 불평해 왔다.

048

Glaciers terminate where the rate of ice loss is equivalent to the forward advance of the glacier.

어휘 glacier 빙하   rate 비율, 속도   equivalent 같은, 동등한   forward 앞으로

빙하는 얼음의 손실 비율이 빙하가 앞으로 나아가는 것과 같을 때 끝난다.

049

Advanced mammals such as monkeys, apes, and humans have brains derived from ancestors that took to living in the trees, where vision mattered more than smell.

어휘 advanced 고급의   ancestor 조상   matter 중요하다

원숭이, 유인원, 인간과 같은 고등 포유류는 후각보다 시각이 더 중요하게 작용했던 나무 위 생활에 익숙해진 조상들로부터 물려받은 뇌를 갖고 있다.

050

Many workers lamented the CEO's decision to resign because of the unfortunate incident.

어휘 resign 사임하다   incident 사건

많은 직원들이 불행한 사건 때문에 사임하기로 한 CEO의 결정을 슬퍼했다.

A. Choose the right answer for the underlined word.

1 Greg lamented that he didn't study enough for the test.

Greg는 시험 공부를 제대로 하지 않은 것을 후회했다.

(A) announced (B) regretted (C) boosted (D) addressed

2 The number of shipping companies mushroomed in the 1870s.

선박 회사들의 수는 1870년대에 급증했다.

(A) attended (B) finished (C) swelled (D) disclosed

3 I simply don't see much opportunity for me to advance my ideas here.

단지 여기에서 나의 아이디어를 제시할 기회가 많아 보이지 않는다.

(A) pay (B) elevate (C) report (D) propose

4 Our mother would yell at us if we grumbled about our food.

우리가 음식에 대해 불평하면 어머니는 우리에게 소리를 지르곤 했다.

(A) asserted (B) resisted (C) complained (D) progressed

5 Her attendance at the rally declared her political allegiance.

그녀는 그 집회에 참석함으로써 자신의 정치적 충성심을 분명히 보여 주었다.

(A) proclaimed (B) improved (C) discussed (D) grieved

6 Many English words derived from Latin.

많은 영어 단어들이 라틴어에서 파생한 것이다.

(A) murmured (B) originated (C) maintained (D) disputed

7 He treats diplomats in the lavish surroundings of his country estate.

그는 자신의 호화스러운 시골 별장에서 외교관들을 접대한다.

(A) entertains (B) dismisses (C) fights (D) promotes

8 The government has agreed to lift restrictions on trade with Britain.

정부는 영국과의 무역에서 규제를 철폐하는 데 동의했다.

(A) handle (B) end (C) mourn (D) snowball

Answers A 1. B 2. C 3. D 4. C 5. A 6. B 7. A 8. B

B. Fill in the blanks.

advance	declare	lift	treat	oppose
mushroom	grumble	terminate	derive	lament

1   He was _____ by a doctor right after the accident.

그는 사고 직후에 의사의 치료를 받았다.

2   The workers _____ because they had to work over the weekend.

직원들은 주말에 일해야 했기 때문에 불평했다.

3   The publisher _____ her $10,000 against future royalties.

출판사는 그녀에게 1만 달러를 향후 저작권료에서 선지급했다.

4   The company's debts _____ as the sales continued to decline.

매출이 계속 감소하면서 그 회사의 부채는 급속히 늘었다.

5   The player's contract was _____ after he was caught lying.

그 선수가 거짓말한 것이 탄로났을 때 그의 계약은 끝났다.

C. Choose the right answer.

1   Robert's parents thought he should _____ in school and finish his education. Robert의 부모님은 그가 학교에 남아 공부를 마쳐야 한다고 생각했다.

(A) grumble   (B) treat   (C) remain   (D) lift

2   I can lend you a hand when you have to _____ this heavy sofa.

네가 이 무거운 소파를 들어올려야 될 때 도와줄게.

(A) lift   (B) advance   (C) derive   (D) terminate

3   The area around the volcano has been _____ a national monument.

그 화산의 주변 지역은 국가 기념물로 공식 지정되어 왔다.

(A) lamented   (B) advanced   (C) treated   (D) declared

4   The teacher _____ the lack of effort from her students.

교사는 학생들의 노력 부족을 한탄했다.

(A) terminated   (B) remained   (C) lamented   (D) derived

B   1. treated   2. grumbled   3. advanced   4. mushroomed   5. terminated
C   1. C   2. A   3. D   4. C

051

You can enjoy pure air and *clean* water at the lake.
그 호수에서는 맑은 공기와 깨끗한 물을 즐길 수 있다.

pure · 순수한 innocent
[pjuər] · 청결한 unspoiled, clean
· 불순물이 섞이지 않은 unadulterated

052

It was such an *easy* question that the answer was obvious to everyone. 그것은 아주 쉬운 질문이라서 정답은 모두에게 분명했다.

obvious · 명백한, 분명한 apparent, evident, clear, indisputable
[ábviəs]

053

The party is informal, so dress casually.
그 파티는 비공식적인 것이다. 그러니 캐쥬얼하게 옷을 입어라.

informal · 비공식의, 약식의 unofficial, unceremonious
[infɔ́ːrməl] · 격식을 차리지 않는, 허물없는 casual, relaxed, free
- informally · 비공식적으로

054

Maria is not only *beautiful* but also has an attractive personality. Maria는 아름다울 뿐 아니라 매력적인 성품도 가지고 있다.

attractive · 매력적인, 관심을 끄는 appealing, inviting, enticing, engaging
[ətrǽktiv] · 아름다운 pretty, beautiful

055

Laziness is the principal or *main* cause of his failure.
게으름이 그가 실패한 가장 큰 주요 원인이다.

principal · 주요한, 주된, 제일의 central, chief, main, major
[prínsəpəl] · 교장, 학장 head teacher, dean
· 원금, 자산 capital, asset

056

Remembering these *important* facts is vital.

이러한 중요한 사실을 기억하는 것이 필수적이다.

vital [váitəl]	(형) 생명의, 생명 유지에 필요한 필수적인, 긴요한 essential, critical, fundamental 생생한, 활기찬 lively, dynamic, vibrant

057

Bob is an apt student who *learns very quickly*.

Bob은 아주 빨리 배우는 총명한 학생이다.

apt [æpt]	(형) 영리한, 이해가 빠른, 재주 있는 smart, capable, gifted ~하기 쉬운, ~하는 경향이 있는 likely, liable, prone, disposed

058

Many animals stay dormant and *inactive* during winter.

많은 동물들은 겨울 동안에는 동면하면서 활동하지 않는다.

dormant [dɔ́ːrmənt]	(형) 잠자는 (듯한) sleeping 동면하는 hibernating 잠재해 있는 inactive, suspended

059

***Not much is known* about this obscure artist.**

이 무명의 예술가에 대해 알려진 것은 많지 않다.

obscure [əbskjúər]	(형) 잘 알려지지 않은, 무명의 unknown 분명하지 않은, 애매한 uncertain, unclear 눈에 띄지 않는 unnoticeable (동) 덮어 감추다 hide, conceal 애매하게 하다 weaken

060

Mark was being equivocal and *didn't give clear* answer.

Mark는 모호한 상태로 확실한 답을 제시하지 않았다.

equivocal [ikwívəkəl]	(형) (태도·상황이) 애매한, 불분명한 ambiguous, vague, uncertain (말의 뜻이) 모호한 oblique - equivocally (부) 애매하게

051

Even before we spend our money, making, advertising, and packaging what we buy can cost a lot in pure water, air, and soil. (2000년 수능 예문 26번)

어휘 advertise 광고하다   package 포장하다

우리의 돈을 쓰기도 전에, 우리가 사는 것을 만들고 광고하고 포장하는 것은 깨끗한 물, 공기, 토양에 많은 대가를 치르게 할 수 있다.

052

It is obvious that scientists study earthquakes to warn people from possible earthquakes.

어휘 earthquake 지진

과학자들은 가능한 지진에 대해 사람들에게 경고하기 위해 지진을 연구하는 것이 분명하다.

053

The ice cream cone, the hamburger, and iced tea were all introduced at the 1904 Louisiana Purchase Exposition informally known as the St. Louis Fair.

어휘 introduce 소개하다   exposition 전시회   fair 품평회

아이스크림콘, 햄버거, 아이스티는 1904년 비공식적으로는 St. Louis Fair로 알려진 Louisiana Purchase Exposition에서 소개되었다.

054

The only long-term solution is to make life in the rural areas more attractive, which would encourage people to stay there. (1996년 기출 수능 예문 49~50번)

어휘 long-term 장기적인   rural 시골의, 농촌의   stay 머무르다

유일한 장기적인 해결책은 농촌 지역의 생활을 더 매력적으로 만들어 사람들이 그곳에 머물도록 장려하는 것이다.

055

The 20-year loan should cost people between $21 million and $30 million with principal and interest.

어휘 loan 대출

20년 대출은 사람들이 원금과 이자로 2,100만~3,000만 달러를 내야 한다.

056 His writing was vital to him because that was the only thing that kept him going despite the harsh reality.

어휘 despite ~에도 불구하고　harsh 가혹한, 무자비한
글쓰기는 가혹한 현실에도 불구하고 그가 버텨낼 수 있게 만든 유일한 것이었기에 그에게 필수적이었다.

057 A drastic change in one part of the environment is apt to cause an equally drastic, but unexpected change somewhere else.

어휘 drastic 급격한, 철저한　unexpected 뜻밖의
환경의 한 부분에서의 급격한 변화는 다른 부분에서 똑같이 급격하지만 뜻밖의 변화를 일으키기 쉽다.

058 In the early spring of 1980, scientists announced the reawakening of the dormant volcano.

어휘 reawaken 다시 깨어나다　volcano 화산
1980년 이른 봄에 과학자들은 그 휴화산의 활동 재개를 발표했다.

059 The old man cactus is so called because of the long, silvery hairs that totally obscure its leafless, columnar stem.

어휘 columnar 원주의, 원형의　stem 줄기
The old man cactus는 잎이 없는 원형 줄기를 완전히 덮고 있는 긴 은백색 털 때문에 그렇게 불린다.

060 Parents who speak equivocally may cause their children to become confused.

어휘 confused 혼란스러워하는
애매하게 말하는 부모들은 자녀들을 혼란스럽게 할 수도 있다.

A. Choose the right answer for the underlined word.

1 It was an <u>obscure</u> mistake that no one really noticed at first.
그것은 처음에는 아무도 알아차리지 못한 눈에 띄지 않는 실수였다.

(A) indisputable (B) robust (C) unnoticeable (D) fundamental

2 The flower is the most <u>attractive</u>, most colorful, and most fragrant part of many plants. 꽃은 많은 식물의 가장 매력적이며 가장 다채롭고 가장 향기로운 부분이다.

(A) clear (B) beautiful (C) innocence (D) vibrant

3 Many cold-blooded animals are <u>dormant</u> during the winter.
많은 냉혈 동물들은 겨울철에 동면한다.

(A) breathing (B) inviting (C) hibernating (D) tending

4 Chemically <u>pure</u> iron has relatively few commercial uses.
화학적으로 순수한 철은 상업적인 쓸모가 비교적 거의 없다.

(A) suspended (B) weakened (C) disposed (D) unadulterated

5 Roger needs to be reminded about the meeting because he is <u>apt</u> to forget. Roger는 잘 잊어버리니까 회의에 대해 상기시켜 주어야 한다.

(A) apparent (B) relaxed (C) essential (D) likely

6 We rushed past the <u>obvious</u>.
우리는 서두르다가 명백한 사실을 지나치고 말았다.

(A) evident (B) unspoiled (C) appealing (D) unceremonious

7 The book is written in an <u>informal</u> way to make the readers understand it easily. 그 책은 독자들이 이해하기 쉽도록 평이한 방식으로 쓰여 있다.

(A) major (B) engaging (C) inactive (D) casual

8 There was nothing <u>equivocal</u> about Mr. Smith's statement.
Smith 씨의 말에 모호한 것은 전혀 없었다.

(A) ambiguous (B) central (C) pretty (D) unofficial

Answers **A** 1. C 2. B 3. C 4. D 5. D 6. A 7. D 8. A

B. Fill in the blanks.

| pure obvious informal attractive principal |
| vital apt dormant obscure equivocal |

1   Silver is a(n) _____ white metal that has a bright shine.
은은 밝은 빛을 내는 순수한 흰색 금속이다.

2   Mr. Daniels grew up in a(n) _____ village.
Daniels 씨는 잘 알려지지 않은 마을에서 자랐다.

3   The new products are displayed in _____ containers.
신제품들은 멋있는 용기에 담겨 전시된다.

4   America's railroads were a(n) _____ part of the war effort.
미국의 철도는 전쟁 노력의 긴요한 부분이었다.

5   Danny was being _____ about what he got on the test.
Danny는 시험에서 몇 점을 받았는지 불분명하게 말했다.

C. Choose the right answer.

1   Rice is the _____ crop for many Asians.
쌀은 많은 아시아인들에게 주요 곡물이다.

(A) principal   (B) dormant   (C) pure   (D) attractive

2   Two sides have reached a(n) _____ agreement.
양측은 비공식적인 합의에 도달했다.

(A) apt   (B) obvious   (C) informal   (D) principal

3   No one is more _____ at math than Peter.
Peter보다 수학을 더 잘하는 사람은 없다.

(A) attractive   (B) apt   (C) vital   (D) pure

4   The virus remains _____ in nerve tissue until activated.
바이러스는 활성화될 때까지는 신경 조직 속에 잠복해 있다.

(A) vital   (B) obscure   (C) equivocal   (D) dormant

B   1. pure   2. obscure   3. attractive   4. vital   5. equivocal
C   1. A   2. C   3. B   4. D

061

Connie doesn't appear to be angry but *seems* worried.
Connie는 화나 보이지는 않지만 걱정스러워하는 것 같다.

appear
[əpíər]

동 나타나다 come into view, emerge, surface
~처럼 보이다 seem
출연하다 perform, act

062

I favor Monday, but Tim *prefers* Tuesday to go on vacation.
나는 휴가 갈 때 월요일을 좋아하지만 Tim은 화요일을 더 좋아한다.

favor
[féivər]

동 ~에 찬성하다 approve, endorse, support
편애하다 prefer
명 호의 kindness, courtesy
편애 preference

063

I oppose his plan but *agree* with his idea.
나는 그의 계획은 반대하지만 그의 아이디어에는 찬성한다.

oppose
[əpóuz]

동 ~에 반대하다 resist, dispute
~에 대항하다 fight, dissent

064

Ron *picked* the black one while I selected the white one.
Ron은 검은색을 고른 반면 나는 흰색을 선택했다.

select
[silékt]

동 선택하다 choose, designate
뽑다 pick
형 정선한 elite, limited, superior

065

The traffic was flowing and *moving* easily this morning.
오늘 아침 교통은 원활하게 소통되고 있었다.

flow
[flou]

동 흐르다 stream, travel, run
통하다, 순환하다 circulate
명 흐름 current

066 **The fire alarm was *set off*, but no one knew who triggered it.** 화재 경보기가 울렸지만 누가 작동시켰는지 아는 사람이 없었다.

trigger   ⑧ 유발하다 set off, cause, generate, spark
[trígər]   ⑲ 방아쇠

067 **The new product's design can *change* and its price can fluctuate.** 신제품의 디자인이 바뀔 수 있으며 가격이 변동될 수 있다.

fluctuate   ⑧ 동요하다 waver, vary, alternate, sway
[flʌ́ktʃuèit]

068 **I *accept* the idea and embrace it knowing how it makes me a better person.** 나는 그 아이디어가 나를 어떻게 나은 사람으로 만들어 준다는 것을 알고 그것을 받아들이고 포용한다.

embrace   ⑧ 포옹하다 hug / 포함하다 include, contain
[imbréis]   맞이하다 receive, welcome
         채택하다 adopt
      ⑲ 포옹 hug

069 **The man manifested his anger by *showing* violent behavior.** 그 사람은 난폭한 행동을 보임으로써 분노를 드러냈다.

manifest   ⑧ 드러내다 display, exhibit, reveal, show
[mǽnəfèst]   ⑱ 명백한, 분명한 apparent, evident, obvious

070 **The farmer built a greenhouse to *grow* and cultivate bananas.** 농부는 바나나를 키우고 재배하기 위해 온실을 지었다.

cultivate   ⑧ (땅을) 갈다 plow
[kʌ́ltəvèit]   재배하다 grow
        계발하다 develop, improve, advance
        장려하다 encourage

061 **Someone's life may appear perfect from the outside, but the reality may be a whole other story.**

(어휘) reality 현실
어떤 사람의 삶은 겉으로는 완벽해 보이겠지만 실상은 완전히 다를 수 있다.

062 **The play found favor with the opening-night audience.**

(어휘) audience 관객, 청중
그 연극은 공연 첫날 밤에 관객들의 호응을 얻었다.

063 **Many people oppose the death penalty because of the possibility of miscarriage of justice.**

(어휘) death penalty 사형   miscarriage of justice 오심
많은 사람들이 오심의 가능성을 이유로 사형 제도를 반대한다.

064 **This time around, the drug company has signed contracts with a select group of wholesalers.**

(어휘) wholesaler 도매상인
최근에 그 제약회사는 선정된 도매업자 그룹과 계약을 체결했다.

065 **If you want not to be noticed, you should go with the flow.**

(어휘) notice 주목하다
당신이 주목받기를 원하지 않는다면 대세를 따라야 할 것이다.

066 The flower bud of a water lily opens at sunset since its opening is triggered by the decreased light.

어휘 bud 봉오리   sunset 일몰   decrease 감소하다   trigger 촉발하다
수련 꽃봉오리는 해질녘에 피어나는데, 그 꽃의 개화는 감소한 빛에 촉발되기 때문이다.

067 A manic-depressive usually fluctuates between great excitement and deep depression.

어휘 manic-depressive 조울병 환자   deep 깊은, 심한   depression 우울함, 의기소침
조울병 환자는 대개 커다란 흥분과 깊은 우울감 사이에서 오락가락한다.

068 Prohibition was embraced with varying degrees of enthusiasm in different parts of the country, and enforced accordingly.

어휘 Prohibition 금주령   enthusiasm 열정   varying 가지각색의   enforce 실행하다
금주령은 그 나라의 서로 다른 분야에서 다양한 정도로 수용되어 그에 따라 시행되었다.

069 Her manifest lack of interest in the project has provoked severe criticism.

어휘 provoke 유발하다   criticism 비판
그 프로젝트에 대한 그녀의 명백한 무관심이 혹독한 비판을 불러일으켰다.

070 Dialects form a part of our identity, and dialectical differences may be cultivated and maintained because we want to be associated with certain groups.

어휘 dialect 방언, 사투리   identity 정체성
방언은 우리 정체성의 일부를 형성하며, 방언 차이는 양성되고 유지되기도 하는데 이것은 우리가 특정 집단과 연계되고 싶어 하기 때문이다.

A. Choose the right answer for the underlined word.

1 The evidence <u>manifests</u> the guilt of the defendant.
그 증거는 피고의 유죄를 분명히 드러낸다.

(A) reveals   (B) advances   (C) dissents   (D) emerges

2 Mr. Cumming <u>favors</u> his youngest son.
Cumming 씨는 막내 아들을 더 좋아한다.

(A) welcomes   (B) hugs   (C) picks   (D) prefers

3 Temperature <u>fluctuates</u> greatly during this time of the year.
연중 이맘때의 기온은 변동이 심하다.

(A) shows   (B) varies   (C) surfaces   (D) disputes

4 We checked the room and everything <u>appeared</u> to be in order.
우리가 그 방을 확인했을 때 모든 것이 정돈되어 있는 것처럼 보였다.

(A) approved   (B) seemed   (C) adopted   (D) improved

5 Many experts <u>opposed</u> the mayor's proposal.
많은 전문가들은 시장의 제안에 반대했다.

(A) endorsed   (B) designated   (C) resisted   (D) wavered

6 When an electric current <u>flows</u> through a wire, a magnetic field appears around the wire. 전류가 전선을 통해 흐를 때, 전선 주변에 자기장이 나타난다.

(A) develops   (B) generates   (C) recieves   (D) travels

7 He could not comprehend how Grant had ever been <u>selected</u> for this mission. 그는 Grant가 어떻게 이 임무에 선발됐는지 이해할 수 없었다.

(A) chosen   (B) supported   (C) sparked   (D) displayed

8 You'll only worry about achieving them, and that will <u>trigger</u> a whole host of new anxieties. 당신은 그것들을 성취하는 것에 대해 걱정하기만 할 것이고, 그것은 새로운 근심거리들을 유발할 것이다.

(A) sway   (B) cause   (C) perform   (D) plow

Answers   A   1. A   2. D   3. B   4. B   5. C   6. D   7. A   8. B

B. Fill in the blanks.

appear	favor	oppose	select	flow
trigger	fluctuate	embrace	manifest	cultivate

1 The river _____ from north to south.
그 강은 북쪽에서 남쪽으로 흐른다.

2 You can be a better writer if you can _____ a love for reading.
독서에 대한 사랑을 키울 수 있다면 너는 나은 작가가 될 수 있다.

3 A full mailbox may _____ a robber to break into your house.
가득 찬 우편함은 도둑이 침입하게 만드는 원인이 될 수 있다.

4 Gas prices _____ all week because of the political troubles in Iran.
이란의 정치 불안 때문에 한 주 내내 기름 값이 요동쳤다.

5 For the most part, Congress and the people _____ the changes that
Roosevelt made. 대부분의 경우 국회와 국민은 Roosevelt 대통령이 일으킨 변화를 수용했다.

C. Choose the right answer.

1 There are more than 10 choices that you can _____ from.
당신이 선택할 수 있는 것이 10가지가 넘는다.

   (A) fluctuate   (B) oppose   (C) select   (D) manifest

2 The wind _____ their journey.
바람은 그들이 여행하기에 좋게 불었다.

   (A) favored   (B) cultivated   (C) appeared   (D) opposed

3 Everything I do will be for my own benefit, as _____ to the benefit
of a company. 내가 하는 모든 것은 나 자신의 이익을 위하고 회사의 이익에 반할 것이다.

   (A) opposed   (B) fluctuated   (C) triggered   (D) selected

4 Surprisingly, most wild animals _____ a fear of humans.
놀랍게도 대부분의 야생 동물들은 인간에 대한 두려움을 나타낸다.

   (A) embrace   (B) manifest   (C) oppose   (D) cultivate

B 1. flows   2. cultivate   3. trigger   4. fluctuated   5. embraced
C 1. C   2. A   3. A   4. B

071

The term is not a often used expression.
그 용어는 흔히 사용되지 않는 표현이다.

term   (명) 용어, 표현 expression, phrase
[təːrm]   조건 condition
                 기간 period / 학기 semester
                 임기 tenure
           (동) 칭하다 call, label

072

Mary grew up receiving all the affection and *love* from her parents. Mary는 부모님으로부터 온갖 애정과 사랑을 받으며 자랐다.

affection   (명) 애정, 애착 tenderness, fondness, attachment
[əfékʃən]

073

Players prefer to play soccer on *grass* fields.
선수들은 잔디 구장에서 축구하기를 더 좋아한다.

field   (명) 들, 벌판 grassland
[fiːld]   현장 site, location
                 분야, 영역 area, subject
                 구장, 필드 ground

074

I went to the library to get materials and *information* for a report. 나는 보고서를 위한 자료와 정보를 구하러 도서관에 갔다.

material   (명) 재료 substance
[mətí(ː)əriəl]   요소 matter, element
                 자료 information
           (형) 물질적인 physical, tangible, corporeal

075

We can protect *nature* by reducing and preventing air pollution in the environment.
우리는 환경에서 대기 오염을 줄이고 예방함으로써 자연을 보호할 수 있다.

environment   (명) 환경 ecology, atmosphere
[inváiərənmənt] 주위 setting, surrounding, conditions

076

The debts became a big burden and a serious *problem*.
빚이 큰 부담이자 심각한 문제가 되었다.

burden   몡 책임, 부담 responsibility, liability
[bɔ́:rdən]   고생 difficulty, hardship
          통 짐을 지우다 hamper, hinder, impede

077

Molly's aspiration is *to become* a successful doctor.
Molly의 포부는 성공적인 의사가 되는 것이다.

aspiration   몡 열망 yearning, longing
[æ̀spəréiʃən]   포부 ambition, hope, goal

078

The summit marked the first time that these two presidents had a meeting. 그 정상 회담은 이 두 대통령이 최초로 만난 것이었다.

summit   몡 정상, 꼭대기 top, peak, apex
[sʌ́mit]   정상 회담 summit talk

079

Upon *approval*, an official sanction letter will be sent to you. 승인과 동시에 공식 허가증이 당신에게 보내질 것이다.

sanction   몡 승인, 인가 approval
[sǽŋkʃən]   제재 penalty
          통 허가하다 allow, approve
          제재하다 penalize

080

We learn the importance of virtues like honesty and righteousness in school.
우리는 학교에서 정직함이나 정의와 같은 미덕들의 중요성을 배운다.

virtue   몡 미덕 morality, integrity
[vɔ́:rtʃuː]   선행 goodness, excellence
          장점 merit, asset

071 The Republican incumbent said he wants to create 250,000 new jobs if elected to a second term.

[어휘] Republican 공화당의   incumbent 현역 의원
그 공화당 현역 의원은 자신이 재선되면 25만 개의 새 일자리를 창출하고 싶다고 말했다.

072 It could mean that I like you. That would be a kind of affection. [1994년 2차 수능 예문 15번]

[어휘] a kind of 일종의
그것은 내가 당신을 좋아한다는 것을 의미할 수도 있다. 그것은 일종의 애정일 것이다.

073 Cornelius Vanderbilt's success in shipping encouraged him to extend his interests into the field of railroad transportation in the early 1860s.

[어휘] shipping 해운업, 선박업   extend 확장하다, 넓히다   transportation 운송, 수송
1860년대 초, 해운업에서의 Cornelius Vanderbilt의 성공은 그의 관심 분야를 철도 운송 분야로 확대하도록 자극했다.

074 The first is the material culture, which is made up of all the physical objects that people make and give meaning to.

[1999년 수능 예문 29번]

[어휘] make up 구성하다, 지어내다
첫째는 물질 문화인데, 그것은 사람들이 만들고 의미를 부여하는 모든 물리적 물체들로 이루어져 있다.

075 He said he also wants to ensure a good environment for children and teachers.

[어휘] ensure 보장하다
그는 자신도 역시 아이들과 교사를 위한 좋은 환경을 보장하고 싶다고 말했다.

076

He is always burdened by the fact that he has to support his entire family.

어휘 support 부양하다

그는 항상 가족 전체를 부양해야 한다는 사실에 부담을 가지고 있다.

077

As nineteenth-century American cultural aspirations expanded, women stepped into a new role as interpreters of art, both by writing works on art history and by teaching art.

어휘 step into ~에 발을 들여놓다   role 역할, 배역   interpreter 해석자, 통역사

19세기 미국의 문화적인 열망이 확산되면서 여성들은 미술사에 대한 작품을 쓰고 미술을 가르치면서 미술 해석자로서의 새 역할을 맡기 시작했다.

078

The Argentine mountain named Aconcagua is the highest summit outside Central Asia.

아르헨티나의 Aconcagua라는 산은 중앙아시아 외곽에서 가장 높은 정상이다.

079

The UN sanctioned Iraq for its failure to comply with the treaty.

어휘 comply with 지키다, 준수하다   treaty 협정, 조약

유엔은 협정을 준수하지 않은 이라크에 제재를 가했다.

080

An open-door policy is regarded as the country's central virtue and a vital means to peace.

어휘 be regarded as ~으로 여겨지다   vital 중요한   means 수단

개방 정책은 그 나라의 중심적인 미덕이자 평화를 위한 긴요한 수단으로 여겨진다.

A. Choose the right answer for the underlined word.

1 The main virtue of the new model is its price.
새 모델의 주요 장점은 가격이다.

(A) expression   (B) merit   (C) responsibility (D) goal

2 Among all societies, legal marriage is usually accompanied by some kind of ceremony that expresses group sanction of the union.
모든 사회에서 법률혼에는 대개 그 결합에 대한 집단의 승인을 표시하는 모종의 예식이 따른다.

(A) hardship   (B) morality   (C) approval   (D) tenure

3 Mr. Connor decided to retire at the summit of his career.
Connor 씨는 그의 경력의 정점에서 은퇴하기로 결정했다.

(A) ecology   (B) difficulty   (C) peak   (D) site

4 What sort of loan term were you interested in?
어떤 종류의 대출 조건에 관심이 있었나요?

(A) condition   (B) yearning   (C) subject   (D) integrity

5 People usually think of their hometown with affection.
사람들은 대개 애정을 가지고 고향을 생각한다.

(A) goodness   (B) setting   (C) element   (D) fondness

6 The native plants and animals have developed many mechanisms to adapt to the desert environment.
토종 식물과 동물은 사막 환경에 적응하기 위해 많은 메커니즘을 발전시켰다.

(A) surrounding   (B) tenderness   (C) location   (D) excellence

7 Forests provide us with building materials and fuels in the form of lumber.
숲은 재목의 형태로 우리에게 건축 재료와 연료를 제공한다.

(A) conditions   (B) assets   (C) grounds   (D) substances

8 Close to one-fifth of the burden of disease in developing countries can be attributed to environmental risks.
개발도상국 전염병 원인의 5분의 1 정도는 환경적 위험 요소 때문이다.

(A) penalty   (B) apex   (C) period   (D) liability

Answers   A 1. B   2. C   3. C   4. A   5. D   6. A   7. D   8. D

B. Fill in the blanks.

term	affection	field	material	environment
burden	aspiration	summit	sanction	virtue

1 She'll explain the techniques in simple _____ .
그녀는 쉬운 용어로 기술적인 것을 설명할 것이다.

2 People consider the judge as a man of _____ .
사람들은 그 판사를 덕을 갖춘 사람이라고 생각한다.

3 A farmer noticed a spot in his _____ that did not grow crops well.
농부는 밭에서 농작물이 제대로 자라지 않는 한 곳을 발견했다.

4 Many people view the holiday as an opportunity to express _____ to friends and family. 많은 사람들은 휴일을 친구와 가족들에게 애정을 표현하는 기회라고 여긴다.

5 These behaviors are a distraction from the learning _____ .
이러한 행동들은 학습 환경에서 벗어나는 것이다.

C. Choose the right answer.

1 The boy's teachers did not think he was college _____ .
그 소년의 선생님들은 그가 대학에 갈 만한 실력이라고는 생각하지 않았다.

(A) field   (B) term   (C) material   (D) virtue

2 Wheel is one of the first and most useful inventions easing the _____ of work. 바퀴는 노동의 부담을 덜어 준 최초이자 가장 유용한 발명품 중의 하나이다.

(A) summit   (B) affection   (C) burden   (D) sanction

3 We were very tired after reaching the _____ .
우리는 산 정상에 도달한 후 아주 피곤했다.

(A) material   (B) environment   (C) aspiration   (D) summit

4 The UN decided to lift _____ against the country.
UN은 그 나라에 대한 제재를 철폐하기로 결정했다.

(A) burdens   (B) virtues   (C) sanctions   (D) materials

B 1. terms   2. virtue   3. field   4. affection   5. environment
C 1. C   2. C   3. D   4. C

081 **Derek** provided **me with a place to sleep and** *gave* **me some food.** Derek은 나에게 잠잘 곳을 제공하고 음식을 주었다.

provide   동 제공하다 supply, furnish, yield
[prəváid]   주다 give, afford

082 **The fireman** rescued **the children but couldn't** *save* **their dog.** 소방관은 아이들은 구했지만 그들의 개는 구하지 못했다.

rescue   동 구조하다, 구하다 save, deliver
[réskju:]   회복하다 recover
       해방시키다 free, liberate
      명 구출, 구조 salvation, deliverance

083 **Sarah** faced **many problems and** *dealt with* **them by herself.** Sarah는 많은 문제들에 직면해 혼자서 그것들을 처리했다.

face   동 직면하다 meet, confront, encounter, tackle
[feis]   명 외관 surface, feature, façade
      측면 aspect

084 **He** labored **up to 12 hours a day at** *work*. 그는 직장에서 하루에 최대 12시간씩 노동했다.

labor   동 노동하다, 애쓰다 toil, struggle, strive, endeavor
[léibər]   명 노동 work
      노력, 수고 effort, toil

085 **Although the government didn't want gas prices to** rise, **they** *went up*. 정부는 기름 값이 상승하는 것을 원하지 않았지만 가격이 올랐다.

rise   동 일어나다 get up
[raiz]   오르다, 상승하다 ascend, soar, increase
      발전하다 progress, advance, improve, develop
      나타나다 emerge, appear

086

The farmer scattered the seeds *over all the field*.
그 농부는 밭 전체에 씨앗을 뿌렸다.

scatter   (동) 뿌리다, 흩뜨리다   spread, disperse, distribute, sprinkle
[skǽtər]

087

I don't recall where I met her, but I do *remember* her name.
그녀를 어디에서 만났는지 기억할 수는 없지만 그녀의 이름은 분명히 기억한다.

recall   (동) 상기하다   remember, recollect
[rikɔ́:l]   되부르다, 소환하다   call back
           (명) (불량 상품의) 회수, 리콜
           회상, 상기   recollection, memory

088

Do you want to *get rid of* insects? Our product will eradicate them right away.
벌레를 없애고 싶습니까? 저희 제품이 즉시 박멸해 드리겠습니다.

eradicate   (동) 근절하다, 박멸하다   eliminate, exterminate
[irǽdəkèit]   뿌리째 뽑다   uproot, wipe out

089

I cherish and *respect* your valuable advices.
나는 너의 귀중한 충고를 존중하고 가치 있게 여긴다.

cherish   (동) 소중히 여기다   value, prize, treasure, revere
[tʃériʃ]

090

He sealed the envelope so that his brother *can't open* it.
그는 형이 열 수 없도록 봉투를 봉했다.

seal   (동) 도장을 찍다, 조인하다   ratify
[si:l]   확정짓다, 확실하게 하다   finalize, secure
        봉인하다, 밀봉하다   enclose, close
        (명) 도장   stamp / 봉인
        바다표범

081

In an experiment on their behavior, baby monkeys were separated from their mothers at birth and provided with artificial mother. (2001년 수능 예문 24번)

(어휘) experiment 실험   behavior 행동, 습성   at birth 출생 시에   artificial 인공의
원숭이들의 행동에 대한 실험에서 새끼 원숭이들은 태어나자마자 어미로부터 분리되어 인공 어미를 제공받았다.

082

The economic crisis called for the federal government to come to the rescue.

(어휘) crisis 위기, 국면   call for 요구하다   federal government 연방 정부
경제 위기는 연방 정부의 구조를 필요로 했다.

083

These are just old problems with new faces.

이것들은 새로운 얼굴을 한 오래된 문제들일 뿐이다.

084

Child labor was first recognized as a social problem with the introduction of the factory system in late 18th-century Great Britain.

(어휘) recognize 인식하다   introduction 도입
미성년자 노동은 18세기 말 영국에 공장 제도가 도입되면서 처음 사회 문제로 인식되었다.

085

With the rise of the "theater of the absurd," trends in scenery design have become eclectic, ranging from realism to surrealism.

(어휘) absurd 부조리(의)   scenery 경치, 무대 배경   eclectic 절충적인, 다방면에 걸친
'부조리 연극'의 출현과 함께 배경 디자인의 경향은 현실주의에서 초현실주의에 이르기까지 다양하게 되었다.

086 **He scattered sand on the floor and tapped ever so softly.**

어휘 tap 가볍게 두드리다
그는 바닥에 모래를 뿌리고 아주 부드럽게 두드렸다.

087 **Studying for an hour a day for a week will result in improved information recall and retention as compared to studying for seven hours straight in one day.**

어휘 retention 보존력, 기억력
일주일에 매일 1시간씩 공부하는 것은 하루에 7시간 연이어 공부하는 것에 비해 정보 회상력과 기억력을 향상시켜 줄 것이다.

088 **The Salk vaccine is a major factor in the fight to eradicate polio.**

어휘 major 주요한   factor 요소, 요인
소크 백신은 소아마비를 근절하기 위한 싸움에서 주요한 요소이다.

089 **In an interview for the BBC, he says his country has "set a good example for the millions of people who still cherish freedom and democracy."**

어휘 millions of 수백만의   democracy 민주주의
BBC와의 인터뷰에서 그는 자기 나라가 자유와 민주주의를 여전히 소중히 여기는 수백만의 사람들에게 좋은 본보기가 되었다고 말한다.

090 **Several countries like Norway and Denmark joined in the campaign to protect whales and seals in their national parks.** [1996년 수능 예문 36번]

어휘 campaign 캠페인
노르웨이와 덴마크 같은 몇몇 나라는 자국의 국립공원 내에서 고래와 바다표범을 보호하기 위한 캠페인에 동참했다.

A. Choose the right answer for the underlined word.

1 The police scattered the crowd.

경찰이 군중을 해산시켰다.

(A) dispersed　　(B) liberated　　(C) supplied　　(D) confronted

2 It rises or falls as the glaciers melt or grow. 〔1994년 1차 수능 예문 35번〕

그것은 빙하가 녹거나 커짐에 따라 오르락내리락한다.

(A) ascends　　(B) uproots　　(C) encloses　　(D) frees

3 I recall a little neighbor boy who was trying to balance on his small bicycle after having his training wheels taken off.

보조 바퀴를 떼어낸 후에 자신의 작은 자전거 위에서 균형을 잡으려고 애쓰던 이웃집 남자아이가 생각난다.

(A) appear　　(B) revere　　(C) recollect　　(D) spread

4 Researchers have suggested that the stress workaholics labor under can lead to some serious health consequences.

연구자들은 일 중독자들이 일하면서 받는 스트레스가 심각한 건강 문제를 일으킬 수 있음을 시사해 왔다.

(A) distribute　　(B) afford　　(C) toil　　(D) advance

5 The intention of Social Security was to eradicate poverty in America.

미국 사회보장제도의 취지는 미국에서 가난을 근절하는 것이었다.

(A) struggle　　(B) eliminate　　(C) improve　　(D) value

6 The new research provides additional support to the already strong arguments against smoking.

새로운 연구 결과는 흡연에 반대하는 기존의 강한 주장에 더욱 힘을 실어 준다.

(A) ratifies　　(B) recovers　　(C) yields　　(D) develops

7 Jake's last-minute goal sealed the victory for his team.

Jake가 마지막 순간에 넣은 골은 그의 팀의 승리를 굳혀 주었다.

(A) soared　　(B) met　　(C) prized　　(D) secured

8 The World Wildlife Foundation has rescued several species of animals since 1961. 〔1996년 수능 예문 36번〕

국제야생동물기금은 1961년 이래로 몇몇 종의 동물을 구해 왔다.

(A) remembered　(B) saved　　(C) furnished　　(D) wiped out

Answers　　**A** 1. A　2. A　3. C　4. C　5. B　6. C　7. D　8. B

B. Fill in the blanks.

> provide   rescue   face   labor   rise
> scatter   recall   eradicate   cherish   seal

1   The new president promised to _____ government corruption.
새 대통령은 정부의 부패를 근절할 것을 약속했다.

2   My things are _____ all around the room and bathroom.
내 물건들이 방과 화장실에 온통 널려 있다.

3   Every year, several parts of the world _____ severe water shortages.
매년 세계 여러 곳이 극심한 물 부족에 직면하고 있다.

4   By the end of the century, temperatures could _____ by more than 10°F all year round in the Northeast.
금세기 말에는 북동부의 연간 기온이 화씨 10도 이상 상승할 가능성이 있다.

5   Can you _____ what she said?
그녀가 무슨 말을 했는지 기억할 수 있니?

C. Choose the right answer.

1   I _____ and value our friendship greatly.
나는 우리의 우정을 매우 소중하고 가치 있게 여긴다.

(A) seal   (B) labor   (C) provide   (D) cherish

2   Salt added to the water used to boil eggs will _____ a cracked egg by coagulating the leaking white.
달걀을 삶을 때 쓰이는 물에 첨가된 소금은 새는 흰자를 응고시킴으로써 금이 간 달걀을 봉해 줄 것이다.

(A) scatter   (B) face   (C) seal   (D) eradicate

3   The book has received negative reviews for _____ the reader with unnecessary details. 그 책은 불필요한 세부 사항으로 독자들을 힘들게 한다는 부정적인 평가를 받고 있다.

(A) cherishing   (B) laboring   (C) eradicating   (D) rising

4   It is also the father's duty to _____ for the physical needs of his family. 가족들의 물리적 필요를 채워 주는 것 역시 아버지의 의무이다.

(A) provide   (B) rescue   (C) scatter   (D) seal

B   1. eradicate   2. scattered   3. face   4. rise   5. recall
C   1. D   2. C   3. B   4. A

091

It was *difficult* and tough decision, but I had to fire my cousin. 그것은 어렵고 힘든 결정이었지만 나는 사촌을 해고해야 했다.

tough
[tʌf]

⟨형⟩ 강인한, 굳센 strong
단단한, 질긴, 튼튼한 hard, resilient
힘든, 어려운 difficult, arduous

092

The basic level requires only *simple* steps.
기초 수준에서는 간단한 단계들만 필요하다.

basic
[béisik]

⟨형⟩ 기초적인 fundamental, elementary
근본의 central, essential, key
기본적인 simple, plain
⟨명⟩ 기본, 원리 fundamental, essential, principle
필수품 necessity

093

You need to *keep up to date* with current events.
너는 현재 일어나는 사건들에 대해 항상 알고 있어야 한다.

current
[kə́:rənt]

⟨형⟩ 현재의 present, existing, recent
최신의 up-to-date, modern, contemporary
⟨명⟩ 흐름 flow, stream
조류, 해류

094

Ron needs to learn to ask appropriate questions at the *right* time. Ron은 적절한 때에 적합한 질문을 하는 것을 배워야 한다.

appropriate
[əpróupriət]
[əpróuprièit]⟨동⟩

⟨형⟩ 적합한 proper, suitable
⟨동⟩ 충당하다 assume
책정하다 expropriate

095

We sell a lot of this model because it is so practical and *useful*. 이 모델은 아주 실용적이고 유용해서 많이 팔린다.

practical
[prǽktikəl]

⟨형⟩ 실용적인 pragmatic, functional, sensible
실제적인, 현실성 있는 realistic, feasible

096

Smoking is detrimental to your health and *harmful* to others. 흡연은 당신의 건강에 해롭고 다른 사람들에게도 유해하다.

detrimental　　형 유해한 harmful, injurious, deleterious
[dètrəméntəl]　　손해가 되는 unfortunate, disadvantageous

097

***Hard work and luck* enabled Jack to make vast *sums of money*.** Jack은 근면함과 행운 덕분에 큰돈을 벌 수 있었다.

vast　　형 거대한 enormous, immense, huge
[væst]　　막대한 great, extensive, considerable

098

You need to be careful with *wild* animals because they can be ferocious. 야생 동물들은 사나울 수도 있기 때문에 조심해야 한다.

ferocious　　형 사나운 savage, fierce
[fəróuʃəs]　　잔인한 cruel

099

It was a deceptive speech because it was full of *misleading* facts. 그 연설은 오도하는 사실이 가득했기 때문에 기만적인 것이었다.

deceptive　　형 기만적인, 현혹하는 misleading, false, deceitful
[diséptiv]　　믿을 수 없는 fake, spurious

100

Bob certainly has a unique personality: there is *no one like him*. Bob은 확실히 독특한 성격을 갖고 있다. 그와 같은 사람은 아무도 없다.

unique　　형 독특한 exceptional, extraordinary, peerless, unparalleled
[juːníːk]

091   **Oaks are strong, long-lived trees with tough wood.**

(어휘) long-lived 장수하는, 수명이 긴
참나무는 목질이 단단해 강하며 장수하는 나무이다.

092   **The movie actor is taking a step back from the silver screen to learn the basics he missed out on in his speedy rise to stardom.**

(어휘) stardom 스타의 자리
그 영화배우는 급히 스타가 되면서 놓친 기초를 익히려고 은막에서 한 걸음 물러나 있을 것이다.

093   **Dangerous waste dumped off the coast of a country is often transported by strong ocean currents to other places all around the globe.**

(어휘) dump 버리다
한 나라의 해안에 버려진 오염 물질들은 강한 해류에 의해 전 세계의 다른 장소들로 운반되는 경우가 많다.

094   **Family-style child-care centers attempt to provide age-appropriate developmental opportunities that assist in fostering development in all areas.**

(어휘) developmental 발전(발육)의, 개발적인   assist 돕다, 원조하다
가정 스타일의 어린이집은 모든 영역에서 발달을 촉진시키는 데 도움이 되는 연령에 적합한 발달 기회를 제공하려고 시도한다.

095   **The practical importance of the numerous applications of weather forecasting cannot be overestimated.**

(어휘) numerous 많은   forecast 예보하다   overestimate 과대평가하다
일기 예보의 무수한 응용의 실제적인 중요성은 아무리 과대평가해도 지나치지 않다.

096

Studies show that when a teenager befriends only one or two people, and spends all of their time with that limited group, it can be detrimental to the person's social health.

어휘 befriend ~와 친구가 되다

연구들은 십대 청소년이 한두 사람과만 친하게 지내며 그 한정된 집단과 시간의 대부분을 보내면, 그 사람의 사회적 건강에 해로울 수 있다는 것을 보여 준다.

097

The vast majority of people believe that it's a good idea to limit smoking in places like bus stops and public parks.

어휘 vast majority of 대다수의   limit 제한하다

대다수의 사람들은 버스 정류장이나 공원 같은 곳들에서 흡연을 제한하는 것이 좋은 아이디어라고 생각한다.

098

Despite their seemingly ferocious appearance, gorillas are very gentle and peace-minded, forest-dwelling giants.

어휘 seemingly 겉보기에는   peace-minded 평화를 추구하는   dwell 거주하다

사나워 보이는 외모에도 불구하고 고릴라는 아주 부드럽고 평화를 사랑하는 숲에 사는 거인들이다.

099

Deceptive labeling of certain types of merchandise is not allowed under the Pure Food and Drug Act of 1906.

어휘 label 라벨을 붙이다   merchandise 상품

특정 유형의 상품에 기만적인 라벨을 붙이는 것은 1906년에 제정된 순수 식품 의약 법안에 의해 금지되고 있다.

100

In his novels, Upton Sinclair showed his unique genius for recreating social history.

어휘 genius 천부적 재능, 천재   recreate 재현하다

Upton Sinclair는 그의 소설에서 사회의 역사를 재현하는 데 있어 독특한 천재성을 보여 주었다.

A. Choose the right answer for the underlined word.

1   The <u>practical</u> contributions of the theory are unquestioned.
그 이론의 실용적 공헌에는 의문의 여지가 없다.

(A) fundamental   (B) extraordinary (C) recent   (D) functional

2   While some bacteria are beneficial, others are <u>detrimental</u> in that they cause disease. 일부 세균은 유익한 반면에, 다른 것들은 질병을 유발하므로 유해하다.

(A) unparalleled   (B) harmful   (C) spurious   (D) difficult

3   Although the job is <u>tough</u>, the pay will be good.
그 일은 고되기는 하겠지만 보수는 괜찮을 것이다.

(A) arduous   (B) savage   (C) elementary   (D) realistic

4   Effective next month, the company is raising the rate for its <u>basic</u> cable television service by $2. 다음 달부터 그 회사는 기본 케이블 TV 서비스 요금을 2달러 인상할 것이다.

(A) pragmatic   (B) simple   (C) cruel   (D) strong

5   Many people at that time thought it would be <u>appropriate</u> to name the planet after him, in recognition of his accomplishments.
그 당시 많은 사람들은 그의 업적을 인정하여 행성에 그의 이름을 따서 붙이는 것을 타당하다고 생각했다.

(A) disadvantageous   (B) suitable   (C) considerable (D) central

6   You are a <u>unique</u> individual who, as an active actor in life's drama, can make things happen.
여러분은 인생 드라마 속의 능동적인 배우로서 상황을 스스로 만들어 나가는 독자적인 개인입니다.

(A) exceptional   (B) immense   (C) key   (D) resilient

7   When cornered, a bobcat is <u>ferocious</u>.
스라소니는 구석에 몰리면 사나워진다.

(A) hard   (B) enormous   (C) fierce   (D) contemporary

8   Don't be fooled by the <u>deceptive</u> advertising.
그 거짓 광고에 속지 마라.

(A) misleading   (B) peerless   (C) proper   (D) extensive

B. Fill in the blanks.

tough	basic	current	appropriate	practical
detrimental	vast	ferocious	deceptive	unique

1   The firemen had a very hard time putting out _____ fire.
소방관들은 사나운 불길을 잡는 데 무척 애를 먹었다.

2   The used car salesman is simply being _____ and misleading.
그 중고차 영업 사원은 단순히 속이고 현혹한다.

3   We need to be _____ about the situation.
우리는 그 상황에 대해 좀 더 현실적일 필요가 있다.

4   Building more nuclear power plants is not the answer to our _____ problem. 더 많은 원자력 발전소를 짓는 것은 현재 우리의 당면 문제에 대한 답이 아니다.

5   Researchers have discovered that dolphins convey _____ emotions such as happiness and sadness.
연구자들은 돌고래가 행복과 슬픔과 같은 기본적인 감정을 표현한다는 것을 알게 되었다.

C. Choose the right answer.

1   It will be really _____ for him to accept the news.
그로서는 그 소식을 받아들이기가 아주 어려울 것이다.

(A) current   (B) deceptive   (C) ferocious   (D) tough

2   The student failed to provide a(n) _____ excuse for his absence.
그 학생은 결석한 것에 대해서 적절한 해명을 하지 못했다.

(A) unique   (B) basic   (C) appropriate   (D) ferocious

3   Taken to an extreme, however, perfectionism can be very _____.
하지만 극한 상태의 완벽주의는 매우 해로울 수 있다.

(A) vast   (B) detrimental   (C) current   (D) practical

4   Jefferson had long dreamed of exploring the _____ land on the other side of the Mississippi. Jefferson은 오랫동안 미시시피 강 너머의 광활한 땅을 탐험하는 것을 꿈꾸어 왔다.

(A) appropriate   (B) tough   (C) detrimental   (D) vast

B   1. ferocious   2. deceptive   3. practical   4. current   5. basic
C   1. D   2. C   3. B   4. D

101

The agency is created to aid, *help* and protect the interests of the middle class. 그 기관은 중산층의 이익을 보호하고 지원하기 위해 창립되었다.

aid
[eid]

통 돕다, 원조하다, 거들다 help, support, assist
명 원조, 도움 assistance, help

102

The Lions *won* the championship by beating the Bears.
라이언스 팀은 베어스 팀을 이겨서 우승을 차지했다.

beat
[biːt]

통 연달아 치다, 두드리다 batter, strike
이기다, 패배시키다 conquer, defeat
명 구타
박자 rhythm

103

Mr. Kline founded a company which *created* many jobs.
Kline 씨는 많은 일자리를 창출한 회사를 설립했다.

found
[faund]

동 설립하다 establish, set up, erect
시작하다 originate, launch
기초를 두다 base

104

He wanted to soak his feet but ended up getting his pants *wet*. 그는 발을 물에 담그고 싶었지만 결국 바지까지 적시게 되었다.

soak
[souk]

동 흠뻑 적시다 drench, saturate, douse
~에 스며들다 penetrate, pervade, permeate
빨아들이다, (지식을) 흡수하다 absorb, understand, grasp

105

Many feel that new law restricts freedom of speech and *limits* people's rights.
많은 사람들은 새 법률이 언론의 자유를 제한하고 사람들의 권리를 제한한다고 느낀다.

restrict
[ristríkt]

동 제한하다, 한정하다 limit, confine, restrain, constrain

106 **The architect refused to *change* or modify his design.**
그 건축가는 자신의 설계를 변경하거나 수정하기를 거절했다.

modify   동 수정하다 change, alter
[mάdəfài]   완화하다, 조절하다 moderate, adjust

107 **His action was justified when the judge *found him not guilty*.** 판사가 그가 무죄라고 판결했을 때 그의 행동은 정당화되었다.

justify   동 정당화하다, 증명하다 rationalize, prove, verify
[dʒʌstəfài]

108 **Everyone wanted Mr. Ellis to facilitate the meeting so that it'll *go smoothly*.**
모든 사람은 Ellis 씨가 회의를 도와 순조롭게 진행되도록 하기를 바랐다.

facilitate   동 용이하게 하다, 돕다, 촉진하다 make easier, expedite, aid, promote
[fəsílitèit]

109 **The survivors fashioned tents and *made* other things from what they had.** 생존자들은 갖고 있던 것으로 텐트와 다른 물건들을 만들었다.

fashion   동 만들다 create, shape, make, construct
[fǽʃən]   명 패션, 유행 fad, trend, vogue
        방식, 양식 mode, style, method, way
        관습 custom, tradition

110 **Two companies will remain partners and collaborate in future projects.** 두 회사는 파트너로 남아 앞으로의 프로젝트에서 협력할 것이다.

collaborate   동 협력하다, 합작하다 cooperate, combine, work together
[kəlǽbərèit]

101 **The federal government allots millions of dollars for emergency aids.**

(어휘) allot 할당하다, 배정하다   emergency 긴급, 긴급용의
연방 정부는 긴급 원조용으로 수백만 달러를 배정하고 있다.

102 **A folk song will often vary its beat or alternate between major and minor keys.**

(어휘) alternate between A and B A와 B 사이를 오가다
포크 송은 박자를 다양하게 바꾸거나 장조와 단조 사이를 왔다 갔다 하는 경우가 많다.

103 **Is the article a complete fabrication or is it founded on reality?**

(어휘) fabrication 조립, 구성
그 기사는 완전히 날조된 것인가 아니면 사실에 근거한 것인가?

104 **It takes time to soak in Professor Johnson's lecture.**

(어휘) lecture 강의
Johnson 교수의 강의를 이해하려면 시간이 걸린다.

105 **For example, the giraffe has adapted to grazing on treetops, but it is specialized and thus restricted to grazing on trees.**

(1994년 2차 수능 예문 34번)

(어휘) adapt 적응시키다   graze 풀을 뜯어먹다
예를 들어 기린은 나무 꼭대기의 잎을 먹는 데 적응했지만 특화되어 나무의 잎을 먹는 것으로 제한되었다.

The texture of sandy soils is generally very difficult to modify because huge amounts of organic material must be added.

[어휘] texture 짜임새, 결   organic 유기의
모래 토양은 엄청난 양의 유기 물질이 첨가되어야만 하기 때문에 일반적으로 바꾸기가 매우 어렵다.

Most importantly, don't try to justify your mistakes by saying that you didn't really mean what you said.

[어휘] mean 뜻하다
가장 중요한 것은 당신이 한 말이 사실은 그런 뜻이 아니었다고 말함으로써 자기 실수를 정당화하려고 하지 않는 것이다.

All levels of government should facilitate the flight of people from the central city into the suburbs.

[어휘] flight 도피, 탈출   suburbs 교외 지역
모든 수준의 정부는 사람들이 중심 도시에서 교외 지역으로 탈출하는 것을 도와야 한다.

He liked the fashion of the simple, sturdy furniture.

[어휘] simple 단순한, 소박한   sturdy 견고한
그는 소박하고 견고한 가구 양식을 좋아했다.

Honey guides, or indicator birds, collaborate with honey badgers in seeking out bee colonies.

[어휘] guide 안내인   indicator 지표, 표지   seek out 찾아내다
일명 '표지 새'라고도 불리는 줄안내새는 벌들이 모여 있는 곳을 찾을 때 오소리와 협력한다.

A. Choose the right answer for the underlined word.

1 Children love to beat on toy drums or empty boxes.

아이들은 장난감 북이나 빈 상자를 두드리기를 무척 좋아한다.

(A) grasp   (B) strike   (C) alter   (D) constrain

2 The cavemen fashioned tools from stones.

석기 시대 원시인들은 돌로 도구를 만들었다.

(A) based   (B) made   (C) defeated   (D) launched

3 Foxes aid the farmer by attacking destructive rodents.

여우들은 해로운 설치류 동물을 공격함으로써 농민들을 돕는다.

(A) saturate   (B) prove   (C) assist   (D) promote

4 The end does not always justify the means.

목적이 항상 수단을 정당화하는 것은 아니다.

(A) rationalize   (B) understand   (C) douse   (D) shape

5 The candidate refused to modify his stand on the tax issue.

그 후보는 세금 문제에 대한 자신의 입장을 바꾸기를 거부했다.

(A) erect   (B) create   (C) narrow   (D) adjust

6 The use of computers in school is facilitated by this realization.

이러한 인식으로 인해 학교에서의 컴퓨터 이용이 활성화되었다.

(A) drenched   (B) constructed   (C) confined   (D) expedited

7 Green plants soak up sunlight and use it, along with water and carbon dioxide, to produce their own food so that they can grow.

녹색 식물은 햇빛을 흡수해 물과 이산화탄소와 함께 사용해 자신이 성장할 수 있도록 영양물을 만들어 낸다.

(A) moderate   (B) set up   (C) originate   (D) absorb

8 By 1900, many municipalities began to restrict the use of automobiles to ensure pedestrian safety.

1900년경에는 여러 지방 자치체들이 보행자의 안전을 보장하기 위해 자동차 사용을 제한하기 시작했다.

(A) combine   (B) aid   (C) conquer   (D) limit

Answers   A   1. B   2. B   3. C   4. A   5. D   6. D   7. D   8. D

B. Fill in the blanks.

aid   beat   found   soak   restrict
modify   justify   facilitate   fashion   collaborate

1 Having the receipt will _____ your refund.
영수증을 갖고 있으면 환불이 용이해질 것이다.

2 The benefits of a gym membership do not _____ the cost.
헬스클럽 회원권의 혜택이 가격을 정당화하지는 않는다.

3 Many volunteers can master skills that _____ them to get ready for
real-world jobs. 많은 자원봉사자들은 실제 취업할 준비를 하는 데 도움이 되는 기술을 숙달할 수 있다.

4 We had to _____ our schedule after the latest delay.
최근의 지연 때문에 우리 일정을 변경해야 했다.

5 Nothing _____ being out on the water on such a beautiful day.
이렇게 날씨 좋은 날에는 물로 나가 있는 것보다 더 좋은 것이 없다.

C. Choose the right answer.

1 Most water _____ into the ground and will eventually become part
of another body of water. 대부분의 물은 땅속으로 스며들어 또 다른 물줄기의 일부가 된다.

(A) facilitates   (B) restricts   (C) beats   (D) soaks

2 The singer _____ with many famous musicians.
그 가수는 많은 유명한 음악가와 함께 일했다.

(A) justified   (B) fashioned   (C) collaborated   (D) founded

3 The use of the Internet was _____ to a certain fields for decades.
수십 년간 인터넷 사용이 특정 분야들에 제한되었다.

(A) soaked   (B) facilitated   (C) restricted   (D) aided

4 The Romans _____ the ancient city of London, the capital of the
United Kingdom, in AD 43. 로마인들이 서기 43년에 영국의 수도인 런던의 고대 도시를 건립했다.

(A) founded   (B) justified   (C) modified   (D) beat

B 1. facilitate   2. justify   3. aid   4. modify   5. beats
C 1. D   2. C   3. C   4. A

111

It was difficult to deny that these *facts* were evidence to set Harry free. 이 사실들이 Harry를 풀려나게 할 증거라는 것은 부인하기 어려웠다.

evidence
[évidəns]
- 명 증거, 증명 proof, verification, confirmation
- 징표, 징후 sign, mark, indication
- 통 입증하다 prove, confirm
- 보여 주다 reveal

112

He has a great faith and *trust* in his friends.
그는 친구들에게 큰 믿음과 신뢰를 지니고 있다.

faith
[feiθ]
- 명 신앙, 믿음 belief, creed
- 신뢰 trust, confidence
- 신념 conviction

113

The *idea* of calling the teacher by his first name is a strange notion to some. 일부에게는 선생님을 이름으로 부르는 아이디어가 특이한 생각이다.

notion
[nóuʃən]
- 명 관념, 개념 conception, view
- 생각 idea, thought
- 의견 opinion

114

We all hope that a high-tech *solution* will be a remedy for our problem. 우리 모두는 첨단 기술 해법이 우리 문제에 대한 해결책이 되기를 희망한다.

remedy
[rémədi]
- 명 치료, 의료 treatment, cure
- 해결책 solution
- 교정 correction
- 통 고치다 correct
- 치료하다 heal, cure

115

The purpose of the medical record is to *keep track of* the patient's history. 진료 기록의 목적은 환자의 병력을 계속 추적하는 것이다.

record
[rékərd]
[rikɔ́:rd] 통
- 명 기록 account, log, report, journal
- 통 기록하다, 등록하다 chronicle, register
- (계기가) 표시하다, 나타내다 register, show, indicate

116

Rob said he reached the peak, but I didn't see him at the mountaintop. Rob은 정상에 도달했다고 말했지만 나는 산꼭대기에서 그를 보지 못했다.

peak
[pi:k]
- 명 산꼭대기 mountaintop, summit, point
- 첨단, 뾰족한 끝 edge
- 절정, 최고도, 정점 height
- 형 최고의, 절정의 climax
- 동 최고도에 이르다 culminate, consummate

117

He is having a difficult time with financial adversity.
그는 재정난으로 어려움을 겪고 있다.

adversity
[ædvə́:rsəti]
- 명 역경, 불행 difficulty, hardship, misfortune

118

I love to smell the aroma of freshly baked bread.
나는 갓 구운 빵 냄새를 맡는 것을 무척 좋아한다.

aroma
[əróumə]
- 명 향기 fragrance, scent, smell, odor

119

I committed the blunder, but I won't make the same mistake again. 나는 큰 실수를 저질렀다. 하지만 다시 같은 실수를 하지 않을 것이다.

blunder
[blʌ́ndər]
- 명 큰 실수 error, slip, mistake, fumble
- 동 큰 실수를 하다 bungle, botch, goof

120

This hiking trail is a difficult course for a beginner.
이 하이킹 트레일은 초보자에게는 어려운 코스이다.

trail
[treil]
- 명 흔적 track, trace
- 오솔길, 등산로 path, track, route, course
- 동 뒤지다, 낙오하다 lag[fall] behind
- 뒤쫓다 chase, follow, pursue

111 But today there is evidence that regular exposure to the ultraviolet rays of sunlight, especially if it results in burns, can be harmful to health. (1996년 수능 예문 21번)

(어휘) exposure 노출   harmful 해로운

그러나 오늘날 일광 자외선에의 정기적인 노출이 특히 화상을 일으킬 경우에 건강에 해로울 수 있다는 증거가 있다.

112 It was through his faith that he was able to overcome the most difficult time in his life.

(어휘) overcome 극복하다   difficult 어려운, 힘든

그가 생애에서 가장 어려운 때를 극복할 수 있었던 것은 바로 그의 신앙을 통해서였다.

113 Biological determinism is a notion that has important philosophical implications and political consequences.

(어휘) determinism 결정론   implication 암시, 함의   consequence 결과, 중요성

생물학적 결정론은 중요한 철학적 함의와 정치적 중요성을 가진 개념이다.

114 Some of technology's negative aspects are extremely hard to remedy.

(어휘) aspect 측면, 양상

과학기술의 부정적 측면들의 일부는 고치기가 극히 어렵다.

115 Raising that kind of money is difficult for someone without a business record because the flow of venture capital has dried up. (1998년 수능 예문 43번)

(어휘) raise 올리다, 모으다   capital 자본(금)   dry up 바싹 마르다, 바닥나다

벤처 자본의 흐름이 고갈되었기 때문에 사업 경력이 없는 사람이 그 정도의 돈을 모으기는 어렵다.

116 He probably travels at a peak time when the airports are crowded and unpleasant. [1994년 2차 수능 예문 44번]

(어휘) crowded 붐비는   unpleasant 불쾌한
그는 아마도 공항이 붐비고 불쾌한 피크타임에 여행하게 될 것이다.

117 A friend will show his or her true colors in times of adversity.

(어휘) show one's true colors 본색을 드러내다
친구는 역경의 시기에 본색을 드러낼 것이다.

118 The aroma of seasoned meat, cooked on barbecue grill, hangs in the air.

(어휘) seasoned 양념을 한, 조미한
바비큐 그릴 위에서 구워진 양념 고기의 냄새가 공기 속에 배어 있다.

119 Diplomatic misunderstandings can often be traced back to blunders in translation.

(어휘) diplomatic 외교상의   misunderstanding 오해, 분쟁   translation 번역, 해석
외교적인 오해는 번역상의 큰 실수에서 비롯되었을 가능성이 많다.

120 Today Mount St. Helens is quiet again, as sightseers walk along wooded trails and view the majesty of the mountain.

(어휘) sightseer 관광객   majesty 웅장함, 장관
요즈음 St. Helens 산이 다시 잠잠해지자 관광객들은 숲길을 산책하고 산의 장관을 감상한다.

A. Choose the right answer for the underlined word.

1　None of the highest <u>peaks</u> in Alaska is of volcanic origin.
알래스카 주의 가장 높은 봉우리들 중에 화산으로 생긴 것은 하나도 없다.

(A) logs　　　　(B) opinions　　　　(C) courses　　　　(D) summits

2　Although Doug is only 20 years old, he experienced many <u>adversities</u> in life. Doug는 20세밖에 안 됐지만 살면서 많은 역경을 겪었다.

(A) mistakes　　(B) hardships　　　(C) heights　　　　(D) corrections

3　You should keep a <u>record</u> of how much you spend in a month.
한 달에 얼마를 쓰는지 계속 기록해야 한다.

(A) error　　　　(B) point　　　　(C) trust　　　　(D) account

4　Historians have found <u>evidence</u> of a tsunami more than 300 feet high along the coast of Crete some 1,600 years BC.
역사가들은 기원전 1,600년경에 크레타 섬 연안에 높이 300피트가 넘는 쓰나미가 덮친 증거를 발견했다.

(A) conception　　(B) proof　　　　(C) edge　　　　(D) fragrance

5　It is widely known that vitamin C is one of the effective <u>remedies</u> for the common cold. 비타민 C는 일반 감기에 효과적인 치료제의 하나로 널리 알려져 있다.

(A) treatments　(B) convictions　(C) reports　　　(D) confirmations

6　He wakes up to the <u>aroma</u> of coffee every morning.
그는 매일 아침 커피 향에 잠을 깬다.

(A) conception　　(B) scent　　　　(C) track　　　　(D) confidence

7　The hurricane left a <u>trail</u> of destruction behind it.
허리케인은 파괴의 흔적을 남겨 두었다.

(A) fumble　　　(B) solution　　　(C) cure　　　　(D) trace

8　The editor was able to catch the reporter's silly <u>blunder</u>.
편집자는 그 기자의 터무니없는 실수를 잡아낼 수 있었다.

(A) verification　(B) slip　　　　(C) odor　　　　(D) thought

B. Fill in the blanks.

evidence	faith	notion	remedy	record
peak	adversity	aroma	blunder	trail

1 The dish has a very strong _____.
그 요리는 향이 무척 강하다.

2 The scientist's _____ in the new discovery was never in doubt.
새로운 발견에 대한 그 과학자의 믿음은 의심의 여지가 없었다.

3 There are many different _____ of love and romance.
사랑과 로맨스에 대해 여러 다른 개념들이 있다.

4 Eating a lot of oranges can be an effective _____ for the common
cold. 오렌지를 많이 먹는 것이 보통 감기에 효과적인 치료법이 될 수 있다.

5 The Inca civilization reached its _____ in 1400s.
잉카 문명은 1400년대에 절정에 달했다.

C. Choose the right answer.

1 As many as one in five women who have heart attacks or are hospitalized
with heart failure has _____ of depression.
심장 발작을 겪었거나 심부전으로 병원에 입원해 있는 여성 5명 중 1명은 우울증 징후를 보인다.

(A) evidence   (B) adversity   (C) faith   (D) notion

2 The instrument used to _____ earthquakes is called a seismograph.
지진을 기록하는 데 사용되는 기구를 지진계라고 부른다.

(A) evidence   (B) record   (C) peak   (D) remedy

3 The home team was _____ 20 to 15.
홈팀이 20대 15로 뒤지고 있었다.

(A) remedying   (B) blundering   (C) recording   (D) trailing

4 Bill is emotionally strong enough to deal with any kind of _____.
Bill은 어떤 종류의 역경도 이겨낼 정도로 감정적으로 강하다.

(A) aroma   (B) notion   (C) adversity   (D) peak

B 1. aroma   2. faith   3. notions   4. remedy   5. peak
C 1. A   2. B   3. D   4. C

121 **I *like* his personality, but I admire his courage more.**
나는 그의 성품을 좋아하지만 그의 용기를 더 높이 평가한다.

admire   동 높이 평가하다, 존경하다 value, respect, esteem
[ədmáiər]   좋아하다 like, appreciate

122 **When birds migrate, they usually *travel* in groups.**
새들은 이주할 때 대개 무리 지어 이동한다.

migrate   동 이동하다 travel, move
[máigreit]   이주하다 emigrate, immigrate
    - migration 명 이동, 이주 relocation, immigration

123 **His lies *damaged*, but not totally ruined their friendship.**
그의 거짓말은 그들의 우정을 손상했지만 완전히 파괴하지는 않았다.

ruin   동 파괴하다 destroy
[rú(:)in]   손상하다 damage

124 **Mr. Williams thought of an idea to boost sales and *increase* profits.** Williams 씨는 매출을 증대시키고 수익을 늘릴 아이디어를 생각해 냈다.

boost   동 끌어올리다, 상승시키다 lift, raise, elevate, improve
[buːst]   격려하다, 후원하다 bolster, support, encourage
    명 끌어올리기, 인상 increase, rise
    도움, 지지, 후원 aid, help, encouragement, endorsement

125 **The teacher can bear the students' laziness but can't *stand* their lies.** 그 교사는 학생들이 게으른 것은 견딜 수 있지만 거짓말하는 것은 참을 수 없다.

bear   동 낳다, 출산하다 produce, yield, give birth, reproduce, breed
[bɛər]   참다, 견디다 endure, stand, tolerate

126

You should call your doctor if the pain *continues* to persist.
통증이 계속 지속되면 의사에게 전화해야 한다.

persist   통 고집하다 persevere, insist, carry on
[pərsíst]   지속하다 continue, endure, remain
- **persistent** 형 끈덕진, 지속적인 constant, determined, steady
- **persistently** 부 집요하게, 지속적으로 continuously, steadily

127

We *focus* on positives and not dwell on negatives.
우리는 긍정적인 것에 초점을 맞추고 부정적인 것을 깊이 생각하지 않는다.

dwell   통 살다, 거주하다 reside, live, inhabit
[dwel]   머무르다 stay, remain, settle
    생각하다 ponder, consider

128

We can't *carry* all these chairs, so we need a truck to haul them. 우리는 이 의자들을 모두 옮길 수 없으므로 그것들을 운반할 트럭이 필요하다.

haul   통 잡아끌다, 끌어당기다 drag, pull, tug
[hɔːl]   운반하다 transport, convey
    명 어획량 catch
    수송량, 화물 freight

129

Everyone expected him to *give up*, but Harry overcame many difficulties.
모든 사람이 Harry가 포기할 것이라고 예상했지만 그는 많은 어려움을 극복했다.

overcome   통 이기다 defeat, beat, triumph
[òuvərkÁm]   극복하다, 정복하다 conquer, surmount
    압도하다 overpower, prevail

130

He bartered rice for salt and *traded* a cow for a horse.
그는 쌀을 소금으로 바꾸고 소를 말로 교환했다.

barter   통 물물 교환을 하다, 교역하다 trade, exchange
[báːrtər]   협상하다 negotiate, haggle
    명 물물 교환, 교역 trade

121 You can attend writing workshops, read the works of writers that you admire, and solicit constructive criticism from more talented writers.

어휘 solicit 바라다, 구하다
당신은 글쓰기 워크숍에 참석해 당신이 좋아하는 작가들이 쓴 작품을 읽고, 더 재능 있는 작가들의 건설적인 비평을 청할 수도 있다.

122 The persecution of Jews led the migration of Soviet Jews to Israel.

어휘 persecution 핍박, 박해   lead to 유발하다
유대인들에 대한 박해 때문에 소련의 유대인들이 이스라엘로 이주하게 되었다.

123 Several dead bodies of unfortunate victims were lying in the streets, while lots of people were searching for their family members and relatives who had disappeared in the ruins.

어휘 unfortunate 불운한   victim 희생자   search for 찾다
불운한 희생자들의 시신 몇 구가 길가에 드러누워 있었고, 반면에 많은 사람들이 폐허 속에서 없어진 가족과 친척을 찾고 있었다.

124 The candidate received a boost on Monday when *The New York Times* endorsed him in an editorial.

어휘 candidate 후보   endorse 지지하다   editorial 사설
그 후보는 월요일에 〈뉴욕타임스〉가 사설에서 그를 지지하자 격려를 받았다.

125 The relationship will get stronger as partners learn to bear and tolerate each other's negative emotional states.

어휘 relationship 관계   emotional 감정의   state 상태
파트너들이 서로의 부정적 감정 상태를 참고 용인해 가면서 서로의 관계가 더욱 견고해질 것이다.

126 Brooks Adams failed to find the universal law of commerce that he persistently sought.

어휘 universal 보편적인　law 법, 규칙　commerce 상업, 통상
Brooks Adams는 자신이 지속적으로 탐구했던 보편적인 통상 법칙을 찾아내지 못했다.

127 As early as the eleventh century, the Pueblo people dwelt in large cities that were constructed from boulders and mud bricks.

어휘 boulder 둥근 돌　mud 진흙　brick 벽돌
이미 11세기에 Pueblo 족 사람들은 둥근 돌과 진흙 벽돌로 건설된 큰 도시들에 거주했다.

128 One gallon of diesel fuel will haul about four times as much by rail as by truck. [1997년 수능 예문 40번]

어휘 fuel 연료　rail 철도
1갤런의 디젤 연료로 철도는 트럭보다 거의 4배를 운반한다.

129 I try very hard to overcome my prejudice, because I realize it limits me. [1998년 수능 예문 54~55번]

어휘 prejudice 편견　limit 제한하다
나는 편견을 극복하려고 매우 열심히 노력하는데, 편견이 나를 제한한다는 것을 알기 때문이다.

130 By producing an excess amount of some household articles, a New England colonial family could barter with other families.

어휘 excess 초과하는, 잉여의　amount 양　household 가족, 세대
일부 가정용 물품을 초과 생산함으로써 뉴잉글랜드 식민지 가정은 다른 가정들과 물물 교환을 할 수 있었다.

A. Choose the right answer for the underlined word.

1 Merkel has <u>bartered</u> away her reform ambitions to occupy the chancellery.
Merkel은 총리 자리를 차지하기 위해 개혁 야망을 팔아넘겼다.

(A) lifted   (B) yielded   (C) traded   (D) pondered

2 I <u>admire</u> his work for its richness and profoundness.
나는 그의 작품을 풍요롭고 깊이가 있어 높이 평가한다.

(A) persevere   (B) endure   (C) triumph   (D) appreciate

3 The researcher spends most of his time in the forest to study tree-<u>dwelling</u> animals. 그 연구자는 나무에 거주하는 동물들을 연구하기 위해 숲에서 대부분의 시간을 보낸다.

(A) inhabiting   (B) damaging   (C) standing   (D) insisting

4 Jane's test scores <u>boosted</u> her confidence.
Jane의 시험 점수가 그녀의 자신감을 높여 주었다.

(A) respected   (B) considered   (C) raised   (D) dragged

5 The walnut is a deciduous tree that <u>bears</u> valuable nuts.
호두나무는 값진 견과를 맺는 낙엽수이다.

(A) prevails   (B) produces   (C) endures   (D) stays

6 During the Civil War, steam-boating on the lower Mississippi River was <u>ruined</u>. 남북 전쟁 동안 미시시피 강 하류의 증기선 운항이 타격을 입었다.

(A) negotiated   (B) destroyed   (C) improved   (D) traveled

7 Speech difficulties may sometimes could be <u>overcome</u> if a person is shown where to place the tongue and teeth to make sounds.
소리를 내기 위해 혀와 이를 어디에 두어야 할지를 보여 준다면 언어 장애는 때때로 극복될 수 있을 것이다.

(A) tolerated   (B) pulled   (C) resided   (D) conquered

8 Raised for its milk, meat, and hide, the reindeer is also used to <u>haul</u> things from place to place. 젖, 고기, 가죽을 얻기 위해 사육되는 순록은 이곳저곳으로 물건을 운반하는 데에도 사용된다.

(A) transport   (B) haggle   (C) exchange   (D) reproduce

Answers   A   1. C   2. D   3. A   4. C   5. B   6. B   7. D   8. A

B. Fill in the blanks.

admire	migrate	ruin	boost	bear
persist	dwell	haul	overcome	barter

1 Martha _____ four children by the time she turned 25.

Martha는 25세가 될 때까지 4명의 아이를 낳았다.

2 Despite the increase last week, the gasoline price is _____ again.

지난주의 인상에도 불구하고 휘발유 값이 다시 오르고 있다.

3 A visa is required for anyone wishing to travel or _____ to the country. 그 나라로 이주하거나 여행하기를 원하는 사람은 누구나 비자가 필요하다.

4 We still _____ and appreciate Leonardo da Vinci's works to this day.

오늘날까지 우리는 레오나르도 다빈치의 작품을 높이 평가하고 감상한다.

5 It is too bad that news media tend to _____ mostly on bad news.

뉴스 매체가 주로 나쁜 소식을 자세히 다루는 경향이 있는 것은 매우 유감이다.

C. Choose the right answer.

1 We arrived with new _____ for the villagers.

우리는 주민들을 위한 새로운 교역품을 갖고 도착했다.

(A) haul   (B) migration   (C) barter   (D) boost

2 Too much debt will not only _____ you but also destroy your family.

지나치게 많은 빚은 당신을 망칠 뿐만 아니라 가정마저 파괴할 것이다.

(A) overcome   (B) bear   (C) ruin   (D) admire

3 Mark usually _____ with the problem until he gets the answer.

Mark는 보통 해답을 구할 때까지 문제와 계속 씨름한다.

(A) persists   (B) overcomes   (C) dwells   (D) barters

4 He is _____ down box after box and really starting to sweat.

그는 상자들을 계속 내리다가 정말로 땀이 나기 시작했다.

(A) admiring   (B) boosting   (C) migrating   (D) hauling

B 1. bore 2. boosted 3. migrate 4. admire 5. dwell

C 1. C 2. C 3. A 4. D

131 **One may expect her recovery from surgery to be** gradual **rather than speedy.**
그녀의 수술 후 회복은 신속하기보다는 점진적일 것으로 예상할 수 있다.

gradual
[grǽdʒuəl]
형 점진적인, 완만한 slow, steady, measured, moderate
- gradually 부 점차, 서서히

132 **The *traffic was so bad* that it took Martha** forever **to get home.** 교통 정체가 너무 심해서 Martha가 집에 도착하는 데 아주 오래 걸렸다.

forever
[fərévər]
형 영원히, 언제나, 오랫동안 constantly, eternally, indefinitely, infinitely
명 오랜 시간, 영원

133 **We feel safe and** secure **in our home.**
우리는 집에서 위험이 없고 안전하다고 느낀다.

secure
[sikjúər]
형 안전한, 위험이 없는 safe, protected, sheltered
동 확보하다 obtain, acquire,
확실하게 하다 assure, guarantee
보호하다 guard, protect

134 **He was an** absolute **ruler because he had *complete* power.**
그는 완전한 권력을 가졌기 때문에 절대적인 통치자였다.

absolute
[ǽbsəlùːt]
형 절대적인 supreme, ultimate
완전한 complete, total, thorough
확실한, 명백한 clear, certain, sure
명 절대적인 것

135 **It was considered people's car because it was *cheap* and** economical. 그 차는 싸고 경제적이었기 때문에 국민차로 여겨졌다.

economical
[ìːkənámikəl]
형 경제적인, 저렴한 inexpensive, cheap, reasonable
절약하는, 검소한 thrifty, frugal

136

He pays attention to every *small* and minute detail.
그는 작고 사소한 모든 세부에까지 관심을 기울인다.

minute   형 미세한, 아주 작은 small, tiny, miniscule, infinitesimal
[mainjúːt]

137

We have diverse students with *different* interests.
우리에게는 관심사가 다른 다양한 학생들이 있다.

diverse   형 다양한, 다른 various, dissimilar, different, distinct
[divə́ːrs]   - diversified 형 다각적인, 다채로운 varied, assorted
     - diversify 동 다양화하다, 다각화하다 vary, mix
     - diversity 명 다양성 difference, distinctiveness, variety

138

It was *wrong* and inappropriate for him to say such a thing.
그가 그런 말을 하는 것은 잘못되었고 부적절했다.

inappropriate   형 부적절한 wrong, unsuitable, improper
[ìnəpróupriət]   - inappropriately 부 부적절하게

139

The situation is indeed very serious, and it is a grave situation. 상황이 실로 매우 심각하여 그것은 중대한 상황이다.

grave   형 중대한 serious, critical, important, significant
[greiv]   엄숙한 solemn, somber
     명 무덤 tomb
     - gravely 부 중대하게

140

Service at this hotel is always *quick* and prompt.
이 호텔의 서비스는 항상 빠르고 신속하다.

prompt   형 신속한, 기민한 quick, rapid, swift, expeditious
[prɑmpt]   시간을 지키는 on time, punctual
     동 자극하다, 유발하다 cause, induce, encourage
     - promptly 부 신속하게, 기민하게

131 You gradually become aware that you are a unique person with your own ideas and attitudes. (1996년 수능 예문 41번)

(어휘) aware 알아차린   unique 독특한   attitude 태도
당신은 점차 자신이 고유한 생각과 태도를 지닌 유일한 사람이라는 것을 알아차리게 된다.

132 She is forever bumping elbows with the person sitting next to her at lunch and having to take off her watch to wind or adjust it.

(어휘) bump ~에 부딪히다   elbow 팔꿈치   adjust 맞추다
그녀는 언제나 점심 식사 시간에 옆에 앉은 사람과 팔꿈치를 부딪치고 손목시계를 벗어 태엽을 감거나 시간을 맞추어야 한다.

133 The novel secured his reputation.

(어휘) reputation 명성
그 소설로 그는 확실하게 명성을 확보했다.

134 One hundred percent, though, is an absolute scandal, and I am not prepared to pay such a large increase. (1998년 수능 예문 18번)

(어휘) prepare 준비하다, 대비하다   increase 증가, 인상   scandal 스캔들, 추문
하지만 100퍼센트 인상은 전혀 터무니없는 것이며 저는 그런 큰 인상분을 지불할 준비가 되어 있지 않습니다.

135 The architect is noted for his economical use of interior space.

(어휘) architect 건축가   be noted for ~으로 유명하다   interior 내부의   space 공간
그 건축가는 실내 공간을 경제적으로 사용하는 것으로 유명하다.

136 The minute water drops settle on everything, including grass, bushes, and trees.

어휘 bush 덤불, 관목숲
미세한 물방울들이 풀, 덤불, 나무를 비롯한 모든 것에 내려앉는다.

137 One of the unique aspects of American society is its diversity.

어휘 unique 독특한   aspect 측면, 양상
미국 사회의 독특한 측면들 중의 하나는 그 사회의 다양성이다.

138 The audience felt that the speaker's remark was inappropriate for such a grave issue.

어휘 audience 청중, 관중   speaker 연설가, 강연자
청중은 그 연사의 발언이 그렇게 중대한 문제에 부적절하다고 느꼈다.

139 This production of *Hamlet* is enough to make Shakespeare turn in his grave.

어휘 production 공연 작품
이번 '햄릿' 공연 작품은 셰익스피어가 무덤 속에서 탄식할 만한 것이다.

140 Later, the discovery of gold in California around 1848 prompted a base unit of United States currency.

어휘 discovery 발견   base unit 기본 단위   currency 통화, 유통
훗날 1848년경에 캘리포니아 주에서 금이 발견되어 미국 통화의 기본 단위가 되는 계기가 되었다.

A. Choose the right answer for the underlined word.

1 Please show up one hour before departure to ensure <u>prompt</u> service.
신속한 서비스를 보장하기 위해 출발 1시간 전까지 와 주십시오.

(A) quick   (B) small   (C) cheap   (D) somber

2 Living things consist of <u>minute</u> structures called cells.
생물은 세포라고 불리는 작은 구조물들로 이루어져 있다.

(A) measured   (B) miniscule   (C) thrifty   (D) protected

3 Even the best-built machine will not run <u>forever</u> without proper maintenance. 최고로 만들어진 기계라도 적절하게 유지되지 않으면 영원히 작동하지는 않을 것이다.

(A) inexpensively (B) infinitely   (C) thoroughly   (D) deliberately

4 I am writing to you about something of <u>grave</u> importance, yet it is often overlooked. 저는 아주 중대하지만 자주 간과되고 있는 사안에 대해 편지를 쓰고 있습니다.

(A) assorted   (B) critical   (C) sheltered   (D) infinitesimal

5 Waiting a few months and then renting a movie may be a far more <u>economical</u> option. 몇 달 기다리고 나서 영화를 빌려 보는 것이 훨씬 더 경제적인 선택일 수도 있다.

(A) supreme   (B) reasonable   (C) dissimilar   (D) unsuitable

6 During the years before the American Civil War, differences between the North and the South <u>gradually</u> came to focus on the question of slavery.
미국의 남북 전쟁이 발발하기 전 여러 해 동안 남북 간의 차이점들이 점차 노예 제도 문제로 집중되어 갔다.

(A) seriously   (B) rapidly   (C) eternally   (D) slowly

7 The New River in North Carolina is <u>inappropriately</u> named because it is five hundred million years old.
노스캐롤라이나 주의 New 강은 이름이 적절하지 않은데, 그 강은 5억 년 되었기 때문이다.

(A) differently   (B) improperly   (C) swiftly   (D) indefinitely

8 'Sound law' is a term devised by linguist August Leskien to describe the supposed <u>absolute</u> regularity of this kind of structural change in language.
'음성 법칙'은 언어학자인 August Leskien이 언어에서의 이러한 종류의 구조적 변화에서 가정되는 절대적 규칙성을 묘사하기 위해 고안한 용어이다.

(A) total   (B) distinct   (C) tiny   (D) consequential

B. Fill in the blanks.

gradual	forever	secure	absolute	economical
minute	diverse	inappropriate	grave	promptly

1 Please be back at the bus _____, so we can get to our next
destination on time. 즉시 버스로 돌아와 주십시오. 그래야 우리가 정시에 목적지에 도착할 수 있습니다.

2 The house was a(n) _____ mess.
그 집은 완전히 엉망진창이었다.

3 Checks in many ways are more _____ than other payment methods.
수표는 여러 면에서 다른 결제 방식보다 더 안전하다.

4 Mary says that she has one tiny and _____ problem with her
homework. Mary는 숙제 하는 데 한 가지 작고 사소한 문제가 있다고 말한다.

5 Even before I sat in the dentist chair, I had to wait _____!
나는 치과 진료실 의자에 앉기도 전에 한참을 기다려야 했다!

C. Choose the right answer.

1 Which type of water heating system is the most _____?
어떤 종류의 온수 난방 시스템이 가장 경제적일까?

(A) gradual   (B) diverse   (C) secure   (D) economical

2 There are many different and _____ opinions on the issue.
그 이슈에 대해 여러 다른 다양한 의견들이 있다.

(A) economical   (B) prompt   (C) absolute   (D) diverse

3 We thought that Mark was _____ injured, but he only twisted his
ankle. 우리는 Mark가 중상을 입었다고 생각했지만 그는 발목을 삐었을 뿐이었다.

(A) securely   (B) gravely   (C) forever   (D) minutely

4 _____ weight loss, achieved through a sensible plan of diet and
moderate exercise, is the healthiest option for most adults.
현명한 다이어트 계획과 적당한 운동을 통해 달성하는 점진적인 체중 감량이 대부분의 성인들에게 가장 건강한 선택 방안이다.

(A) Prompt   (B) Gradual   (C) Inappropriate (D) Secure

B 1. promptly   2. absolute   3. secure   4. minute   5. forever
C 1. D   2. D   3. B   4. B

141 **Mr. Cummings *said no* to interviews and declined to answer questions.** Cummings 씨는 인터뷰에 동의하지 않고 질문에 답하기를 거절했다.

decline
[dikláin]
- ⑧ 거절하다, 사절하다 refuse, reject
- 하락하다, 감소하다 decrease, fall
- 쇠퇴하다 weaken, deteriorate
- ⑲ 경사, 내리막 slope
- 몰락, 쇠퇴 downfall, deterioration

142 **After *creating* a new department, Mr. Johnson established new rules.** 새 부서를 창설한 후에 Johnson 씨는 새로운 규칙을 만들었다.

establish
[istǽbliʃ]
- ⑧ 설립하다, 창립하다 create, organize, institute, found, set up

143 **Bob tried to prevent the accident from happening, but *couldn't stop* it.** Bob은 사고 발생을 예방하려고 노력했지만 막지 못했다.

prevent
[privént]
- ⑧ 막다 avoid, impede, avert
- 방해하다 hinder, interfere, obstruct

144 **He tried very hard to obtain the information, but couldn't *get* it.** 그는 정보를 얻으려고 매우 열심히 노력했지만 얻지 못했다.

obtain
[əbtéin]
- ⑧ 얻다, 획득하다 achieve, acquire, get, procure, secure

145 **We need to change the current *rules* that govern the election.** 우리는 선거를 관리하는 현행 규정을 바꾸어야 한다.

govern
[gʌ́vərn]
- ⑧ 다스리다, 지배하다 rule, reign, dominate, dictate
- 통제하다, 관리하다, 좌우하다 control, regulate

146 **The teacher *pointed out* the chapter 2 and underscored its importance.** 선생님은 2장을 가리키며 그것의 중요성을 강조했다.

underscore   통 강조하다 emphasize, stress, underline
[ʌ́ndərskɔ̀ːr]

147 **You should have yielded and *let* the other car *go* first.**
너는 양보해서 다른 차가 먼저 가도록 했어야 했다.

yield   통 산출하다, 생산하다 produce, bear, generate
[jiːld]   항복하다 surrender, give in
            양보하다 give way
          명 생산량, 산출량, 수확량 harvest, produce, output
            수익 profit, return

148 ***Two* companies merged to *form one* giant company.**
두 회사가 합병해 한 거대 회사가 되었다.

merge   통 합병하다, 합치다 combine, unite, join, fuse
[məːrdʒ]

149 **Hard work breeds success and *develops* confidence.**
근면함은 성공을 낳고 신뢰를 발전시킨다.

breed   통 낳다 give birth, reproduce
[briːd]   생산하다 generate
            기르다 raise, rear, nurture
          명 종류, 혈통, 품종 lineage, race, species

150 **When did I grant the permission? I never *agreed* to it.**
내가 언제 허락했지? 나는 절대 찬성하지 않았는데.

grant   통 주다, 수여하다 give, award
[grænt]   허락하다, 승인하다 allow, permit
          명 허가 permission
            보조금, 장학금 subsidy, scholarship, fellowship

141   **After his seventieth birthday he went into a decline.**

(어휘) go into a decline 쇠퇴하다
70회 생일이 지난 후에 그는 쇠약해졌다.

142   **Over the thousands of years Native Americans had established traditions rich with myths and legends that highlighted their religious beliefs.**

(어휘) myth 신화   legend 전설   highlight 강조하다   religious 종교적인
수천 년 동안 아메리카 원주민들은 그들의 종교적 믿음을 강조하는 신화와 전설이 풍부한 전통을 확립해 왔다.

143   **There is sufficient food to feed humans worldwide, at least to prevent death by starvation.**

(어휘) sufficient 충분한   starvation 굶주림
전 세계 인구를 먹일 만큼 충분한 식량이 적어도 아사를 막을 정도는 있다.

144   **If students are lucky enough to get a part-time job in their area of study, they obtain invaluable real-life experiences.**

(어휘) invaluable 아주 귀중한   experience 경험
학생들이 운 좋게 자기 전공 분야에서 시간제 일자리를 얻을 경우 소중한 실전 경험을 습득한다.

145   **All his decisions have been solely governed by sincere desire to help the needy.**

(어휘) solely 오로지   sincere 성실한, 진실한   the needy 빈곤한 사람들
그의 모든 결정은 오로지 빈곤한 사람들을 돕겠다는 진실한 욕구에 의해 좌우되어 왔다.

146   The speaker used many different graphs to underscore the point that he was making.

어휘 point 요점

그 강연자는 그가 주장하는 요점을 강조하기 위해 여러 다른 그래프를 사용했다.

147   Scientists are beginning to experiment with different genetic combinations that could increase the yield of a crop like corn.

어휘 experiment 실험하다   genetic 유전자의

과학자들은 옥수수 같은 곡물의 생산량을 늘릴 수 있는 다양한 유전자 조합을 실험하기 시작했다.

148   Historical novels merge historical facts and fiction to create interesting plots.

어휘 historical 역사적인   fiction 허구   plot 줄거리, 구상

역사 소설은 역사적 사실과 허구를 합쳐 흥미로운 줄거리를 만들어 낸다.

149   Animal protection groups turn their backs for a moment, and the breed disappears.

어휘 moment 순간   disappear 사라지다

동물 보호 그룹들이 잠시 등을 돌리면 그 종은 사라진다.

150   They receive the state grants for the university, and attend state-training programs if they lose their jobs.

[1994년 1차 수능 예문 26번]

어휘 receive 받다, 받아들이다

그들은 주에서 주는 대학 학비 보조금을 받으며, 실직하면 주 교육 프로그램에 참여한다.

A. Choose the right answer for the underlined word.

1 Turn on your turn signal and <u>merge</u> with oncoming traffic.
방향 지시등을 켜고 다가오는 차량들과 합류하시오.

(A) impede   (B) nurture   (C) decrease   (D) join

2 Jenny <u>yielded</u> to the temptation and ate the last piece of cake.
Jenny는 유혹에 넘어가 남은 마지막 케이크 한 조각을 먹었다.

(A) created   (B) surrendered   (C) regulated   (D) allowed

3 Last week's fire <u>underscores</u> the necessity of observing safety rules.
지난주의 화재는 안전 규칙 준수의 필요성을 강조한다.

(A) organizes   (B) combines   (C) deteriorates   (D) emphasizes

4 Without Social Security Numbers, one would be unable to <u>obtain</u> work, attend school, or live in the U.S. legally.
사회 보장 번호가 없이는 미국에서 합법적으로 일자리를 얻고 학교에 다니거나 생활할 수 없을 것이다.

(A) decrease   (B) obstruct   (C) produce   (D) get

5 Henry Ford <u>established</u> a 40-hour workweek and a minimum wage for his employees. Henry Ford는 자기 회사 직원들을 위해 40시간 주당 근로 시간과 최소 임금제를 만들었다.

(A) dominated   (B) instituted   (C) awarded   (D) secured

6 The Chukchi of the Siberian Arctic <u>bred</u> reindeer as a source of food.
시베리아 북극의 추크치 족은 식량 공급원으로 순록을 길렀다.

(A) acquired   (B) raised   (C) united   (D) stressed

7 Warming up before you begin exercising will <u>prevent</u> injury and muscle cramping. 운동을 시작하기 전에 준비운동을 하면 부상이나 근육 경련을 예방할 수 있다.

(A) avoid   (B) fuse   (C) found   (D) bear

8 The colonists obtained a charter that <u>granted</u> them the right to settle in the New World. 식민지 개척자들은 신세계에 정착할 권리를 부여해 주는 설립 허가서를 취득했다.

(A) averted   (B) gave   (C) procured   (D) combined

Answers   A 1. D   2. B   3. D   4. D   5. B   6. B   7. A   8. B

B. Fill in the blanks.

decline	establish	prevent	obtain	govern
underscore	yield	merge	breed	grant

1 Laws should be passed to _____ the wishes of the public.
법은 대중의 소원을 들어주기 위해 통과되어야 한다.

2 Beware of two freeway entrance lanes _____ into one.
2개의 고속도로 진입로가 1개로 합쳐지는 것을 조심하시오.

3 The latest failure _____ the challenge facing our nation.
최근의 실패는 우리나라가 직면하는 어려움을 강조하고 있다.

4 She _____ herself as a leading surgeon.
그녀는 일류 외과 의사로 자리 잡았다.

5 Mr. Robertson's credit card was _____.
Robertson 씨의 신용 카드가 승인 거부되었다.

C. Choose the right answer.

1 He changed his job to _____ a better income.
그는 나은 소득을 얻기 위해 직장을 바꾸었다.

(A) decline   (B) underscore   (C) establish   (D) obtain

2 Many critics claimed that the new mayor is too inexperienced to _____
effectively. 많은 비평가들이 신임 시장은 경험이 너무 없어서 효과적으로 다스릴 수 없다고 주장했다.

(A) generate   (B) underline   (C) govern   (D) fall

3 Unfortunately, no one was willing to _____ one's seat to an old lady.
안타깝게도 아무도 할머니에게 자리를 양보하고 싶어 하지 않았다.

(A) obtain   (B) yield   (C) merge   (D) govern

4 This dog is very expensive because it's a pure _____.
이 개는 순종 혈통이기 때문에 매우 비싸다.

(A) breed   (B) decline   (C) yield   (D) grant

B 1. grant   2. merging   3. underscores   4. established   5. declined
C 1. D   2. C   3. B   4. A

151

I *trust* Vince because he has a *strong sense of* duty.
나는 Vince가 책임감이 강하기 때문에 그를 신뢰한다.

duty   명 의무, 책임 responsibility, obligation
[dʲúːti]   임무, 직무 assignment, task
       관세, 세금 custom, tariff, tax

152

You are not my foe *but* my *friend*.
너는 나의 적이 아니라 친구다.

foe   명 원수, 적수, 반대자 enemy, opponent, adversary, antagonist
[fou]

153

Vitamins are essential for the normal growth and *development*.
비타민은 정상적인 성장과 발달에 필수적이다.

growth   명 성장, 발육 development, evolution, advance
[grouθ]   증가, 확장 increase, surge, rise

154

What is your *goal* or aim in life?
네 삶의 목표는 무엇이니?

aim   명 목표 goal, purpose, object
[eim]   동 겨냥하다 point, direct
       ~하려고 노력하다, 갈망하다 aspire to, try for

155

Ellen has *perfect* skin *without* a single flaw.
Ellen은 티 하나 없는 완벽한 피부를 지니고 있다.

flaw   명 흠, 결점 defect, blemish, fault
[flɔː]

156

Your destiny is not set because you can change your *future*.
네가 네 미래를 바꿀 수 있으니까 네 운명이 정해진 것은 아니야.

destiny   명 운명 fate, fortune, lot
[déstəni]

157

He is considered an expert in the realm of politics and in other *fields*. 그는 정치 영역과 기타 분야들에서 전문가로 여겨진다.

realm   명 범위, 영역 area, field, region, domain
[relm]   영토 territory, domain

158

Bob formed a bad *habit* which was a tendency to oversleep in the morning. Bob은 아침에 늦잠 자는 경향인 나쁜 버릇이 생겼다.

tendency   명 경향, 성향 inclination, propensity, penchant
[téndənsi]   버릇 habit

159

The city has many amenities like *recreational centers and golf courses*. 그 도시에는 레크리에이션 센터와 골프장 같은 편의 시설이 많다.

amenity   명 기분 좋음, 쾌적함, 편의 시설 comfort, convenience, facility, service
[əménəti]

160

He didn't leave any trace, not even one *footprint*.
그는 어떤 흔적도, 심지어 발자국 하나도 남기지 않았다.

trace   명 발자국 footprint
[treis]   자취, 흔적 track, trail
        동 추적하다 chase, pursue
        조사하다 investigate

Words in Reading

151 **They spent their days off duty in hiking and fishing.**

(어휘) day off 비번, 휴일   hiking 하이킹   fishing 낚시
그들은 근무가 없는 날들을 하이킹과 낚시를 하며 보냈다.

152 **One type of cobra sprays venom into the eyes of a foe instead of biting it.**

(어휘) spray 내뿜다   instead of ~ 대신에   bite 물다, 쏘다
코브라의 한 종류는 적을 무는 대신에 적의 눈에 독을 뿜어 댄다.

153 **In a laboratory study conducted at Stanford University, the same changes in plant growth patterns were brought about by touching plants twice a day.**

(어휘) laboratory 연구실   pattern 패턴, 양식   bring about 초래하다
스탠퍼드 대학교에서 실시한 실험실 연구에서 하루에 두 번 식물을 만져 줌으로써 식물 성장 패턴에 동일한 변화들이 일어났다.

154 **The peace talks aim to end the conflict between North and South Korea.**

(어휘) end 끝내다   conflict 충돌, 대립
그 평화 회담은 남북한 간의 대립을 끝내는 것을 목표로 한다.

155 **You may think if you allow friends to see your flaws, they'll like you less. But they may like you more.**

(어휘) allow 허용하다
당신은 친구들이 당신의 결점을 보도록 허용하면 그들이 당신을 덜 좋아할 것이라고 생각할지도 모른다. 하지만 그들이 당신을 더 좋아할 수도 있다.

156 Vincent believes that destiny has chosen him, especially, to complete this dangerous journey.

[어휘] especially 특별히   dangerous 위험한   journey 여행, 여정
Vincent는 운명이 특별히 이 위험한 여정을 마치도록 자신을 선택했다고 믿는다.

157 It's still a man's world out there – at least in the realm of Nobel science prizes.

[어휘] at least 적어도, 최소한   prize 상
여전히 남자의 세계인 곳이 있다. 적어도 노벨 과학상의 분야가 그렇다.

158 This has a tendency to lower the barriers separating him from others. [1994년 2차 수능 예문 48번]

[어휘] lower 낮추다   barrier 장벽   separate 분리하다, 가르다
이것은 그를 다른 사람들과 갈라놓는 장벽을 낮춰 주는 경향이 있다.

159 The amenities of civilization are left behind when an individual embarks on a camping trip in a remote area.

[어휘] leave behind 남겨 두다   embark on ~에 나서다   remote 멀리 떨어진
한 개인이 멀리 떨어진 지역에서의 캠핑 여행에 나설 때 문명 사회의 안락함은 뒤에 남겨지게 된다.

160 Nineteenth-century scholars tried to trace the origins of modern languages to ancient Hebrew.

[어휘] scholar 학자   origin 기원   modern 현대의
19세기 학자들은 현대 언어들의 기원을 고대 히브리어에서 찾으려고 노력했다.

A. Choose the right answer for the underlined word.

1   The primary aims of government should be three: security, justice, and conservation. (1995년 수능 예문 41번)
정부의 일차 목표는 세 가지, 즉 안보, 정의, 보존이 되어야 한다.

(A) territories   (B) customs   (C) purposes   (D) enemies

2   The growth of the pharmaceutical industry during the twentieth century has been astonishing. 20세기 동안 제약 업계의 성장은 눈부셨다.

(A) lot   (B) fault   (C) development   (D) obligation

3   The mayor's foes insist that he took bribes from various construction companies. 그 시장의 적수들은 시장이 여러 건설 회사로부터 뇌물을 받았다고 주장한다.

(A) opponents   (B) defects   (C) tracks   (D) habits

4   He wants to be in control of his own destiny.
그는 자신의 운명을 좌우하고 싶어 한다.

(A) fate   (B) comfort   (C) field   (D) object

5   Small flaws in an object show that it is handmade.
한 물건의 작은 흠들은 그것이 손으로 만들어졌음을 보여 준다.

(A) assignments   (B) blemishes   (C) antagonists   (D) tariffs

6   These are some of new amenities that are available at our hotel.
이것들이 저희 호텔에서 이용하실 수 있는 새 위락 시설의 일부입니다.

(A) domains   (B) facilities   (C) adversaries   (D) surges

7   One negative thing about him is his tendency to talk too much.
그의 한 가지 단점은 말을 너무 많이 하는 경향이다.

(A) rise   (B) goal   (C) propensity   (D) region

8   In 1863, a group of miners drilled 40 feet into the ground to find traces of gold. 1863년에 한 무리의 광부들이 금의 흔적을 찾기 위해 지하 40피트까지 파 내려갔다.

(A) fortunes   (B) trails   (C) tasks   (D) evolutions

Answers   A 1. C   2. C   3. A   4. A   5. B   6. B   7. C   8. B

B. Fill in the blanks.

duty	foe	growth	aim	flaw	
destiny	realm	tendency	amenities	trace	

1 The governor's _____ is to increase state income.

그 주지사의 목표는 주의 수입을 늘리는 것이다.

2 This log cabin has all the basic _____.

이 통나무 집은 모든 기본 편의 시설을 갖추고 있다.

3 No one will believe that it's his _____ to be poor.

그가 가난해질 운명이라고 믿을 사람은 아무도 없다.

4 The bank robber disappeared without a(n) _____.

그 은행 강도는 흔적도 없이 사라졌다.

5 You need protein for _____ and to repair cells.

성장과 세포의 회복을 위해 단백질이 필요하다.

C. Choose the right answer.

1 The biggest _____ wasn't the opposing team but was the weather.

최대의 적은 상대 팀이 아니라 날씨였다.

(A) realm   (B) growth   (C) tendency   (D) foe

2 It is the _____ of the court to make sure that the jury system work properly. 배심원 제도가 제 기능을 할 수 있도록 만드는 것은 법원의 의무이다.

(A) destiny   (B) duty   (C) amenity   (D) growth

3 The new theory goes beyond the _____ of science.

그 새 이론은 과학의 영역을 초월한다.

(A) foe   (B) flaw   (C) realm   (D) aim

4 He has a(n) _____ to be late to social occasions.

그는 사교 행사에 지각하는 경향이 있다.

(A) tendency   (B) aim   (C) trace   (D) amenity

B   1. aim   2. amenities   3. destiny   4. trace   5. growth

C   1. D   2. B   3. C   4. A

161   **The *conclusion* of the game was determined by the last-minute goal.** 그 경기의 결과는 마지막 순간의 골로 결정되었다.

     determine   통 결정하다 decide, settle on, control
     [ditə́ːrmin]   결론짓다 conclude, establish

162   **The researcher *watched* and observed the animal days and nights.** 그 연구자는 그 동물을 밤낮으로 지켜보며 관찰했다.

     observe   통 관찰하다, 감시하다 watch. monitor
     [əbzə́ːrv]   (명절을) 축하하다, 쇠다 celebrate, commemorate, honor
                 지키다, 준수하다 follow, obey

163   **The organization promotes and *advances* the idea of sharing.** 그 단체는 나눔의 정신을 장려하고 증진한다.

     promote   통 진전시키다 advance, further
     [prəmóut]   촉진하다, 증진하다 champion, encourage, advocate
                 진급시키다, 승진시키다 raise, upgrade, elevate
                 홍보하다, 선전하다 advertise, publicize

164   **My test scores satisfied me and *pleased* my parents.**
내 시험 점수에 나는 만족했고 부모님은 기뻐하셨다.

     satisfy   통 만족시키다 please, gratify
     [sǽtisfài]   충족시키다 meet
                 채우다 fill

165   **The debate *continued* and lasted for three hours.**
그 토론은 3시간 동안 계속 이어졌다.

     last   통 계속하다, 지속하다 continue, remain
     [læst]   견디다, 유지되다 endure, persevere
                 형 마지막의, 최후의 final, ultimate

166

The police pursued the robber but couldn't *catch* him.
경찰들이 도둑을 뒤쫓았지만 잡을 수 없었다.

pursue
[pərsúː]

(동) 뒤쫓다, 추적하다 chase, follow, trail
추구하다 yearn, desire
실행하다, 진행하다 proceed, conduct, carry on

167

Frank worked hard to refine his skills and *improve* his conditions. Frank는 기술을 연마하고 자신의 조건을 개선하기 위해 열심히 일했다.

refine
[rifáin]

(동) 순화하다, 정제하다 purify, filter, process
세련되게 하다, 다듬다, 개량하다 polish, improve, cultivate

168

Cindy portrayed Mary as mean, but Mark *described* her as nice. Cindy는 Mary를 비열하다고 묘사했지만 Mark는 그녀를 친절하다고 평했다.

portray
[pɔːrtréi]

(동) 그리다, 묘사하다 depict, describe, characterize, render

169

The speech was really inspiring and *moving*.
연설은 정말 고무적이고 감동적이었다.

inspiring
[inspáiəriŋ]

(형) 고무하는, 격려하는 uplifting, encouraging, moving
- inspire (동) 고무하다, 격려하다 motivate, move, encourage
영감을 주다 arouse, kindle, prompt

170

Anthony claims to tend his plants but doesn't *take care of* them. Anthony는 자신의 화초들을 돌본다고 주장하지만 보살피지 않는다.

tend
[tend]

(동) ~하는 경향이 있다, ~하기 쉽다 incline, be inclined, be likely
지키다, 돌보다 look after, attend, care for

Words in Reading

161 **Scientists in England studied 100 newborn babies to determine how much time they spent looking at pictures of attractive people as compared to unattractive people.**

(어휘) attractive 매력적인 as compared to ~에 비해
영국의 학자들은 신생아 100명을 대상으로 그들이 매력 없는 사람들에 비해 매력적인 사람들의 사진을 들여다보는 데 얼마나 많은 시간을 보내는지를 알아보기 위한 연구를 했다.

162 **Even though scientists have learned to observe earthquakes better than in the past, they have not learned to predict exactly when the next one will come.**

(어휘) predict 예측하다
과학자들이 지진을 과거보다 더 잘 관측하는 법을 익히기는 했지만 다음 지진이 정확하게 언제 오게 될지를 예측하는 법은 익히지 못했다.

163 **We specialize in producing dynamic video content to promote your idea or business.**

(어휘) specialize 전문으로 하다 dynamic 역동적인
우리는 당신의 아이디어나 비즈니스를 홍보하는 역동적인 비디오 콘텐트 제작을 전문으로 하고 있습니다.

164 **Full-time students must satisfy this requirement by the beginning of their second semester, while part-time students must fulfill it by the beginning of their third semester.**

(어휘) requirement 요건 semester 학기 fulfill 완수하다
정규 학생들은 2학기 초까지 이 요건을 충족시켜야만 하며 비정규 학생들은 3학기 초까지 그것을 완수해야만 합니다.

165 **The Depression in the United States lasted until the beginning of the Second World War.**

(어휘) depression 불경기, 불황
미국의 대공황은 제2차 세계 대전 초까지 지속되었다.

166

They support a woman's right to pursue her goals and dreams, whether she wants to be an astronaut, athlete, banker, or mother.

어휘 right 권리   dream 꿈, 이상

그들은 여자들이 우주 비행사, 운동선수, 은행가 아니면 어머니가 되고 싶든지 간에 자신의 목표와 꿈을 추구할 여성의 권리를 옹호한다.

167

The hurricane was a wake-up call to refine our national energy policy.

어휘 wake-up call 잠을 깨우는 전화, 주의를 환기시키는 것   policy 정책

그 허리케인은 우리의 국가적인 에너지 정책을 재정비하라는 경고였다.

168

He wanted me to know he'd do everything he could to portray my father accurately.

어휘 accurately 정확하게

그는 우리 아버지의 초상을 정확하게 그리기 위해 자신이 할 수 있는 모든 것을 하려 한다는 것을 내가 알기 원했다.

169

The laborers were inspired by a belief in a better future.

어휘 laborer 노동자   belief 믿음

노동자들은 더 좋은 미래에 대한 믿음으로 고무되었다.

170

Children's books tend to reinforce the stereotype of women in society.

어휘 reinforce 강화하다   stereotype 전형

어린이 책들은 사회 속의 전형적인 여성상을 강화하는 경향이 있다.

A. Choose the right answer for the underlined word.

1   The defendant's lawyer underlined portrayed him as a victim.
    피고측 변호사는 그를 희생자로 묘사했다.

    (A) met   (B) established   (C) depicted   (D) encouraged

2   Unfortunately, this wonderful weather will not last as we are going to have some heavy rain by the afternoon.
    안타깝게도 오후에 많은 양의 비가 내릴 예정이므로 이 멋진 날씨는 지속되지 않을 것입니다.

    (A) attend   (B) trail   (C) kindle   (D) continue

3   Elderly African-Americans tend to have stronger and larger social networks than white Americans.
    나이든 미국 흑인들은 미국 백인들보다 더 강력하고 더 큰 사회 네트워크를 갖는 경향이 있다.

    (A) endure   (B) incline   (C) arouse   (D) render

4   There are many factors which determine how sound can be heard.
    소리가 들릴 수 있게 하는 방식을 결정짓는 많은 요인들이 있다.

    (A) decide   (B) obey   (C) publicize   (D) persevere

5   There are certain rules of behavior that you should observe when visiting someone in the hospital. 입원 중인 사람을 방문할 때 지켜야 할 특정한 행동 규칙들이 있다.

    (A) follow   (B) proceed   (C) motivate   (D) describe

6   The words that poets use can inspire you and stir your soul.
    시인들이 사용하는 말들은 영감을 주고 혼을 자극할 수 있다.

    (A) purify   (B) gratify   (C) move   (D) desire

7   The falcon is a type of hawk that is trained to pursue game in the sport called falconry. 팔콘은 매의 일종으로 매사냥이라는 스포츠에서 사냥감을 뒤쫓도록 훈련받는다.

    (A) commemorate (B) advance   (C) chase   (D) conclude

8   Thomas Edison made every attempt to refine it by testing different types of filaments. Thomas Edison은 다양한 종류의 필라멘트를 시험하면서 그것을 개선하기 위한 모든 시도를 했다.

    (A) characterize (B) lean   (C) fill   (D) improve

Answers   A 1. C   2. D   3. B   4. A   5. A   6. C   7. C   8. D

B. Fill in the blanks.

determine	observe	promote	satisfy	last
pursue	refine	portray	inspire	tend

1 The article _____ the player as selfish.
   그 기사는 그 선수를 이기적이라고 묘사했다.

2 We hope, over time, his style will be _____.
   우리는 그의 스타일이 시간이 지나면서 세련되기를 바란다.

3 The festival _____ three weeks.
   그 축제는 3주 동안 지속되었다.

4 The hearty meal _____ his hunger.
   풍성한 식사가 그의 허기를 충족시켰다.

5 The doctor needs to get an MRI to _____ the extent of my injury.
   의사는 내 부상의 정도를 판정하기 위해 MRI 사진을 찍어야 한다.

C. Choose the right answer.

1 The Aleutian goose mates for life, but only the female _____ the
   eggs. 캐나다기러기는 평생 동안 짝을 짓지만 암컷들만이 알을 돌본다.

   (A) observes   (B) determines   (C) refines   (D) tends

2 Modern Western culture may _____ one particular ideal of female
   beauty. 현대 서구 문화는 한 가지 특정한 여성미의 전형을 조장하는지도 모른다.

   (A) promote   (B) last   (C) satisfy   (D) pursue

3 I want you to _____ her reaction to the judge's question.
   판사의 질문에 대한 그녀의 반응을 지켜보기 바랍니다.

   (A) portray   (B) satisfy   (C) inspire   (D) observe

4 Students needed to be _____ to do their best.
   학생들은 최선을 다하도록 자극받을 필요가 있었다.

   (A) determined   (B) inspired   (C) portrayed   (D) promoted

B 1. portrayed   2. refined   3. lasted   4. satisfied   5. determine
C 1. D   2. A   3. D   4. B

171   **Bob *studied so much* that he actually is** anxious **to take the test.** Bob은 공부를 아주 많이 했기 때문에 실제로 시험을 치고 싶어 한다.

anxious   (형) 걱정하는, 염려하는, 불안해하는 nervous, worried, concerned
[ǽŋkʃəs]   갈망하는 eager, keen
                 - anxiety (명) 걱정, 근심, 불안 uneasiness, concern, worry

172   **It is important to be** precise **and *clear-cut* when you are writing a report.** 보고서를 쓸 때는 정확하고 명쾌한 것이 중요하다.

precise   (형) 명확한, 정밀한, 정확한 clear, exact, accurate
[prisáis]   엄격한 strict, rigid
                 바로 그 very
                 - precisely (부) 정밀하게

173   **These two subjects are closely** related**, but also are *different* from each other.** 이 두 주제는 밀접하게 관련되어 있지만 또한 서로 다르다.

related   (형) 관계 있는, 관련된 relevant, linked, associated, pertinent
[riléitid]   친척 관계인, 동족의 akin, kindred

174   **People *like* the new supermarket because its *prices* are** reasonable**.** 사람들은 가격이 적당해서 새로 생긴 슈퍼마켓을 좋아한다.

reasonable   (형) 합리적인, 분별 있는 rational, sensible
[ríːzənəbl]   정당한 fair, justifiable
                 적당한, 비싸지 않은 low, cheap, moderate

175   **Losing his job made Rick feel** vulnerable **and *helpless*.**
Rick은 실직하자 자신이 허약하고 무능하게 느껴졌다.

vulnerable   (형) 공격받기 쉬운, 취약한 susceptible, unprotected, weak
[vʌ́lnərəbl]   노출되어 있는 exposed, open

176

The land was so barren that *no animal lived* on it.
그 땅은 너무 황량해서 아무 동물도 살지 않았다.

barren   형 척박한, 황량한 desolate, empty, desert, inhospitable
[bǽrən]   열매를 맺지 못하는, 불임의 unproductive, fruitless, infertile

177

The *rich* uncle *left Jason* substantial inheritance.
그 부자 삼촌은 Jason에게 상당한 유산을 남겨 주었다.

substantial   형 상당한 significant, considerable, sizeable, extensive
[səbstǽnʃəl]   - substantially 부 상당히

178

He is not only a prominent scientist but also a *famous* musician. 그는 저명한 과학자일 뿐만 아니라 유명한 음악가이기도 하다.

prominent   형 중요한 important, major
[prámənənt]   저명한 famous, renowned
     눈에 잘 띄는, 두드러진 noticeable, obvious

179

Victor said harsh and *unkind* things to Mary, making her cry. Victor는 Mary에게 가혹하고 불친절한 말을 해서 그녀를 울렸다.

harsh   형 가혹한, 무자비한 unkind, cruel
[hɑːrʃ]   (환경이) 혹독한 severe, bleak, inhospitable
     거친, 조잡한 rough, abrasive

180

It was *pointless* and futile to change Zack's mind.
Zack의 마음을 바꾸는 것은 무의미하고 소용없었다.

futile   형 무익한, 헛된, 소용없는 useless, pointless, fruitless, vain
[fjúːtəl]

171 It was a kind of election revolution achieved through the impassioned desires of the Korean people who were anxious for the beginning of a new age.

[어휘] election 선거   revolution 혁명   impassioned 열정적인   desire 욕구
그것은 새 시대의 시작을 간절히 바랐던 한국 국민들의 열렬한 욕구를 통해 이루어진 일종의 선거 혁명이었다.

172 The nerve fibers in the brain insulate themselves in such a way that the baby begins to hear sounds very precisely.

[어휘] nerve 신경   fiber 섬유   insulate 차단하다
뇌 속의 신경 섬유가 스스로를 절연시켜 그 아기는 소리를 아주 정밀하게 듣기 시작한다.

173 Demand hinges on the price of the goods, the prices of related products, and consumers' incomes and tastes.

[어휘] hinge on ~에 따라 결정되다   goods 상품   product 제품   income 소득
수요는 상품의 가격, 관련 제품의 가격, 소비자들의 소득과 취향에 따라 결정된다.

174 A person who feels bad with reasonable regularity will enjoy the occasional period of feeling good far more than somebody who feels so often that he is bored by it.   〔1997년 수능 예문 28번〕

[어휘] regularity 규칙적임   occasional 때때로의, 가끔의   bore 지루하게 하다
적당히 규칙적으로 기분이 나쁜 사람은 너무 자주 기분이 좋아 싫증을 내는 사람보다는 가끔 맞는 기분 좋을 때를 훨씬 더 많이 즐길 것이다.

175 Cheetah reproduction has slowed in recent years, and the whole species is vulnerable.

[어휘] reproduction 번식   species 종
최근 수년 동안 치타의 번식 속도가 느려져 종 전체가 취약한 상태이다.

176 Efficient irrigation can convert a barren, infertile wasteland into agricultural land and forest area.

(어휘) efficient 효율적인　irrigation 관개　convert 변화시키다　infertile 메마른
효과적인 관개는 척박하고 메마른 황무지를 농경지와 숲 지역으로 바꿀 수 있다.

177 Tuition at American universities varies substantially, depending on the type of institution and its endowment.

(어휘) tuition 수업료, 등록금　institution 기관, 단체　endowment 기부(금)
미국 대학교의 수업료는 학교와 기부금의 종류에 따라 매우 다양하다.

178 Gothic architecture was used in building many castles, palaces, town halls, universities, and to a less prominent extent, private houses.

(어휘) architecture 건축　castle 성
고딕 양식 건축은 많은 성, 궁전, 시청, 대학교, 그리고 덜 알려져 있지만 개인 집을 짓는 데 사용되었다.

179 In India, people living up in the mountains wear the wool from cashmere goats to protect themselves from harsh conditions.

(어휘) protect 보호하다
인도에서는 산 속 높은 곳에 사는 사람들이 혹독한 환경으로부터 자신을 보호하기 위해 캐시미어 염소의 털로 만든 옷을 입는다.

180 What we observed was basically a futile attempt to establish a democratic form of government there.

(어휘) attempt 시도　democratic 민주적인
우리가 지켜본 것은 요컨대 그곳에 민주적 형태의 정부를 세우려는 헛된 시도였다.

A. Choose the right answer for the underlined word.

1 These qualities are especially important for wealthy and <u>prominent</u> families. 이러한 자질들이 부유하고 유명한 가정들에는 특히 중요하다.

(A) severe   (B) renowned   (C) keen   (D) rational

2 Young people are <u>vulnerable</u> to the influence of radio and television.
젊은이들은 라디오와 TV의 영향을 받기 쉽다.

(A) noticeable   (B) susceptible   (C) bleak   (D) rough

3 Annie Oakley became famous as one of the world's most <u>precise</u> sharpshooters. Annie Oakley는 세계에서 가장 정확한 명사수 중의 한 명으로 유명해졌다.

(A) moderate   (B) accurate   (C) major   (D) vain

4 Large areas of Alaskan land remain <u>barren</u> due to harsh climate.
알래스카 땅의 넓은 지역들이 혹독한 기후 때문에 불모지로 남아 있다.

(A) desolate   (B) useless   (C) cheap   (D) rigid

5 The main reason is that the speed of communication has increased <u>substantially</u>. 주요 원인은 통신 속도가 상당히 빨라져 왔다는 것이다.

(A) weakly   (B) considerably   (C) clearly   (D) obviously

6 Ancient Greek heroes would use <u>harsh</u> soaps and other substances to bleach and redden their hair.
고대 그리스의 영웅들은 거친 비누와 다른 물질들을 사용해 머리를 탈색하고 붉게 물들였다.

(A) cruel   (B) germane   (C) abrasive   (D) unproductive

7 The trip to Paris was costly, tiring, and completely <u>futile</u>.
파리 여행은 비용이 많이 들고 피곤하며 완전히 무익하다.

(A) justifiable   (B) fruitless   (C) deserted   (D) unprotected

8 The company is really <u>anxious</u> to get its new product on the market as soon as possible. 그 회사는 가능한 한 빨리 신제품을 시장에 내놓고 싶어 한다.

(A) inhospitable   (B) eager   (C) relevant   (D) significant

Answers   A   1. B   2. B   3. B   4. A   5. B   6. C   7. B   8. B

B. Fill in the blanks.

> anxious precise related reasonable vulnerable
> barren substantial prominent harsh futile

1 The porpoise is _____ to the whale and dolphin.
상괭이는 고래와 돌고래의 친척이다.

2 An accountant needs to be very _____ when dealing with numbers.
회계사는 숫자를 다룰 때 매우 정확해야 한다.

3 There are _____ evidences that he committed the crime.
그가 그 범죄를 저질렀다는 상당한 증거가 있다.

4 The pioneers were able to cultivate land that was utterly _____.
개척자들은 완전히 척박한 땅을 개간할 수 있었다.

5 Young children and senior citizens are encouraged to get a shot because they are most _____ to flu.
어린이와 노약자들은 독감에 가장 취약하기 때문에 예방 주사를 맞을 것을 권한다.

C. Choose the right answer.

1 His excuse for coming to the class late was _____.
수업에 지각한 것에 대한 그의 변명은 적당했다.

(A) reasonable　(B) futile　(C) precise　(D) barren

2 I am still _____ about whether we have enough food to feed everyone. 모든 사람을 먹일 수 있을 만큼 충분한 음식이 있는지 나는 여전히 걱정스럽다.

(A) precise　(B) anxious　(C) prominent　(D) substantial

3 We all considered the punishment to be too _____.
우리 모두는 그 처벌이 너무 가혹하다고 여겼다.

(A) barren　(B) reasonable　(C) harsh　(D) related

4 The church tower is the most _____ feature in our town.
교회 탑은 우리 도시에서 가장 두드러진 특징이다.

(A) substantial　(B) precise　(C) vulnerable　(D) prominent

B 1. related 2. precise 3. substantial 4. barren 5. vulnerable
C 1. A 2. B 3. C 4. D

181 **I *checked* and confirmed my hotel reservation.**
나는 호텔 예약을 체크하고 확인했다.

confirm   ⑧ 확인하다 prove, check, verify
[kənfə́:rm]   확실하게 하다, 확증하다 affirm, approve, authorize
    더욱 굳게 하다, 강화하다 strengthen, secure, reinforce

182 **Don't *believe* or assume that what you read in the newspaper is always true.**
신문에서 읽는 것이 항상 사실이라고 믿거나 간주하지 마라.

assume   ⑧ 가정하다, 간주하다 think, believe, suppose
[əsjú:m]   떠맡다 take up, undertake
    가장하다 fake, feign

183 **He was defeated in the election and this was the second time that he *lost*.** 그가 선거에서 패배했는데, 이번이 두 번째 진 것이다.

defeat   ⑧ 패배시키다, 처부수다 beat, crush, conquer, subdue
[difí:t]   좌절시키다 frustrate, thwart
    ⑲ 승리 conquest, beating
    패배, 실패 loss, failure, setback

184 **Randy used to *live* here, but now resides the other side of the town.** Randy는 이곳에 살았지만 지금은 시내 반대 편에 거주한다.

reside   ⑧ 살다, 거주하다 live, dwell, inhabit
[rizáid]   존재하다 be present, exist

185 **Jill spread the news about Erica by *telling almost everyone in the class*.** Jill은 학급의 거의 모든 사람에게 이야기해 Erica에 대한 뉴스를 퍼뜨렸다.

spread   ⑧ 펴다, 뻗다, 늘이다 extend, stretch, expand
[spred]   퍼뜨리다, 분포시키다 publish, disperse, scatter, distribute
    ⑲ 확산, 퍼뜨림 expansion, increase, diffusion

186

Don't pile your clothes all over the place. *Put them together in one basket.* 사방에 옷을 쌓아 두지 마라. 한 바구니 안에 함께 담아라.

pile   图 쌓다, 축적하다, 모으다 heap, stack, put together, collect,
[pail]   圐 더미, 다량 heap, stack, accumulation
                  큰돈, 재산 fortune, wealth

187

He not only exceeded the coach's expectation but also *topped* his own. 그는 코치의 기대를 넘어섰을 뿐 아니라 본인의 예측도 능가했다.

exceed   图 초과하다, 넘어서다 go over, surpass, beat, top
[iksíːd]

188

The new heater emits bright red light but fails to *produce* heat. 새 히터는 밝은 붉은 빛을 내지만 열을 내지는 않는다.

emit   图 내뿜다, 발산하다 give off, release, discharge, secrete, give out
[imít]

189

The result stunned Bob but didn't *shock* Adam.
그 결과에 Bob은 깜짝 놀랐지만 Adam은 충격을 받지 않았다.

stun   图 기절시키다, 멍하게 하다 knock out, daze, stupefy
[stʌn]   깜짝 놀라게 하다 shock, astonish, bewilder, astound
           - stunning 圀 놀랄 만큼 아름다운

190

Mark was devoted to his work, *spending all his time* at the office. Mark는 사무실에서 모든 시간을 보내며 일에 몰두했다.

devoted   圀 충실한, 헌신적인 dedicated, committed, faithful, devout
[divóutid]   - devote 图 바치다, 몰두하다 dedicate, commit, reserve
            - devotion 圐 헌신, 전념, 애착 dedication, commitment, affection

181 **Professor Franklin's theory has been confirmed by other scientists.**

어휘 theory 이론
Franklin 교수의 이론은 다른 과학자들에 의해 확증되었다.

182 **A show about crimes and criminals can help people understand that they need to be careful, and not just assume everyone has good intentions.**

어휘 crime 범죄   criminals 범죄자   intention 의도
범죄와 범죄자들에 대한 프로그램은 사람들이 조심할 필요가 있으며 그냥 모든 사람이 선의를 갖고 있다고 생각해서는 안 된다는 것을 이해하는 데 도움이 된다.

183 **These days children are often encouraged and even forced to defeat their friends cruelly in order to win the first prize.**

어휘 encourage 부추기다   cruelly 무참하게   in order to ~하기 위해
요즘 아이들은 심지어 1등상을 받기 위해 친구들을 무참하게 짓밟도록 부추김을 받는 경우도 많다.

184 **There is no greater power than that which resides in the dictator in this country.**

어휘 dictator 독재자
이 나라에서는 그 독재자에게 있는 권력보다 더 큰 권력은 전혀 없다.

185 **European Union officials this week declared the spread of bird flu from Asia to Europe a "global threat."**

어휘 declare 선언하다   bird flu 조류 독감   threat 위협
이번 주에 유럽연합 관리들은 아시아에서 유럽으로의 조류 독감 확산을 '세계적 위협'이라고 선언했다.

186 The tables inside the Southside Church were piled high with food, bedding and clothing this morning – donations for families who lived in the apartment building that burned last night.

어휘 bedding 침구류 donation 기증(품)

오늘 아침에 Southside 교회 안의 테이블들에는 음식, 침구류, 의류가 높이 쌓여 있었는데, 그것들은 지난밤 불이 난 아파트 건물에 살던 가정들을 위해 기증된 물품들이었다.

187 During severe storms, the capacity of the soil to absorb water may be exceeded by the amount of rainfall.

어휘 capacity 수용력 exceed 능가하다

폭풍우가 심할 때는 토양의 물 흡수 능력이 강우량에 미치지 못할 수도 있다.

188 As they are flying, bats emit high-frequency sound waves that are mostly beyond the range of human hearing.

어휘 bat 박쥐 high-frequency 고주파의 sound wave 음파

박쥐들은 비행하면서 대부분 인간의 청취 영역을 넘어서는 고주파음을 낸다.

189 The school community was stunned by the announcement that the principal had resigned after admitting he had lied about his qualifications.

어휘 principal 교장 resign 사임하다 admit 인정하다 qualifications 자격 요건

학교 사회는 그 교장이 자신의 자격 요건에 대해 거짓말을 한 것을 시인하고 나서 사임했다는 발표에 깜짝 놀랐다.

190 They devoted themselves to hours of unpaid work for the poor and helpless, never minding that few appreciated what they were doing for society. [1998년 수능 예문 52~53번]

어휘 helpless 무력한 mind 꺼리다 appreciate 알아주다

그들은 가난하고 의지할 데 없는 사람들을 위해 무보수로 여러 시간 일하는 데 전념했으며 그들이 사회를 위해 하고 있는 일을 알아주는 사람이 거의 없어도 개의치 않았다.

A. Choose the right answer for the underlined word.

1 Movie stars are no longer required to <u>reside</u> in a particular place.
영화배우들은 더 이상 특정한 곳에 살아야 할 필요가 없다.

(A) frustrate   (B) thought   (C) dwell   (D) bewilder

2 Problems have <u>piled</u> one on top of the other.
문제들이 겹겹이 쌓여 있다.

(A) proved   (B) reserved   (C) distribute   (D) stacked

3 Cathode <u>emits</u> electrons in a controlled environment.
음극은 통제된 환경에서 전자를 방출한다.

(A) beats   (B) tops   (C) discharges   (D) thwarts

4 Please sign here to <u>confirm</u> that you picked it up.
그것을 찾아가셨다는 확인으로 여기에 서명해 주세요.

(A) disperse   (B) believe   (C) verify   (D) secrete

5 Once its supply lines were broken, it took little time for the army to be <u>defeated</u>. 일단 보급로가 끊어지자 그 군대는 오래 가지 않아 패배했다.

(A) lived   (B) approved   (C) conquered   (D) astounded

6 Grouses and peacocks <u>spread</u> their tail feathers out and walk around noticeably, in an attempt to draw a mate.
뇌조와 공작 수컷은 짝을 유인하기 위한 시도로 꽁지깃을 펼쳐 눈에 띄게 돌아다닌다.

(A) fake   (B) heap   (C) feign   (D) extend

7 For the purpose of this drill, we will <u>assume</u> that an evacuation has been ordered. 이 훈련의 목적을 위해 우리는 대피 명령이 내려진 것으로 가정할 것입니다.

(A) subjugate   (B) suppose   (C) expand   (D) authorize

8 Death Valley is one of the hottest places in the world, and it is not unusual to have daytime temperatures that <u>exceed</u> 120°F.
Death Valley는 세계에서 가장 더운 지역 중의 하나여서 낮 시간대 온도가 화씨 120도를 넘는 게 보통이다.

(A) astonish   (B) surpass   (C) stretch   (D) inhibit

Answers   A   1. C   2. D   3. C   4. C   5. C   6. D   7. B   8. B

B. Fill in the blanks.

confirm	assume	defeat	reside	spread
pile	exceed	emit	stun	devote

1 The world population will _____ 8 billion by 2030.
세계 인구는 2030년에 80억이 넘을 것이다.

2 Many people _____ that the scientist worked all his life on the invention. 많은 사람들은 그 과학자가 평생 동안 그 발명품을 연구했다고 생각했다.

3 Global warming is caused by pollutants _____ from automobiles and factories. 지구 온난화는 자동차와 공장에서 나오는 오염 물질에 의해 발생한다.

4 You'll never become a great writer unless you _____ a lot of time to the practice of writing. 작문 연습에 많은 시간을 들이지 않으면 절대로 훌륭한 작가가 되지 못할 것이다.

5 In democracy, power supposedly _____ with the people.
민주주의 국가에서 권력은 가정상 국민에게 있을 것이다.

C. Choose the right answer.

1 The early returns _____ his hopes of election.
초기 투표 결과는 그의 선거에 대한 희망을 좌절시켰다.

(A) pile   (B) assume   (C) reside   (D) defeated

2 Many early Christians risked their lives to _____ the word of the gospel. 많은 초기 그리스도인들은 복음의 말씀을 전파하는 데 생명을 걸었다.

(A) assume   (B) stun   (C) spread   (D) devote

3 He made a _____ on Wall Street during the 1990s.
1990년대에 그는 월스트리트에서 큰돈을 벌었다.

(A) pile   (B) defeat   (C) devotion   (D) spread

4 Amelia looked _____ in the red dress.
빨간 드레스를 입은 Amelia는 무척 아름다워 보였다.

(A) assuming   (B) exceeding   (C) stunning   (D) emitting

B 1. exceed   2. assumed   3. emitted   4. devote   5. resides
C 1. D   2. C   3. A   4. C

191

Every car is required to have safety devices like *seatbelts and airbag*. 모든 차에는 안전벨트와 에어백 같은 안전 장치가 필요하다.

device
[diváis]

명 궁리, 계획, 책략 plot, scheme, plan
고안물, 장치 gadget, machine, tool

192

The most difficult task for a college graduate is to find a *job*.
대학 졸업자에게 가장 어려운 과제는 직장을 구하는 것이다.

task
[tæsk]

명 과제, 일 duty, assignment, job, work, business
동 일을 맡기다 charge, assign, entrust

193

He has earned a *total* sum of $90,000 this year.
그는 올해 총 9만 달러를 벌었다.

sum
[sʌm]

명 금액, 액수 amount, quantity, volume
합계, 총계, 전부 total, aggregate, whole
요점, 요지, 개요 point, gist, essence
동 합계하다, 계산하다 calculate, estimate
요약하다 summarize

194

Mr. Jackson has the resources and *skills* to finish the task.
Jackson 씨는 그 일을 완수할 기술과 재주를 가지고 있다.

resource
[rí:sɔ̀:rs]

명 (-s) 자원, 재원 materials, funds, assets, wealth
수완, 재주 skill, ability, ingenuity

195

The fireman had the courage *to risk his life* to save others.
그 소방관은 다른 사람들을 구하기 위해 목숨을 거는 용기가 있었다.

courage
[kə́:ridʒ]

명 용기, 배짱 bravery, nerve, fortitude, valor

196

The speech had a big impact and *influence* on students.
그 연설은 학생들에게 커다란 충격과 영향을 주었다.

impact
[ímpækt]
- 명 충돌, 격돌 collision, crash
- 충격, 영향, 효과 shock, influence, effect
- 동 충돌하다, 충격(영향)을 주다 strike, crash, affect

197

A habitat is a wild animal's *home* such as a forest or a river.
서식지는 숲이나 강과 같은 야생 동물의 안식처이다.

habitat
[hǽbitæt]
- 명 환경, 거주지, 서식지 home, environment, surrounding, dwelling

198

The origin of the universe is a mystery because no one knows how it *started*.
우주의 기원은 그것이 어떻게 시작되었는지 아무도 모르기 때문에 미스터리이다.

origin
[ɔ́(:)ridʒin]
- 명 기원, 유래, 시초, 근원 beginning, start, source
- 발생 genesis, birth

199

He was a pioneer who developed the system *for the first time.* 그는 최초로 그 시스템을 개발한 개척자이다.

pioneer
[pàiəníər]
- 명 개척자, 선구자 innovator, originator
- 동 개척하다, 선도하다 develop, start, initiate, take the lead

200

I have a strong *emotional* attachment to my family.
나는 가족에 대한 정서적 애착이 강하다.

attachment
[ətǽtʃmənt]
- 명 애정, 애착 fondness, liking, affection
- 첨부 파일

191 The capacity to store and distribute information has increased through the use of computers and other devices.

〔1998년 수능 예문 27번〕

(어휘) capacity 능력, 수용력   distribute 분배하다, 배포하다
컴퓨터와 다른 장비의 이용을 통해 정보의 저장과 배포 능력이 증대되어 왔다.

192 If the charter has failed, the parliament will be temporarily tasked with drawing up a new draft on which to vote.

(어휘) charter 헌장, 강령   parliament 국회   temporary 한시적인   draft 초안
만약 그 강령이 통과되지 못하면 의회는 투표에 부칠 새 초안을 마련하는 일을 임시적으로 맡게 된다.

193 In statistics, the mathematical mean is obtained by dividing the sum of a group of scores by the number of scores.

(어휘) statistics 통계학, 통계   mathematical 수학의   mean (산술) 평균
통계학에서 수학적인 평균은 한 그룹의 득점의 합계를 득점 수로 나누어 얻는 것이다.

194 Even while making political statement, Ben Shahn was in full command of his technical resources.

(어휘) political 정치적인   in full command 충분히 발휘하여   technical 기술적인
Ben Shahn은 정치 연설을 하고 있을 때에조차 자신의 기술적 수완을 충분히 발휘했다.

195 Through Miss Sullivan's help, Helen Keller learned to communicate with others, and others benefited from her unique insights and courage.

(어휘) benefit 이익을 얻다   unique 독특한   insight 통찰력
Sullivan 씨의 도움을 통해 Helen Keller는 다른 사람들과 의사소통하는 법을 배웠고 다른 사람들은 그녀의 독특한 통찰력과 용기에서 유익을 얻었다.

196 We must all do our part to reduce our environmental impact and make the world a cleaner and better place for all of us to live.

어휘 reduce 줄이다   environmental 환경적인
환경에 미치는 영향을 줄이고 세상을 우리 모두가 살기에 더 깨끗하고 나은 곳으로 만들기 위해 우리는 모두 자기 역할을 해야만 한다.

197 The long-term threat to the survival of elephants is the loss of their natural habitat.

어휘 long-term 장기적인   threat 위협   survival 생존   natural 자연의
코끼리 생존에 대한 장기적인 위협은 자연 서식지를 잃는 것이다.

198 Hubble's concept of the expanding universe brought us closer to understanding the origins of the universe and laid the foundation on which modern astronomy builds.

어휘 concept 개념   expand 확장하다   foundation 기초   astronomy 천문학
허블의 우주 팽창 개념은 우리가 우주의 기원을 이해하는 데 한 걸음 더 다가가게 했으며 현대 천문학이 세워지는 기초를 놓았다.

199 He pioneered the use of semiconductors in navigation and control systems.

어휘 semiconductor 반도체   navigation 항해, 운항
그는 항법과 제어 시스템에 반도체를 처음 사용했다.

200 If you get an e-mail with attachment from a stranger, it is best that you don't open it.

모르는 사람에게 첨부 파일이 있는 이메일을 받으면 열지 않는 것이 최선이다.

A. Choose the right answer for the underlined word.

1   The crocodile's habitat is in the waters and lowlands of southeastern United States. 악어의 서식지는 미국 남동부의 하천과 저지대에 있다.

(A) genesis   (B) inclination   (C) home   (D) ability

2   Industrial Revolution had irreversible impacts on society.
산업혁명은 사회에 되돌릴 수 없는 영향을 미쳤다.

(A) influences   (B) births   (C) fortitudes   (D) dwellings

3   Some schools don't have enough resources to educate their students properly. 일부 학교들은 학생들을 적절하게 교육할 만한 충분한 재원을 갖고 있지 않다.

(A) skills   (B) essences   (C) plots   (D) assets

4   Some people have a special attachment to old stamps.
일부 사람들은 옛날 우표에 특별한 애착을 갖고 있다.

(A) asset   (B) effect   (C) affection   (D) surrounding

5   The police face a very difficult task dealing with the increase in violent crime. 경찰은 폭력 범죄의 증가를 다루는 매우 어려운 과제에 직면해 있다.

(A) responsibility (B) plan   (C) strike   (D) assignment

6   In ancient Greece, the lighter hair colors symbolized honor and courage.
고대 그리스에서는 더 밝은 머리 색이 명예와 용기를 상징했다.

(A) desire   (B) valor   (C) amount   (D) connection

7   Historians trace the origin of ice cream to the 4th century B.C., and agree that ice cream was invented in Italy.
역사가들은 아이스크림의 기원을 기원전 4세기까지 거슬러 찾고 있으며 아이스크림이 이탈리아에서 발명되었다는 데 동의한다.

(A) environment   (B) project   (C) beginning   (D) collision

8   A truly great symphony orchestra creates a unified harmonious sound, where the whole is greater than the sum of its parts.
진정으로 훌륭한 교향악단은 통일된 화음을 만들어 내어 그 속에서 전체는 부분들의 총합보다 더 훌륭하다.

(A) originator   (B) source   (C) total   (D) job

Answers   A 1. C   2. A   3. D   4. C   5. D   6. B   7. C   8. C

B. Fill in the blanks.

device	task	sum	resource	courage
impact	habitat	origin	pioneer	attachment

1 He has a strong _____ to his hometown.
그는 고향에 대해 애착이 강하다.

2 If writing seems like a difficult _____, start small by writing in a diary regularly. 작문이 어려운 일처럼 보인다면 규칙적으로 일기를 쓰는 작은 것부터 시작하라.

3 Destruction of _____ is the biggest threat to wildlife.
서식지 파괴는 야생 동물들에게 가장 큰 위협이다.

4 Interestingly, the name 'French fries' does not signify the country of
_____. 흥미롭게도 '프렌치 프라이'라는 이름은 그것이 만들어진 나라를 의미하지는 않는다.

5 When Dr. Sally Ride was young, she had no idea that she would one day become a(n) _____ in space travel.
Sally Ride 박사는 어렸을 때 자신이 우주 여행의 개척자가 될 줄은 전혀 생각하지 못했다.

C. Choose the right answer.

1 The student was able to _____ up his point in a clear fashion.
그 학생은 명확한 방식으로 자신의 점수 합계를 낼 수 있었다.

(A) task   (B) impact   (C) sum   (D) pioneer

2 The captain made the announcement to turn off all electrical _____.
기장은 모든 전자 기기의 전원을 끄라는 안내 방송을 했다.

(A) resource   (B) device   (C) courage   (D) sum

3 The decision may _____ your whole career.
그 결정이 너의 전체 경력에 영향을 줄 수도 있다.

(A) impact   (B) pioneer   (C) sum   (D) task

4 You certainly have a lot of _____ to talk to the teacher like that.
너는 확실히 선생님께 그렇게 말할 만큼 많은 용기가 있어.

(A) courage   (B) device   (C) origin   (D) device

B 1. attachment   2. task   3. habitat   4. origin   5. pioneer
C 1. C   2. B   3. A   4. A

201 **Zach *told the truth* by admitting that he broke the window.**
Zach가 자신이 창문을 깼다고 시인하며 사실을 말했다.

admit   동 들이다, 입장(입학)을 허가하다 let in, accept
[ədmít]   인정하다, 시인하다, 자백하다 acknowledge, concede

202 **Even though the accident did occur, he said it never *happened*.** 사고가 발생했음에도 불구하고, 그는 절대 그런 일이 없었다고 말했다.

occur   동 일어나다, 발생하다 happen, arise, take place
[əkə́ːr]

203 **Mr. Lin settled in New York and *lived* there for the rest of his life.** Lin 씨는 뉴욕에 정착해 남은 생애 동안 그곳에 살았다.

settle   동 ~에 정착하다, 정주하다 inhabit, live
[sétl]   해결하다 resolve
            정하다, 결정하다 decide

204 **The prosecutor battled injustice and *fought* corruptions.**
검사는 불의와 투쟁하고 부패와 싸웠다.

battle   동 싸우다 fight, clash
[bǽtl]   투쟁하다 struggle, strive
           명 전투 combat
            투쟁, 싸움 struggle, fight

205 **The agency tries its best to *help* and assist the poor.**
그 기관은 가난한 사람들을 도와주고 지원하기 위해 최선을 다한다.

assist   동 돕다, 거들다 help, aid, expedite, facilitate
[əsíst]

206

Relatives would *get together* and friends would gather in our house all the time.

우리 집에서는 친척들이 함께 어울리고 친구들이 모여들곤 했다.

gather   통 모으다, 모이다 assemble, collect
[gǽðər]   수확하다 harvest, pick, reap
                추정하다, 이해하다 assume, infer
             명 수확 harvest

207

The announcement intended to arouse and *excite* public opinion and support.

그 발표는 대중의 생각과 지지를 일깨우고 각성시키기 위한 것이었다.

arouse   통 깨우다, 눈뜨게 하다 awaken, wake up
[əráuz]   환기시키다, 자극하다 stimulate, excite, provoke

208

It started to dawn so we had to *begin* our day.

날이 밝아 왔고 우리는 하루를 시작해야 했다.

dawn   통 날이 새다, 밝아지다
[dɔːn]   시작하다 start, begin, commence
              점점 분명해지다 become clear
          명 새벽, 여명 daybreak, sunrise
              처음, 시작 beginning, start

209

I was going to execute the general's order but Ed ended up *carrying it out*. 내가 장군의 명령을 실행하려고 했지만 결국 Ed가 이행했다.

execute   통 실행하다 carry out, do, administer
[éksəkjùːt]   제작하다, 창작하다 create, make, produce
                연주하다, 연기하다 perform, play
                사형에 처하다 put to death
    - execution 명 사형 death penalty / 실행, 실시 carrying out

210

The mayor was criticized for shifting positions and *changing* policies.

시장은 자리를 바꾸고 정책을 변경한 것에 대해 비난을 받았다.

shift   통 이동하다, 바꾸다 move, change, alter, modify
[ʃift]   명 변경, 이동, 변천 change, alteration
             교대 시간, 교대 근무조

201 Well, I'm really happy for you, although I must admit that I'm a little envious, too.

(어휘) envious 부러워하는

음, 나는 너 때문에 정말 행복하다. 나도 네가 좀 부럽기는 하지만 말이야.

202 When such role conflicts occur, you need to do more important things first. (2001년 수능 예문 47번)

(어휘) role 역할   conflict 충돌, 갈등

그러한 역할 갈등이 발생할 때 당신은 더 중요한 것들을 먼저 할 필요가 있다.

203 Martha finally settled on one blouse in particular, as it was the right color and had an interesting pattern on it.

(어휘) in particular 특히   pattern 무늬

Martha가 마침내 특별한 어떤 블라우스 하나를 골랐는데, 그것은 적합한 색깔에 흥미로운 무늬가 있었거든.

204 He was ready to do battle for his beliefs.

(어휘) belief 믿음, 신념

그는 자신의 신념을 위해 싸울 준비가 되어 있었다.

205 The most popular use of the tail for these amphibians is to assist them in swimming straight.

(어휘) popular 인기 있는, 대중적인   amphibian 양서류   straight 일직선으로

이 양서류들에게 꼬리의 가장 일반적인 용도는 똑바로 헤엄치는 것을 돕는 것이다.

206 **I gather that you're going to graduate next semester.**

[어휘] graduate 졸업하다 semester 학기
네가 다음 학기에는 졸업할 거라고 생각해.

207 **In a bullfight, it is the movement, not the color, of objects that arouses the bull.**

[어휘] bullfight 투우 bull 황소
투우에서 황소를 자극하는 것은 물체의 색이 아니라 움직임이다.

208 **With the dawn of space exploration, the notion that atmospheric conditions on Earth may be unique in the solar system was strengthened.**

[어휘] exploration 탐사, 탐험 atmospheric 대기의 strengthen 강화하다
우주 탐사가 시작되면서 지구의 대기 조건은 태양계에서 유일할 것이라는 의견이 더욱 강해졌다.

209 **These skilled craftspeople could fashion the stone into bold images, or they could execute fine details of patterns.**

[어휘] fashion 만들다 bold 뚜렷한 image 형상 fine 정교한
이 숙련된 장인들은 돌로 뚜렷한 형상을 만들거나 정교한 문양을 제작할 수 있었다.

210 **The shifting layers of the earth's center continue to make earthquakes inevitable.**

[어휘] shifting 이동하는 layer 층, 지층 inevitable 피할 수 없는
지구 중심부의 이동하는 지층들은 지진을 계속 피할 수 없게 만든다.

A. Choose the right answer for the underlined word.

1   Is there anything else I can <u>assist</u> you with?
    더 도와 드릴 것은 없습니까?

    (A) stimulate   (B) modify   (C) administer   (D) help

2   He <u>battled</u> his way to the top of his profession.
    그는 자신의 직업 분야에서 정상의 자리에 오르려고 노력했다.

    (A) provoked   (B) began   (C) struggled   (D) moved

3   Too many students were <u>admitted</u> under early admission programs.
    너무 많은 학생들이 수시 전형에서 합격되었다.

    (A) aided   (B) assembled   (C) accepted   (D) arose

4   The noise <u>aroused</u> me from sleep.
    그 소음 때문에 잠에서 깨어났다.

    (A) picked   (B) awakened   (C) created   (D) welcomed

5   Widespread commercial use of the Internet did not <u>occur</u> until the early
    1990s. 인터넷의 광범위한 상업적 이용은 1990년대 초가 되어서야 일어난 일이다.

    (A) let in   (B) inhabit   (C) take place   (D) start

6   Moving continuously, a glacier <u>gathers</u> the rocks and other materials in its
    path. 빙하는 계속 이동하며 진로에 있는 암석들과 다른 물질들을 끌어모은다.

    (A) acknowledges   (B) collects   (C) changes   (D) clashes

7   It <u>dawned on</u> me that I needed to work harder if I wanted to be promoted.
    승진하고 싶으면 더 열심히 해야 한다는 생각이 들었다.

    (A) concluded on   (B) became clear to   (C) excited to   (D) facilitated with

8   He could have caught the ball if he had <u>shifted</u> his position sooner.
    그가 더 빨리 자리를 옮겼다면 공을 잡을 수 있었을 텐데.

    (A) altered   (B) produced   (C) quarreled   (D) conceded

B. Fill in the blanks.

admit	occur	settle	battle	assist
gather	arouse	dawn	execute	shift

1 He _____ his guilt.
그는 자신의 유죄를 인정했다.

2 Please _____ him in moving the furniture.
그가 가구 옮기는 것을 도와주세요.

3 You may also be able to visit these places and _____ facts for yourself. 이런 곳들을 찾아가 네 스스로 사실들을 수집할 수 있을 거야.

4 The serial killer was _____ at midnight.
그 연쇄 살인범은 한밤중에 처형되었다.

5 Why were you not able to _____ in and get down to work?
왜 마음을 다잡고 일을 시작하지 못하는 거야?

C. Choose the right answer.

1 Because he is a night person, John prefers to work during the evening _____ . John은 야행성이기 때문에 저녁 근무 시간대에 일하는 것을 더 좋아한다.

(A) dawn   (B) execution   (C) gather   (D) shift

2 The captain's speech _____ the players.
주장의 연설은 선수들을 각성시켰다.

(A) aroused   (B) occurred   (C) assisted   (D) settled

3 Photosynthesis takes place primarily in plant leaves, and little to none _____ in stems. 광합성은 주로 식물 잎에서 일어나며 줄기에서는 거의 발생하지 않는다.

(A) occurs   (B) settles   (C) shifts   (D) admits

4 More firefighters are needed to _____ these forest fires.
이 산불들과 싸우려면 더 많은 소방관들이 필요하다.

(A) admit   (B) assist   (C) arouse   (D) battle

B 1. admitted   2. assist   3. gather   4. executed   5. settle
C 1. D   2. A   3. A   4. D

211 **It was a *perfect* ending to the flawless performance.**
완벽한 공연에 맞는 흠잡을 데 없는 마무리였다.

flawless   휑 흠집 없는 intact, whole
[flɔ́ːlis]   결점 없는, 완벽한 perfect, faultless, unblemished

212 **He has sufficient experiences to do the job *well*.**
그는 그 일을 잘할 만한 충분한 경험이 있다.

sufficient   휑 충분한, 적당한 adequate, enough, ample, satisfactory, suitable
[səfíʃənt]

213 ***Almost everyone* in the department is involved in this widespread scandal.**
그 부서의 거의 모든 사람이 널리 퍼진 이 스캔들에 연루되어 있다.

widespread   휑 널리 퍼진, 광범위한 general, common, extensive, pervasive
[wáidspréd]

214 **He made a considerable amount of money *enough* to retire at the age of 25.** 그는 25세에 은퇴하기에 충분할 만큼 상당한 액수의 돈을 벌었다.

considerable   휑 상당한, 중요한 great, major, sizable, substantial, significant
[kənsídərəbl]

215 **He likes a firm mattress more than a *soft* one.**
그는 푹신한 매트리스보다 딱딱한 것을 더 좋아한다.

firm   휑 단단한, 견고한 hard, solid
[fəːrm]   확고한, 단호한 definite, certain, fixed

216 **He made the fatal mistake which caused him to *die*.**
그는 자신을 죽게 만든 치명적인 실수를 저질렀다.

fatal
[féitəl]
> 혱 치명적인 deadly, lethal, terminal

217 **Tom swam in a *clam* and placid lake.**
Tom은 평온하고 조용한 호수에서 수영했다.

placid
[plǽsid]
> 혱 잔잔한, 조용한, 차분한 still, quiet, calm, serene, tranquil

218 **It is essential that you remember these *important* dates for the test.** 시험에 필요한 이 중요한 날짜들을 기억해 두는 게 필수적이야.

essential
[isénʃəl]
> 혱 필수적인 vital, indispensable
> 본질적인, 근본적인 fundamental, basic
> 몡 요점, 핵심 fundamental
> 필수품 necessity, requisite

219 **He felt *lonely and afraid* because he lived in such a desolate area.** 그는 매우 황량한 지역에 살았기 때문에 외롭고 무서웠다.

desolate
[désəlit]
> 혱 황폐한, 사람이 살지 않는 deserted, uninhabited, barren
> 버려진 forsaken

220 **The soup has a distinctive taste which can be *remembered for a long time*.** 그 수프는 오랫동안 기억될 수 있는 독특한 맛이 있다.

distinctive
[distíŋktiv]
> 혱 뚜렷이 구별되는, 독특한 different, unique, distinguishing

211 A flawless diamond is worth a great deal more than one with imperfections.

(어휘) worth ~의 가치가 있는　imperfection 불완전함, 결함
흠 없는 다이아몬드는 결함 있는 것보다 훨씬 더 큰 가치가 있다.

212 These two brave explorers left with twenty men and sufficient supplies for three years.

(어휘) explorer 탐험가　supplies 보급품
이 두 용감한 탐험가들은 남자 20명과 3년간 사용하기에 충분한 보급품과 함께 떠났다.

213 As both a religion and a social force, Puritanism has had a widespread influence in the United States.

(어휘) religion 종교　force 세력　influence 영향, 작용
종교이자 사회 세력인 청교도주의는 미국에서 광범한 영향을 미쳐 왔다.

214 Mary Mapes Dodge exercised considerable influence on children's literature in the late nineteenth century.

(어휘) exercise 행사하다, 휘두르다
Mary Mapes Dodge는 19세기 말 아동 문학에 상당한 영향력을 행사했다.

215 As governor of Massachusetts, Calvin Coolidge became a national figure because of his firm opposition to the 1919 police strike.

(어휘) governor 주지사　figure 인물　opposition 반대　strike 파업
매사추세츠 주의 주지사였던 Calvin Coolidge는 1919년의 경찰 파업에 대한 단호한 반대로 전국적인 인물이 되었다.

216 A team of researchers has found that immunizing patients with bee venom instead of with the bees' crushed bodies can better prevent serious and sometimes fatal sting reactions.

(어휘) immunize 예방 접종하다   venom 독액   sting (벌의) 독침   reaction 반응
한 연구팀은 분쇄한 벌의 몸통보다는 벌의 독액을 환자들에게 접종하는 것이 심각하거나 때로는 치명적인 독침 반응을 보다 더 잘 예방할 수 있다는 것을 알아냈다.

217 From an airplane, the grasslands of the western prairie appear almost as uniform as a placid sea.

(어휘) uniform 같은 모양의, 한결같은
항공기에서 보면 서부 대초원 지대의 초원들은 잔잔한 바다처럼 거의 한결같아 보인다.

218 Concentrate on essentials rather than details.

(어휘) concentrate 집중하다
지엽적인 것보다 핵심에 집중해.

219 Large areas of Alaskan land remain desolate due to harsh climate.

(어휘) remain 여전히 ~이다   due to ~으로 인해
알래스카 땅의 넓은 지역이 혹독한 기후로 인해 여전히 황량한 채로 남아 있다.

220 The fact that Hawaii is the only state with two United States senators of Asian-American descent can be attributed to Hawaii's distinctive demographic profile.

(어휘) descent 가계, 출신   be attributed to ~의 덕분이다   demographic 인구 통계의
하와이가 상원 의원 2명이 아시아계 미국인 출신인 유일한 주라는 사실은 하와이의 독특한 인구 구성 특징 덕분일 것이다.

A. Choose the right answer for the underlined word.

1 It has a long neck and flies with <u>widespread</u> wings.
그것은 긴 목을 가지고 있으며, 넓게 편 날개로 날아다닌다.

    (A) terminal   (B) extensive   (C) basic   (D) uninhabited

2 Despite a <u>flawless</u> game plan, the team ended losing the game by 10 points. 흠잡을 데 없는 경기 계획에도 불구하고, 그 팀은 결국 10점 차로 그 경기에서 졌다.

    (A) satisfactory   (B) major   (C) certain   (D) perfect

3 Discipline is <u>essential</u> in an army.
군기는 군대에서 필수적이다.

    (A) quiet   (B) vital   (C) sizable   (D) general

4 One aspirin should be <u>sufficient</u> to relieve the pain.
아스피린 한 알이면 통증을 완화하는 데 충분할 것이다.

    (A) faultless   (B) adequate   (C) definite   (D) forsaken

5 A <u>considerable</u> number of people went to the last night's concert.
상당한 수의 사람들이 어젯밤에 열린 콘서트에 갔다.

    (A) enough   (B) satisfied   (C) substantial   (D) fundamental

6 The family moved from a <u>desolate</u> town in New Mexico to New York City.
그 가족은 뉴멕시코 주의 황량한 도시에서 뉴욕 시로 이사했다.

    (A) calm   (B) different   (C) pervasive   (D) deserted

7 Exercise keeps your muscles <u>firm</u> and strengthens your heart and lungs.
운동은 근육을 단단하게 유지해 주고 심장과 폐를 강화해 준다.

    (A) significant   (B) ample   (C) hard   (D) unblemished

8 Driving and texting can lead to a <u>fatal</u> accident.
운전하면서 문자를 보내는 것은 치명적인 사고로 이어질 수 있다.

    (A) lethal   (B) indispensable   (C) distinguishing   (D) great

Answers   A   1. B   2. D   3. B   4. B   5. C   6. D   7. C   8. A

B. Fill in the blanks.

> flawless sufficient widespread considerable firm
> fatal placid essential desolate distinctive

1 He is a man of _____ importance in this town.
그는 이 도시에서 상당히 중요한 인물이다.

2 Franklin Roosevelt had enjoyed _____ support from the public.
Franklin Roosevelt는 대중으로부터 광범위한 지지를 얻었다.

3 It is called Yellow Lake because of its _____ color.
그곳의 독특한 색깔 때문에 `Yellow Lake`라고 불린다.

4 The lawyer made a(n) _____ closing argument.
그 변호사는 흠잡을 데 없는 최종 변론을 했다.

5 Luckily, he was able to avoid a(n) _____ injury.
다행히 그는 치명적인 부상은 피할 수 있었다.

C. Choose the right answer.

1 My family enjoyed vacationing at this quiet and _____ resort.
우리 가족은 이 조용하고 평온한 리조트에서 휴가를 즐겼다.

(A) placid   (B) desolate   (C) essential   (D) considerable

2 A series of floods left the area totally _____.
연이은 홍수로 그 지역은 완전히 황폐하게 되었다.

(A) widespread   (B) distinctive   (C) desolate   (D) flawless

3 One of the most _____ concepts in the world of economics is supply and demand. 경제학계에서 가장 중요한 개념 중의 하나는 수요와 공급이다.

(A) sufficient   (B) essential   (C) firm   (D) fatal

4 Some people believe a _____ handshake means the person is of strong character. 어떤 사람들은 손을 꼭 쥐고 악수하는 사람은 개성이 강한 사람이라고 생각한다.

(A) considerable (B) firm   (C) flawless   (D) placid

B 1. considerable   2. widespread   3. distinctive   4. flawless   5. fatal
C 1. A   2. C   3. B   4. B

221

The dam was built to block the water flow and *stop* the flood waters. 그 댐은 물길을 차단해 홍수를 막기 위해 세워졌다.

block
[blɑk]
- (동) 방해하다, 차단하다, 막다 inhibit, prevent, confine, impede
- (명) 장애(물) barrier, hindrance, obstacle
- (도시의) 블록 neighborhood

222

The teacher highlighted and *stressed* what was on chapter 2. 그 교사는 2장에 있는 것을 강조했다.

highlight
[háilàit]
- (동) 두드러지게 하다, 강조하다 accentuate, emphasize, stress
- (명) 가장 중요한 부분 focal point

223

To illustrate my points, I *showed* the audience several pictures. 내 말의 요지를 설명하기 위해 나는 청중에게 사진 몇 장을 보여 주었다.

illustrate
[íləstrèit]
- (동) 보여 주다 represent, depict, portray
- 설명하다, 예시하다 explain, demonstrate

224

The medicine relieved the pain, but didn't *reduce* the temperature. 그 약은 통증은 완화해 주었지만 열을 내려 주지는 못했다.

relieve
[rilíːv]
- (동) 경감하다, 완화하다 reduce, lessen, alleviate, ease
- 해방하다, 구원하다 free
- 구제하다 aid
- 해임하다, 박탈하다 dismiss

225

He agreed to investigate the accident and *find out* who is responsible. 그는 그 사고를 조사해 누구 책임인지 밝혀내는 것에 동의했다.

investigate
[invéstəgèit]
- (동) 조사하다 search, inquire, probe, scrutinize
- 연구하다 study, research
- investigation (명) 조사, 연구, 심사 inquiry, search, review

226

The scientist's new theory was *accepted* and adopted.
그 과학자의 새 이론이 받아들여져 채택되었다.

adopt   통 채택하다, 받아들이다 endorse, ratify, sanction, take on, accept
[ədápt]   양자로 삼다

227

**Bob *is doing well* in every subject, but he especially excels
in math.** Bob은 모든 과목에서 잘하고 있지만 특히 수학에서 뛰어나다.

excel   통 능가하다 exceed, surpass, eclipse
[iksél]   뛰어나다, 탁월하다 be outstanding, shine
    - **excellence** 명 우월, 우수 distinction, brilliance
    - **excellent** 형 뛰어난, 탁월한 exceptional, outstanding

228

The fans applauded and *praised* the players' effort.
팬들은 선수들의 노력에 박수갈채하고 칭찬했다.

applaud   통 박수갈채하다 clap, cheer
[əplɔ́ːd]   성원하다 hail
    칭찬하다 praise, laud

229

**Cathy wanted to resolve the problem with Mindy, but she
couldn't *work it out*.**
Cathy는 Mindy와 함께 그 문제를 해결하고 싶었지만 그렇게 할 수가 없었다.

resolve   통 해결하다 find a solution for, solve, settle
[rizálv]   결심하다 decide, determine
    명 의지 will, conviction
    결심, 결의 resolution

230

Samantha endured the pain and *kept on* playing the game.
Samantha는 통증을 참으며 경기를 계속했다.

endure   통 견디다, 참다 stand, bear
[indjúər]   (고난을) 경험하다 experience, suffer, undergo
    계속되다, 지속하다 last, continue

221 His stubbornness is a block to all my efforts.

어휘 stubbornness 고집　effort 노력
그의 고집이 내 모든 노력을 허사로 만든다.

222 "Oh, that's the highlight of my life," Dunkin said.

"아! 그때가 바로 내 생애에서 가장 중요한 때였어."라고 Dunkin이 말했다.

223 Dora and her friends illustrate that being able to speak another language is valuable and should be embraced.

어휘 language 언어　embrace 포용하다
Dora와 그녀의 친구들은 다른 언어를 말할 수 있다는 것은 소중하며 포용되어야 한다는 것을 보여준다.

224 Eating healthy foods, exercising daily, and finding healthy ways to relieve stress can add years to your life.

어휘 add 더하다
건강에 좋은 음식을 먹고 매일 운동하고 스트레스를 푸는 건강한 방식들을 찾는 것이 수명에 몇 년을 더해 줄 수 있다.

225 The Crab Nebula, a striking formation in the constellation Taurus, may be the most thoroughly investigated object of modern astrophysical science.

어휘 striking 눈에 띄는, 인상적인　object 대상　astrophysical 천체물리학의
황소자리에서 인상적인 형태를 하고 있는 게성운은 현대 천체물리과학에서 가장 철저하게 조사한 대상일 것이다.

226

Another character whose name has been adopted into the language is that of Atlas, a giant from Greek mythology who supported the heavens on his shoulders.

어휘 giant 거인　Greek mythology 그리스 신화　heaven 하늘

그 이름이 언어 속에 받아들여진 또 다른 인물은 Atlas인데, 그는 양어깨에 하늘을 떠받치고 있던 그리스 신화에 나온 거인이다.

227

Babe Didrikson Zaharias excelled in basketball, baseball, and track in her youth and later became a champion golfer.

어휘 track 육상 경기

Babe Didrikson Zaharias는 젊었을 때 농구, 야구, 육상 경기에서 뛰어났으며 나중에는 골프 챔피언이 되었다.

228

The ideal listener has been humorously described as a person who applauds vigorously.

어휘 ideal 이상적인　describe 묘사하다　vigorously 활기차게, 힘차게

이상적인 청자는 열성적으로 박수갈채하는 사람이라고 익살맞게 묘사되어 왔다.

229

But the team showed resolve, intensity, patience and most importantly, an ability to finish strong in a tight contest.

어휘 intensity 격렬함, 열성　patience 인내

그러나 그 팀은 의지, 열성, 인내 그리고 가장 중요하게 막상막하의 접전에서 이길 수 있는 능력을 보여 주었다.

230

Ron and Adam believe that their friendship will endure forever.

어휘 friendship 우정

Ron과 Adam은 자신들의 우정이 영원히 지속될 것이라고 믿었다.

A. Choose the right answer for the underlined word.

1   People living in the Middle East have to <u>endure</u> the blazing sun almost all
    year round. 중동에 사는 사람들은 거의 일 년 내내 이글거리는 태양을 견뎌야 한다.
    (A) confine   (B) scrutinize   (C) lessen   (D) bear

2   In economics, graphs are used to <u>illustrate</u> functions.
    경제학에서 도표는 상관관계를 보여 주기 위해 사용된다.
    (A) exceed   (B) sanction   (C) explain   (D) inhibit

3   People <u>applauded</u> the President's decision to veto the bill.
    국민들은 그 법안에 거부권을 행사하기로 한 대통령의 결정을 칭찬했다.
    (A) stood   (B) lauded   (C) alleviated   (D) emphasized

4   Robert has a very analytical mind and <u>excels</u> in problem solving.
    Robert는 매우 분석적인 정신을 갖고 있어 문제 해결에 뛰어나다.
    (A) demonstrates (B) shines   (C) probes   (D) determines

5   Try to stay calm and make sure that oncoming traffic is not <u>blocked</u> by
    your car. 계속 침착하게 있으면서 당신 차가 다가오는 차들을 막지 않도록 하세요.
    (A) impeded   (B) suffered   (C) searched   (D) hailed

6   Neck and shoulder massages can <u>relieve</u> tension.
    목과 어깨의 마사지가 긴장을 풀어 줄 수 있다.
    (A) reduce   (B) eclipse   (C) ratify   (D) depict

7   Wildlife rangers <u>investigated</u> to see whether or not a koala has been taken
    illegally. 야생생물 보호구역 감시원들은 불법적으로 반출되는 고알라가 없는지 조사했다.
    (A) cheered   (B) inquired   (C) clapped   (D) stressed

8   They blame the mayor and council for not acting sooner to <u>resolve</u> the
    conflict before it got out of hand.
    그들은 시장과 의회가 더 빨리 행동해 분쟁이 걷잡을 수 없게 되기 전에 해결하려고 하지 않는 것을 비난한다.
    (A) ease   (B) enact   (C) settle   (D) bear

B. Fill in the blanks.

> block   highlight   illustrate   relieve   investigate
> adopt   excel   applaud   resolve   endure

1 I'm _____ to see that there is nothing negative that came back from the blood test. 나는 혈액 검사 결과 부정적인 것은 아무것도 없다는 것을 알게 되어 안도했다.

2 From 1950, she _____ numerous orphans of all races as 'an experiment in brotherhood.' 1950년부터 그녀는 '형제애 속의 실험'으로서 모든 인종의 수많은 고아들을 입양했다.

3 I really _____ your company for being so progressive.
당신의 회사가 그렇게 진보적이라니 찬사를 보냅니다.

4 He said the earthquake had caused landslides at different places, which in turn had _____ roads. 그는 지진이 여러 곳에서 산사태를 일으키는 바람에 도로들이 막혔다고 말했다.

5 UN inspectors were not permitted to _____ the facilities thoroughly.
UN 사찰단은 그 시설을 철저하게 감시하도록 허가받지 못했다.

C. Choose the right answer.

1 When I was young, I didn't _____ either in sports or in music.
나는 어릴 적에 스포츠나 음악 어느 것에도 뛰어나지 못했다.

(A) illustrate   (B) adopt   (C) excel   (D) investigate

2 I'll _____ all of your issues as soon as possible.
가능한 한 네 모든 문제를 해결해 줄게.

(A) relieve   (B) resolve   (C) highlight   (D) block

3 His plays have _____ for more than three centuries.
그의 연극은 300여 년 동안 공연되어 왔다.

(A) applauded   (B) endured   (C) adopted   (D) resolved

4 The cooperation was also mutually _____ in the sense of deepening the trade-economic ties. 교역 및 경제 유대를 강화하는 의미에서 양국 간의 협력 역시 강조되었다.

(A) highlighted   (B) excelled   (C) investigated   (D) endured

---

B   1. relieved   2. adopted   3. applaud   4. blocked   5. investigate
C   1. C   2. B   3. B   4. A

231

He rose to a position of influence and *power* very quickly.
그는 매우 빠르게 영향력과 권세가 있는 지위로 올라갔다.

influence   몡 세력, 권세 power
[ínfluəns]   영향(력), 효과 effect, impact
           통 ~에게 영향을 주다 convince, persuade

232

Uncle Rob told us many *stories* and tales when we were young. Rob 아저씨는 우리가 어렸을 때 많은 이야기와 설화를 들려주었다.

tale   몡 이야기, 설화 story, narrative, legend
[teil]   소문 gossip, rumor

233

***Uncontrolled desire* would lead to greed.**
욕구를 통제하지 못하면 탐욕으로 이어지게 된다.

greed   몡 탐욕, 욕심 desire, craving, longing, avarice
[griːd]

234

This *part* of the country is the coldest region in the country.
그 나라의 이곳이 그 나라에서 가장 추운 지역이다.

region   몡 지역, 지방 area, place, district, province
[ríːdʒən]   영역 domain
        - regional 톙 지역적인 local, provincial, parochial

235

Mark couldn't keep up with his school *work* because of a heavy course load. Mark는 과중한 학습량 때문에 학교 수업을 따라갈 수 없었다.

load   몡 화물 cargo
[loud]   부담, 짐 burden
        과제 assignment
        통 짐을 싣다 pack, stack
        (총포에) 장전하다

236 He retired at the height of his career because he wanted to leave when he was *on top*.

정상에 있을 때 떠나고 싶었기 때문에 그는 직업 생활의 절정기에 은퇴했다.

height
[hait]
- 명 높이, 고도 altitude
- 키, 신장 stature
- 절정, 정점 top, peak, pinnacle, summit

237 Rob's running pace is so *fast* that I can't keep up with him.

Rob의 달리는 속도가 워낙 빨라 나는 그를 따라잡을 수 없다.

pace
[peis]
- 명 걷는 속도, 보조 speed, rate, tempo
- 걸음, 보폭 footstep
- 동 천천히 걷다 walk, stride, stroll

238 Some people want success without exercising the discipline and *self-control* needed.

어떤 사람들은 필요한 규율과 자기 절제를 훈련하지 않은 채 성공을 원한다.

discipline
[dísəplin]
- 명 규율, 훈육 regulation / 징계, 징벌 punishment
- 훈련, 단련 training, practice / 절제력 self-control, restraint
- 동 징계하다, 훈육하다 punish
- 훈련하다, 다스리다 train

239 The military exercise can be understood as a threat or *warning*. 군사 훈련은 위협이나 경고로 이해될 수 있다.

threat
[θret]
- 명 위협, 경고 intimidation, terror, warning
- 징조, 조짐 sign, omen
- 위험 danger
- threaten 동 위협하다 intimidate

240 He had a hard time hiding his *dislike* and contempt for her lies. 그는 그녀의 거짓말에 대해 혐오와 경멸을 숨기기 힘들었다.

contempt
[kəntémpt]
- 명 경멸, 멸시, 모욕 dislike, disrespect, disdain
- 무시 disregard

231   **Outside factors influenced her to resign.**

(어휘) factor 요인, 요소   resign 사임하다
외부적인 요인들이 그녀가 사임하는 데 영향을 미쳤다.

232   **Among them was the tale of a priest who called on a member, and mentioned he hadn't seen her in church recently.**

(1998년 수능 예문 36번)

(어휘) priest 사제, 신부   mention 언급하다   recently 최근에, 요즈음
그것들 중에는 한 신부가 어느 교인을 방문해서는 요즘 교회에서 보지 못했다고 말했다는 이야기가 있었다.

233   **It would appear once again greed by the oil companies is at the reason these price increases.**

(어휘) reason 이유   increase 증가하다
이러한 가격 상승이 원유 회사들의 탐욕 때문이라는 것이 다시 한 번 드러날 것이다.

234   **There are, to be sure, regional differences in what are considered suitable clothes.** (1994년 1차 수능 예문 37번)

(어휘) clothes 옷, 의복
확실히 적절한 옷으로 간주되는 것에는 지역 차이가 있다.

235   **The police officer got shot when he was trying to load his gun.**

(어휘) get shot 총에 맞다
그 경찰관은 권총에 장전하려 하고 있을 때 피격당했다.

236 During the height of the Great Depression, Franklin Roosevelt won the elections of 1932 and 1936 by a landslide.

(어휘) Great Depression (미국의) 대공황   election 선거   landslide 산사태, 압도적 승리
대공황의 절정기에 Franklin Roosevelt는 1932년과 1936년 선거에서 압도적인 표차로 승리했다.

237 American small businesses set a record pace of borrowing to start and expand their companies over the first three months of the current fiscal year.

(어휘) expand 확장하다   current 현행의, 지금의   fiscal year 회계 연도
미국의 소기업들은 회계 연도의 첫 3개월 동안 회사 설립과 확장을 위한 자금 대출에 기록적인 속도를 냈다.

238 The student was disciplined for lying to the principal.

(어휘) principal 교장
그 학생은 교장에게 거짓말한 것 때문에 징계를 받았다.

239 Almost all railroads face serious problems that threaten to drive them out of business. [1997년 수능 예문 40번]

(어휘) railroad 철도   face 직면하다   drive out 몰아내다
거의 모든 철도가 사업을 중단하도록 위협하는 심각한 문제들에 직면하고 있다.

240 When the witness refused to answer the judge's question, she was arrested for contempt of court.

(어휘) witness 목격자, 증인   judge 판사   arrest 체포하다   court 법정
증인이 판사의 질문에 답하기를 거절했을 때 그녀는 법정 모독죄로 체포되었다.

A. Choose the right answer for the underlined word.

1 The rescue worker displayed <u>contempt</u> for his own safety.

그 구조 요원은 자신의 안전을 무시했다.

(A) summit   (B) warning   (C) disregard   (D) legend

2 It was an unfortunate result of the <u>greed</u> of the owner.

그것은 주인의 탐욕이 낳은 불행한 결과였다.

(A) avarice   (B) burden   (C) punishment   (D) power

3 The polar <u>regions</u> are generally covered with ice and snow.

극지방은 일반적으로 얼음과 눈으로 덮여 있다.

(A) disdains   (B) rates   (C) terrors   (D) provinces

4 This time I think I have the <u>discipline</u> to stick with it and practice every day.

이번에는 내가 그것을 매일 지키고 실천할 수 있는 자제력이 있다고 생각한다.

(A) domain   (B) restraint   (C) cargo   (D) pinnacle

5 Realizing he had to hurry so he would not be late for the meeting, he picked up his <u>pace</u>. 회의에 늦지 않으려면 서둘러야 한다는 것을 깨닫자 그는 속도를 내었다.

(A) desire   (B) control   (C) area   (D) speed

6 Men who served in the army tend to exaggerate when they tell <u>tales</u> about their army years. 군에서 복무한 사람들은 자신의 군대 시절에 대해 이야기할 때 과장하는 경향이 있다.

(A) regulations   (B) signs   (C) stories   (D) places

7 The professor decided to take some of the <u>load</u> off the students when they began to complain. 그 교수는 학생들이 불평하기 시작했을 때 과제를 좀 줄여 주기로 결정했다.

(A) peak   (B) assignment   (C) effect   (D) disrespect

8 Once there is a <u>threat</u> to its supply, however, water can quickly become the only thing that matters. (2002년 수능 예문 27번)

그러나 일단 공급에 차질이 생기면, 물은 금세 중요한 유일한 것이 될 수 있다.

(A) danger   (B) narrative   (C) regimen   (D) district

Answers   **A**   1. C   2. A   3. D   4. B   5. D   6. C   7. B   8. A

B. Fill in the blanks.

influence	tale	greed	region	load
height	pace	discipline	threat	contempt

1 From the look of the sky, there is a(n) _____ of rain.

하늘 모양을 보니 비가 올 조짐이 있다.

2 It just takes a little _____ to save up for a vacation.

휴가에 필요한 돈을 저축하려면 약간의 자제력이 필요하다.

3 Paul Bunyan has been the subject of numerous _____.

Paul Bunyan은 수많은 이야기의 주인공이 되어 왔다.

4 The _____ of the fence makes the garden very secluded.

담장 높이 때문에 그 정원은 아주 한적했다.

5 We must not let _____ and selfishness govern America any longer.

우리는 더 이상 탐욕과 이기심이 미국을 지배하게 해서는 절대 안 된다.

C. Choose the right answer.

1 He was driving while under the _____.

그는 술에 취한 상태에서 운전하고 있었다.

(A) height   (B) contempt   (C) place   (D) influence

2 The _____ had become virtually ungovernable.

그 지역은 사실상 통제할 수 없게 되었다.

(A) threat   (B) region   (C) tale   (D) discipline

3 Some lawyers seem to be held in _____.

일부 변호사들은 경멸을 받는 것 같다.

(A) contempt   (B) discipline   (C) greed   (D) tale

4 Planes can decrease maximum takeoff weights by reducing the fuel _____, the cargo, or the number of passengers.

비행기는 연료 적재량, 화물, 승객 수를 줄여 최대 이륙 중량을 줄일 수 있다.

(A) greed   (B) threat   (C) height   (D) load

B 1. threat   2. discipline   3. tales   4. height   5. greed

C 1. D   2. B   3. A   4. D

241 **I have nothing to *hide* or conceal from the police.**
나는 경찰에게 아무것도 숨기거나 감출 게 없다.

conceal   ⑧ 감추다, 숨기다 hide, cover, mask, obscure
[kənsíːl]

242 **The sudden *change* in weather will alter the schedule.**
갑작스런 날씨 변화로 일정이 변경될 것이다.

alter   ⑧ 바꾸다, 개조하다 change, modify, adjust, amend, revise
[ɔ́ːltər]

243 **They often collided because they *disagreed* about almost everything.** 그들은 거의 모든 것에 의견이 맞지 않았기 때문에 자주 충돌했다.

collide   ⑧ 부딪치다, 충돌하다 bump, crash
[kəláid]   ~와 일치하지 않다, 상충하다 clash, conflict

244 **When a shark dies, it *doesn't* float.**
상어는 죽으면 떠오르지 않고 가라앉는다.

float   ⑧ 뜨다, 떠다니다, 흘러가다 stay afloat, hover, drift
[flout]   제안하다, 제시하다 suggest, propose, present
    ⑲ 부유물
    (퍼레이드의) 장식 차량[수레]

245 **Tom helped me *build* a tree house because he had constructed one before.**
Tom은 전에 나무 위의 집을 지은 적이 있기 때문에 내가 한 채를 짓는 것을 도와주었다.

construct   ⑧ 건설하다, 세우다 build, erect, raise
[kənstrʌ́kt]   구성하다, 고안하다 compose

246

It is critical that you *organize* and assemble your thoughts before you begin writing.
글을 쓰기 시작하기 전에 생각을 정리해 조합하는 것이 매우 중요하다.

assemble　　⑧ 모으다, 집합시키다 gather, amass, collect
[əsémbl]　　　조립하다 put together, make, build up
　　　　　　　정리하다 organize
　　　　　　- assembly ⑲ 의회 congress / 모임, 집회 meeting, gathering

247

He claims to forecast the future, but can't *predict* anything accurately. 그는 미래를 예측한다고 주장하지만 아무것도 정확하게 예측할 수 없다.

forecast　　⑧ 예상하다, 예측하다 predict, anticipate, foretell, foresee
[fɔ́:rkæ̀st]　⑲ 예측, 예보 prediction, anticipation

248

He treasures all his trophies, but he *values* this one the most. 그는 자신의 모든 트로피를 소중히 여기지만 이것을 가장 가치 있게 여긴다.

treasure　　⑧ 소중히 여기다, 간직하다 prize, value, cherish, adore
[tréʒər]　　⑲ 보물 valuables, gem, jewel

249

He had struggled in the math class and *failed* it.
그는 수학 시간에 애쓰다가 낙제를 했다.

struggle　　⑧ 투쟁하다, 싸우다 fight, battle, wrestle
[strʌ́gl]　　　애쓰다, 고투하다 strive, labor, toil
　　　　　　⑲ 투쟁, 분투 fight, battle
　　　　　　　노력, 수고 exertion, labor, toil

250

Once the Internet was *connected*, the remote village was linked to the outside world.
일단 인터넷이 연결되자 그 외딴 마을은 바깥 세계와 연결되었다.

link　　　　⑧ 연결하다, 연계시키다 connect, relate, associate
[liŋk]　　　⑲ 고리, 연결 connection, tie, relationship

241 The president is trying to conceal the full extent of the corruption in his administration.

(어휘) extent 범위, 정도   corruption 부패   administration 행정부
대통령은 자기 행정부 내의 모든 범위의 부패를 숨기려고 애쓰고 있다.

242 Rising global temperatures will alter climate patterns all over the globe, upsetting the delicate balance of the world's ecosystems.

(어휘) global 전 세계의   upset 뒤엎다   delicate 섬세한   ecosystem 생태계
상승하는 세계 기온은 전 세계의 기후 패턴을 바꾸어 세계 생태계의 민감한 균형을 무너뜨릴 것이다.

243 Whale sharks are not aggressive, but they have been known to collide with boats.

(어휘) aggressive 공격적인
고래상어는 공격적이지는 않지만 배에 부딪치는 것으로 알려져 왔다.

244 Approaching the tree in which many soldiers had been hanged, he thought he saw something white floating in the middle of the tree. [2002년 수능 예문 39번]

(어휘) approach 다가가다   hang 교수형에 처하다
많은 병사들이 교수형 당했던 나무에 다가가면서 그는 그 나무 한가운데로 허연 것이 떠다니는 것을 보았다고 생각했다.

245 Virginia Tech's veterinary college is seeking donations to construct a memorial for police dogs killed in the line of duty.

(어휘) veterinary 수의학의   seek 찾다, 구하다   donation 기부(금)   memorial 기념비
버지니아 공대 수의과 대학에서는 임무 수행 중에 목숨을 잃은 경찰견들을 위한 기념비를 세우기 위한 기부금을 모으고 있는 중이다.

246

Freedom of expression includes the rights to freedom of speech, press, assembly.

[어휘] freedom 자유   expression 표현
표현의 자유는 언론, 출판, 집회의 자유에 대한 권리를 포함한다.

247

Allen Pearson, who headed a forecast center for years, tells about a lady who was not pleased with the warning system.

[2001년 수능 예문 44번]

[어휘] head 이끌다   please 기쁘게 하다   system 체계
여러 해 동안 기상 센터를 지휘했던 Allen Pearson이 경보 체계에 만족하지 않았던 한 여성에 대해 이야기한다.

248

In the legends of the American West, Paul Bunyan's most treasured possession was Babe the Blue Ox, whose horns were said to span a distance of 42 ax handles.

[어휘] horn 뿔   span (범위가) ~에 걸치다
미국 서부의 전설들 속에서 Paul Bunyan이 가장 아끼던 소유물은 Babe the Blue Ox였는데, 그것의 뿔은 42개의 도끼 자루 길이에 달했다고 한다.

249

The story of Eleanor Roosevelt's struggle for independence is far better known now than it was during her lifetime, thanks largely to the work of her biographer Joseph P. Lash.

[어휘] independence 독립   largely 주로   biographer 전기 작가
Eleanor Roosevelt의 독립 투쟁 이야기는 그녀가 살아 있을 때보다 지금 훨씬 더 잘 알려져 있는데, 이는 대부분 그녀의 전기 작가인 Joseph P. Lash의 작품 덕분이다.

250

For the first time ever, our program will provide the link between learning English and preparing for the test.

생전 처음으로 우리 프로그램은 영어 학습과 시험 준비 사이의 연결 고리를 제공해 줄 것이다.

A. Choose the right answer for the underlined word.

1 The Federal Reserve has no timetable to <u>alter</u> its policy.

연방 은행은 정책을 변경할 계획을 가지고 있지 않다.

(A) modify　　　(B) bump　　　(C) value　　　(D) amass

2 An increase in skin cancer has been <u>linked</u> to the depletion of the ozone layer. 피부암의 증가는 오존층의 파괴와 연관되어 있다.

(A) labored　　　(B) composed　　　(C) hovered　　　(D) connected

3 You can't <u>conceal</u> the truth from the public for a long time.

당신은 오랫동안 대중에게 진실을 숨길 수 없다.

(A) raise　　　(B) obscure　　　(C) foresee　　　(D) change

4 A large crowd <u>assembled</u> in the park to watch the firework.

많은 군중이 불꽃놀이를 보려고 공원에 모여들었다.

(A) prized　　　(B) conflicted　　　(C) related　　　(D) gathered

5 The two ships <u>collided</u> in thick fog causing many casualties.

배 두 척이 짙은 안개 속에서 충돌해 많은 사상자를 냈다.

(A) masked　　　(B) resisted　　　(C) crashed　　　(D) built

6 We will always <u>treasure</u> every moment with your family.

우리는 당신 가족과 함께한 모든 순간을 항상 소중히 생각할 것입니다.

(A) adjust　　　(B) propose　　　(C) cherish　　　(D) drift

7 Trevor's cabin was soon flooded and began to <u>float</u> down the river.

Trevor의 오두막은 곧 홍수에 휩쓸려 강에 떠내려가기 시작했다.

(A) drift　　　(B) hide　　　(C) amend　　　(D) structure

8 Large passenger planes often carry weather instruments with which to <u>forecast</u> storms. 커다란 여객기는 폭풍우를 예측하기 위해 흔히 기상 장비를 휴대하고 다닌다.

(A) predict　　　(B) collect　　　(C) revise　　　(D) fight

B. Fill in the blanks.

> conceal   alter   collide   float   construct
> assemble   forecast   treasure   struggle   link

1 The new bridge will _____ the island to the mainland.
새로운 다리가 그 섬과 육지를 연결하게 될 것이다.

2 Dynamite enabled people to _____ roads more easily.
다이너마이트는 도로를 더 쉽게 건설할 수 있게 해 주었다.

3 I've been trying to _____ this bike all afternoon.
나는 오후 내내 이 자전거를 조립하려고 애쓰고 있다.

4 Through biotechnology, scientists can _____ the genetic make-up of foods. 생명공학을 통해 과학자들은 식품의 유전자 구조를 변형할 수 있다.

5 He _____ to get up after sleeping for only two hours.
그는 거의 2시간만 자고 난 후에 잠자리에서 일어나려고 안간힘을 썼다.

C. Choose the right answer.

1 Alex was doing his best to _____ his anxiety before the job interview. Alex는 취업 면접을 앞두고 초조함을 숨기는 데 최선을 다하고 있었다.

(A) conceal   (B) construct   (C) alter   (D) link

2 The _____ says it'll be cloudy and cold in the morning.
기상 예보에 따르면 아침에는 흐리고 추울 것이라고 한다.

(A) float   (B) treasure   (C) forecast   (D) assembly

3 The Republican Party _____ with the Democratic Party over the proposed bill. 공화당은 상정된 법안에 대해 민주당과 충돌했다.

(A) struggled   (B) concealed   (C) construct   (D) collided

4 A boxfish can move its fins back and forth at the same time so it can _____ and hover in place. 거북복은 제자리에 떠 있으려고 지느러미를 동시에 앞뒤로 움직인다.

(A) alter   (B) assemble   (C) collide   (D) float

B 1. link   2. construct   3. assemble   4. alter   5. struggled
C 1. A   2. C   3. D   4. D

251 **Lois is still bitter and *angry* about what Olivia said.**
Lois는 Olivia가 한 말에 대해 아직도 분개하고 화가 나 있다.

bitter   혱 가혹한, 격렬한 harsh, severe, fierce
[bítər]   분개하는, 매우 불쾌한 resentful, angry
             신랄한 acrid, biting

252 **It was *stupid* and foolish to lie about your test score.**
시험 점수에 대해서 거짓말한 것은 멍청하고 어리석은 짓이었다.

foolish   혱 어리석은, 지각 없는 unwise, imprudent
[fú:liʃ]   바보 같은 stupid
            우스운 ridiculous

253 **He came from a very *poor* and humble background.**
그는 아주 가난하고 미천한 집안 출신이다.

humble   혱 겸손한, 겸허한 modest, unassuming, unpretentious
[hΛmbl]   변변찮은 common, plain, simple
            동 낮추다, 비하하다 disgrace, humiliate

254 **Jack didn't give an immediate answer because he *wanted time to think*.** Jack은 생각할 시간을 원했기 때문에 즉시 대답하지 않았다.

immediate   혱 당장의, 즉시의 instant, prompt
[imí:diət]   직접 접해 있는, 아주 가까운 nearest, adjacent
            직접적인, 직계의 closest

255 **I was looking for a temporary housing to stay *for a few days*.** 나는 며칠 동안 머물 임시 숙소를 찾고 있었다.

temporary   혱 일시적인 short-term, brief, momentary, transient
[témpəreri]   임시의 makeshift

256

We are living in a critical time because *important* things are happening. 우리는 중요한 일들이 일어나고 있기 때문에 중대한 시대에 살고 있는 것이다.

critical
[krítikəl]

형 비판적인 fault-finding, disparaging
중대한, 결정적인 important, crucial, decisive
위험한, 위급한 grave, dangerous

257

He is the foremost expert in the field with *many years of experience*. 그는 다년간의 경험을 지닌 그 분야의 최고 전문가이다.

foremost
[fɔ́ːrmòust]

형 맨 앞의, 첫 번째의 first
일류의, 주요한 chief, leading, principal
부 맨 먼저, 첫째로 chiefly, principally

258

After a week of extreme heat, it started to cool down *rapidly*. 일주일의 폭염 후에 날씨가 급속도로 시원해지기 시작했다.

extreme
[ikstríːm]

형 극도의, 극심한 intense, ultimate, utmost
극단적인, 과격한 excessive, fanatical
- extremely 부 극도로, 매우

259

After a fruitless search, Mark realized that it was *useless* looking for his keys.
찾는 데 허탕을 친 후에 Mark는 열쇠를 찾는 것이 쓸데없는 짓이라는 것을 깨달았다.

fruitless
[frúːtlis]

형 무익한, 헛된 unproductive, ineffective, useless, vain, futile
- fruitlessly 부 헛되이, 보람 없이

260

Living in such a solitary condition makes Henry very *lonely*.
그런 외로운 환경 속에 사는 것이 Henry를 아주 외롭게 만든다.

solitary
[sálitèri]

형 혼자의, 고독한, 외로운 alone, lone
고립된, 외딴 isolated, remote

251 The bitter rivals engaged in a public battle against one another that included threats of lawsuits and accusations of unfair use of taxpayer money.

(어휘) lawsuit 소송 accusation 고발, 고소 unfair 부당한 taxpayer 납세자
그 지독한 적수들은 납세자의 돈을 부당하게 사용한 것을 소송과 고발을 하겠다고 위협하는 등 서로에 대한 공개적인 싸움을 벌였다.

252 It was commonly felt that the purchase of Alaska by the United States in 1867 was foolish.

(어휘) purchase 구입, 매입
1867년에 미국이 알래스카를 매입한 것은 일반적으로 어리석은 짓으로 여겨졌다.

253 Lions was humbled by Bears' defense.

(어휘) defense 방어
라이언스 팀은 베어스 팀의 수비에 참패를 당했다.

254 It is recommended that all activity in the immediate coastal areas be suspended as a precaution.

(어휘) recommend 권하다 suspend 보류하다 precaution 예방 조치, 조심
사고 예방책으로서 연안 인접 지역에서의 모든 활동을 중단할 것을 권고한다.

255 Recent studies on early separation of children from their mothers indicated that children do not usually suffer permanent harm from this temporary experience.

(어휘) separation 분리 indicate 나타내다, 보여 주다 permanent 영구적인
아이들을 엄마에게서 일찍 분리시키는 것에 대한 최근 연구들은 아이들이 대개 이러한 일시적인 경험으로 영구적인 해를 입지는 않는다는 것을 보여 준다.

256 The studies released today are likely to be hotly debated within the circles of physicians and insurers because they come at a critical time.

어휘 release 발표하다　debate 토론하다　physician 내과 의사　insurer 보험업자
오늘 발표된 연구는 중대한 시기에 나왔기 때문에 내과 의학계와 보험업계 간에 열띤 토론의 대상이 될 것 같다.

257 In 1965, California replaced New York as the foremost state in the export of manufactured goods.

어휘 replace 대체하다　export 수출　manufactured goods 제조품, 공산품
1965년에 캘리포니아 주는 공산품 수출의 1등 주로서 뉴욕을 대체했다.

258 Hyenas have four toes on each foot, long fore legs, claws that do not retract, and extremely powerful jaws and teeth.

어휘 hyena 하이에나　claw 발톱　retract 움츠러들다　jaw 턱
하이에나는 발마다 발가락 4개가 있으며 긴 앞다리, 움츠러들지 않는 발톱, 아주 강력한 턱과 이를 가지고 있다.

259 Grounded whales often struggle fruitlessly to reenter deep water.

어휘 grounded 좌초된　struggle 몸부림치다　deep 깊은, 심오한
육지로 밀려온 고래들은 흔히 깊은 바다로 다시 들어가려고 몸부림치지만 아무 소용이 없다.

260 The higher primates are special because, by their nature, they have a propensity to be social rather than solitary.

어휘 primate 영장류　propensity 경향, 성향
고등 영장류는 선천적으로 혼자보다 여럿이 함께 어울리기를 더 좋아하는 성향이 있기 때문에 특별하다.

A. Choose the right answer for the underlined word.

1 In my <u>humble</u> opinion, you are wrong.
제 부족한 소견으로는 당신이 틀렸습니다.

(A) futile   (B) modest   (C) lone   (D) ridiculous

2 This is only a <u>temporary</u> measure.
이것은 잠정적인 조치일 뿐이다.

(A) grave   (B) unproductive   (C) excessive   (D) short-term

3 It would be <u>foolish</u> to spend that much money on a car.
차에 그렇게 많은 돈을 쓰는 것은 바보 같은 짓이다.

(A) unpretentious   (B) imprudent   (C) instant   (D) severe

4 My effort to change Dick's mind proved <u>fruitless</u>.
Dick의 마음을 바꾸려는 내 노력이 쓸데없다는 것이 밝혀졌다.

(A) faultfinding   (B) ineffective   (C) biting   (D) alone

5 He was considered the <u>foremost</u> American novelist in the 1950s.
그는 1950년대 미국 최고의 소설가로 여겨졌다.

(A) decisive   (B) common   (C) leading   (D) acrid

6 Hyenas may be active day or night and live <u>solitary</u> lives or live in packs.
하이에나는 낮이나 밤에 활동할 수 있으며 혼자 생활하거나 떼를 지어 생활한다.

(A) isolated   (B) adjacent   (C) ultimate   (D) momentary

7 Please be advised that the coastal areas may experience <u>extreme</u> wave activity. 연안 지역들은 매우 높은 파도가 칠 가능성이 있음을 알려 드립니다.

(A) intense   (B) chief   (C) important   (D) simple

8 With the <u>immediate</u> family dead or moved away, no one else cared where the body lay. 직계 가족의 사망이나 이주로 그 시신이 어디에 누워 있는지에 대해 다른 사람들은 아무도 관심이 없었다.

(A) transient   (B) vain   (C) closest   (D) unwise

Answers   A   1. B   2. D   3. B   4. B   5. C   6. A   7. A   8. C

B. Fill in the blanks.

| bitter foolish humble immediate temporary |
| critical foremost extreme fruitless solitary |

1 After losing his family, the author led a(n) _____ life.

가족을 잃은 후 그 작가는 외롭게 살았다.

2 Greg made a(n) _____ and silly mistake.

Greg는 바보 같고 어리석은 실수를 저질렀다.

3 It was a(n) _____ attempt to make peace with the enemy.

적과 화해하려는 것은 헛된 시도였다.

4 Mr. Erickson is one of the most _____ and dependable people I know. Erickson 씨는 내가 아는 사람들 중에서 가장 겸손하고 믿을 만한 사람이다.

5 A flash flood is caused by the _____ rainfall.

극심한 폭우로 돌발적인 홍수가 발생했다.

C. Choose the right answer.

1 Patience is _____, but it bears sweet fruit.

인내는 쓰지만 달콤한 열매를 맺는다.

(A) bitter   (B) foolish   (C) foremost   (D) solitary

2 Pain is _____, but victory is forever.

고통은 일시적이나 승리는 영원하다.

(A) fruitless   (B) temporary   (C) extreme   (D) humble

3 First and _____, the leading cause of fire-related deaths in the home is careless smoking. 다른 무엇보다도 가정에서의 화재 관련 사망의 첫째 원인은 부주의한 흡연이다.

(A) immediate   (B) humble   (C) solitary   (D) foremost

4 When leaving one's country, it is _____ to take along all important documents. 자기 나라를 떠날 때는 모든 중요한 서류를 가져가는 것이 필수적이다.

(A) temporary   (B) critical   (C) foolish   (D) bitter

B 1. solitary   2. foolish   3. fruitless   4. humble   5. extreme

C 1. A   2. B   3. D   4. B

261

He did not *give up* his future or abandon his family.
그는 미래를 포기하거나 가족을 버리지 않았다.

abandon   통 버리고 떠나다 leave, desert, forsake
[əbǽndən]   단념하다, 포기하다 give up, surrender, relinquish

262

Eating fish can help you *focus* and concentrate.
생선을 먹으면 집중하고 전념하는 데 도움이 될 수 있다.

concentrate   통 모으다, 집합시키다; 모이다, 집합하다 gather, collect, assemble
[kánsəntrèit]   ~에 집중하다, 전념하다 focus
   명 농축물
   - concentration 명 집중

263

I *bought* my books at the bookstore, but Rob acquired them online. 나는 책들을 서점에서 샀지만 Rob은 온라인에서 구입했다.

acquire   통 얻다, 취득하다 get, gain, obtain, secure, procure
[əkwáiər]   습득하다, 배우다 learn, pick up, master

264

Sam overlooked the problem which he doesn't usually *miss*. Sam이 평소에는 실수하지 않는 문제를 놓쳤다.

overlook   통 못 보고 넘어가다, 간과하다 miss, neglect
[óuvərlùk]   눈감아주다 ignore, forgive, excuse
   내려다보다 have a view over

265

I *let* you play outside, but I didn't permit you to break a window. 바깥에서 노는 것은 허락했지만 창문을 깨라고는 하지 않았다.

permit   통 허락하다, 허가하다, 용인하다 allow, admit, let, sanction
[pə́:rmit]   명 허가증 license, certificate

266 **It is difficult to *predict* when a disaster will occur, but the fire was a tragedy foretold.**
재난이 발생하리라는 것을 예측하기는 어렵지만 그 화재는 예견된 비극이었다.

foretell   통 예언하다, 예고하다 predict, forecast, anticipate
[fɔ:rtél]

267 **He surpassed his own expectation and *beat* his rival.**
그는 자신의 예상을 넘어 경쟁자를 이겼다.

surpass   통 능가하다, 넘다, ~보다 뛰어나다 outdo, top, beat, exceed
[sərpǽs]

268 **The governor advocated and *supported* the bill.**
주지사는 그 법안을 옹호하고 지지했다.

advocate   통 지지하다, 옹호하다 support, promote
[ǽdvəkeit]   추천하다 recommend
[ǽdvəkət]명   명 옹호자, 지지자 supporter, proponent, defender
                   대변자 spokesman

269 **Elle *was busy* because she was engaged in many different activities.** Elle은 여러 다른 활동에 관여했기 때문에 바빴다.

engage   통 관여시키다, 끌어들이다 involve, absorb, immerse
[ingéidʒ]   (눈길·관심을) 끌다, 사로잡다
                 고용하다 employ, hire
                 종사하다, 관여하다 participate in, join in

270 **When the teacher dictates words to her class, she *says* them very clearly.** 그 교사는 학생들에게 단어를 받아쓰게 할 때 매우 명확하게 말한다.

dictate   통 받아쓰게 하다
[díkteit]   규정하다, 지시하다 prescribe, determine
                 요구하다 require, demand

261 The 21st Amendment repealed the 18th in 1933, and by 1966 all states had also abandoned Prohibition.

[어휘] amendment (미국 헌법) 수정 조항   repeal 무효화하다   Prohibition 금주령
1933년에 수정 조항 21조가 18조를 무효화하여 1966년에는 모든 주에서도 금주령을 폐지했다.

262 Goethe once said to his wife, "I've never seen an artist with more power of concentration than this musician."

(2000년 수능 예문 31번)

Goethe는 "나는 이 음악가보다 더 집중력이 강한 예술가를 본 적이 없어."라고 아내에게 말한 적이 있다.

263 U.S. companies are fast learning how to team up with foreign competitors to crack markets and acquire technology.

[어휘] competitor 경쟁자   crack 침투하다, 파고들다   technology 기술
미국 회사들은 시장 진출과 기술 습득을 위해 외국 경쟁사들과 협력하는 방법을 빨리 배우고 있다.

264 They overlook these drawbacks and do not recognize that the real, human contact is being replaced by a less personal network.

[어휘] drawback 결점
그들은 이러한 결점들을 간과하고 진짜 사람들 간의 접촉이 덜 개인적인 네트워크로 대체되고 있음을 인식하지 못하고 있다.

265 In fact, police do issue permits to qualified hunters and advise hikers to wear bright, colorful clothing during hunting season. (2002년 수능 예문 42번)

[어휘] qualified 자격 있는, 면허가 있는   issue 발급하다
사실, 경찰은 사냥철에는 자격 있는 사냥꾼들에게 허가증을 발급하고 있으며 하이킹을 하는 사람들에게 밝고 화려한 색의 옷을 입도록 권장하고 있다.

266 We cannot accurately foretell how much of the carbon dioxide released by factories as waste will remain permanently in the atmosphere.

어휘 carbon dioxide 이산화탄소　release 배출하다　atmosphere 대기
우리는 공장에서 폐기물로 방출되는 이산화탄소가 얼마나 많이 대기 중에 영구적으로 남게 될지 정확히 예측할 수 없다.

267 There is always excitement at the Olympic Games when a previous record of performance is surpassed.

어휘 excitement 흥분, 짜릿함　previous 이전의　performance 성과, 성적
이전의 성적 기록을 능가하게 되는 올림픽 대회에서는 항상 짜릿함이 있다.

268 Shirley Chisholm has been one of the foremost advocates of welfare legislation since the 1960s.

어휘 welfare 복지
Shirley Chisholm은 1960년대 이후 가장 주요한 복지법 제정 옹호자 중의 한 사람이었다.

269 We engage in auditory communication when we talk with others face-to-face or over the telephone.

어휘 auditory 청각의
우리가 다른 사람들과 대면하거나 전화로 이야기할 때는 청각적인 의사소통에 관여하는 것이다.

270 Many think that the realities of geography and climate are going to dictate major changes in the way the city is rebuilt and protected.

어휘 reality 실제　geography 지리, 지형
많은 사람들은 실제의 지리와 기후가 그 도시의 재건과 보호 방식에 중대한 변화를 요구할 것이라고 생각한다.

A. *Choose the right answer for the underlined word.*

1 Eating is not <u>permitted</u> in the concert hall.
콘서트홀에서는 음식을 먹는 것이 허용되지 않는다.

(A) predicted   (B) surrendered   (C) allowed   (D) encouraged

2 It would be a lie if someone claims to <u>foretell</u> the future.
어떤 사람이 미래를 예언한다고 하면 그것은 거짓말일 것이다.

(A) absorb   (B) forsake   (C) obtain   (D) forecast

3 Some students cannot <u>engage</u> in other activities and keep their grades to a satisfactory level. 일부 학생들은 다른 활동에 참가하며 성적을 만족스러운 수준으로 유지할 수 없다.

(A) participate   (B) collect   (C) require   (D) leave

4 The Iranian minister concluded, "Iran will not <u>abandon</u> its right to develop nuclear technology." 그 이란의 장관은 "이란은 핵 기술을 개발할 권리를 포기하지 않을 것이다."라고 결론을 내렸다.

(A) support   (B) secure   (C) relinquish   (D) let

5 Experts predict that China will <u>surpass</u> Germany by next year to become the world's third-largest economy.
전문가들은 중국이 내년에는 독일을 능가해 세계에서 3번째의 경제 대국이 될 것이라고 예측한다.

(A) hold   (B) exceed   (C) excuse   (D) demand

6 Modern dance teachers <u>concentrate</u> on helping students to express the concepts of space time and energy through dance.
현대 무용 교사들은 학생들이 춤을 통해 시공간과 에너지의 관념들을 표현하도록 돕는 데 집중한다.

(A) recommend   (B) hire   (C) focus   (D) anticipate

7 It is better to obey the posted speed limit than to let traffic <u>dictate</u> your speed. 교통량이 속도를 정하게 하는 것보다는 정해진 속도 제한을 지키는 것이 낫다.

(A) determine   (B) procure   (C) top   (D) beat

8 In fact, the experience you <u>acquired</u> as a volunteer may give you an extra advantage over others. 사실, 자원봉사자로서 얻는 경험은 다른 사람들보다 자신에게 더 큰 이익을 줄 수 있다.

(A) deserted   (B) consolidated   (C) immersed   (D) gained

Answers   **A**   1. C   2. D   3. A   4. C   5. B   6. C   7. A   8. D

B. Fill in the blanks.

| abandon concentrate acquire overlook permit |
| foretell surpass advocate engage dictate |

1 We do not _____ the change in any way.

우리는 어떤 방식의 변화도 지지하지 않는다.

2 We already _____ our goal for this month.

우리는 이번 달 목표를 이미 초과 달성했다.

3 You are not _____ to bring anything with you to the test.

시험장에는 아무것도 가져올 수 없다.

4 I can't _____ my luggage here at the airport.

공항에 내 짐을 버리고 갈 수는 없다.

5 I want to _____ particularly on the violent content in videogames, movies, and the Internet. 나는 특히 비디오게임, 영화, 인터넷에 나오는 폭력적인 내용에 집중하고자 한다.

C. Choose the right answer.

1 Our company is being _____ by a competitor.

우리 회사는 경쟁사에 매각된다.

(A) concentrated (B) advocated   (C) permitted   (D) acquired

2 Jason lives on a hill which _____ the Daytona River.

Jason은 Daytona 강이 내려다 보이는 언덕 위에 살고 있다.

(A) surpasses   (B) concentrates (C) overlooks   (D) permits

3 You should not let your brother _____ your life.

형이 네 인생을 좌우하도록 놔두면 안 된다.

(A) advocate   (B) acquire   (C) dictate   (D) engage

4 The novel _____ her attention and interest.

그 소설은 그녀의 주의와 흥미를 끌었다.

(A) engaged   (B) overlooked   (C) foretold   (D) abandoned

B 1. advocate   2. surpassed   3. permitted   4. abandon   5. concentrate
C 1. D   2. C   3. C   4. A

271

Don't be too concerned with the *number* and the quantity.
수와 양에 대해서는 너무 신경 쓰지 마라.

| quantity | 명 양, 분량, 수량 amount, number, volume |
| [kwántəti] | 다량, 다수 abundance |

272

The governmental network could not be used for commercial purposes **unless the *goal* was related to research or education.**
정부 네트워크는 목적이 연구와 교육과 관련된 것이 아니라면 상업 용도로 사용될 수 없었다.

| purpose | 명 목적, 용도 goal, aim, objective, end |
| [pə́ːrpəs] | 의도, 취지 intention, motive |

273

The husband thought it was a perfect spot**, but the wife didn't like the *location*.**
남편은 그곳을 최적의 장소로 생각했지만 아내는 그곳을 좋아하지 않았다.

spot	명 반점, 얼룩 mark, stain
[spɑt]	장소, 지점 place, site, location
	동 발견하다, 찾아내다 detect, discover, find, locate

274

I'm sure today is *kind* of an anniversary of some sort.
오늘이 무슨 기념일인 것은 분명해.

sort	명 종류, 부류 kind, type, category
[sɔːrt]	성격, 성질 character, nature
	동 분류하다, 구분하다 separate, isolate, classify
	가려내다 screen

275

She is a *writer* by occupation.
그녀는 직업 작가이다.

| occupation | 명 직업, 업종 job, work, vocation, profession |
| [àkjupéiʃən] | 점유, 점령 occupancy, invasion |

276   **A strong bond was formed between two childhood *friends*.**
유년기의 두 친구 사이에 강한 유대감이 형성되었다.

bond
[band]
- 명 유대, 결속 tie, connection, alliance
  맹약, 계약 agreement, contract, pledge
  채권 security
- 동 결속시키다 unite
  접착시키다 adhere

277   ***Nothing was decided* because there was a conflict of opinions.** 의견 충돌이 있어 아무것도 결정되지 않았다.

conflict
[kánflikt]
- 명 분쟁, 논쟁 dispute, dissension
  불일치, 충돌, 갈등 discord, friction, clash
  싸움, 투쟁, 전투 battle, struggle, combat
- 동 대립하다, 충돌하다, 모순되다 clash, disagree, differ, collide

278   **The advent of the Internet *started* the process of globalization.** 인터넷의 출현으로 세계화 과정이 시작되었다.

advent
[ǽdvent]
- 명 도래, 출현, 등장 coming, appearance, arrival, dawn

279   **Mr. Hunter placed emphasis on honesty whereas Mr. Fox *stressed* responsibility.**
Hunter 씨는 정직을 강조한 반면에 Fox 씨는 책임감을 역설했다.

emphasis
[émfəsis]
- 명 강조 stress
  중요성 importance, significance

280   **Everyone admires Mr. Logan's consistency: he *never missed* work in 10 years.**
모든 사람이 Logan 씨의 일관성을 존경한다. 그는 10년 동안 한 번도 결근한 적이 없다.

consistency
[kənsístənsi]
- 명 일관성 uniformity, constancy, steadiness
  일치, 조화 agreement, harmony
- consistent 형 변함없는, 일관된 steady, constant
  일치하는 agreeing, harmonious

271 There is also a quantity discount, which is offered to individuals who order large quantities of a product.

(2001년 수능 예문 31번)

[어휘] discount 할인(액)   individual 개인
수량 할인도 있는데, 그것은 많은 양의 상품을 주문하는 개인들에게 제공된다.

272 Tattooing is the practice of inserting pigment underneath the surface of the skin for decorative, religious, identification, or other purposes.

[어휘] tattoo 문신, 문신하다   insert 삽입하다   pigment 색소   identification 일체감
문신은 장식, 종교, 일체감 또는 기타 목적으로 피부 표면 아래에 색소를 삽입하는 관행이다.

273 Then suddenly from that very spot, rocks, dirt, and melted rock flew hundreds of feet into the air.

[어휘] dirt 먼지   melted rock 용암
그때 갑자기 바로 그 지점에서 암석, 먼지, 용암이 공중으로 수백 피트 높이로 날아올랐다.

274 "Oh," the blind man said, "then it must be a wet sort of color."

(1994년 1차 수능 예문 46~47번)

[어휘] blind man 맹인
그 맹인 남자는 "아, 그렇다면 그것은 분명히 일종의 마르지 않은 색깔일 거야."라고 말했다.

275 Since Sam has never been unhappy with his occupation, he cannot understand the attitude of those who have no desire to take up any occupation. (1998년 수능 예문 41번)

Sam은 자기 직업에 불만이었던 적이 한 번도 없었기 때문에, 직업을 얻으려는 욕구가 전혀 없는 사람들의 태도를 이해하지 못한다.

276　The role of the primary caretaker is important, but a year-old baby can also easily bond with secondary caretakers.

어휘 role 역할　primary 1차적인　caretaker 양육자　secondary 2차적인
1차 양육자의 역할이 중요하지만 한 살짜리 아기는 2차 양육자와도 쉽게 유대를 형성할 수 있다.

277　Different biologists, analyzing the same data, may arrive at wholly different and sometimes conflicting interpretations.

어휘 biologist 생물학자　analyze 분석하다　interpretation 해석
다양한 생물학자들은 같은 데이터를 분석해 완전히 다르고 때로는 상충되는 해석에 도달하기도 한다.

278　Prior to the advent of urban centers and the high population densities, the peddler played an important role in bringing goods and services to individuals living in remote areas.

어휘 prior to ~ 전에　urban center 도심지　density 밀도　peddler 행상인
도심지와 높은 인구 밀도의 출현 이전에는 행상인이 외딴 지역에 사는 사람들에게 상품과 서비스를 공급하는 데 중요한 역할을 했다.

279　This system reflects Japan's emphasis on respect and establishes rules on how people of different relationships may speak with each other.

어휘 reflect 반영하다　establish 제정하다, 확립하다
이 제도는 일본의 존중에 대한 강조를 반영하며 다양한 관계의 사람들이 서로에게 말할 수 있는 방식에 대한 규칙을 정하고 있다.

280　The result was consistent with the doctor's diagnosis.

어휘 result 결과　diagnosis 진단
그 결과는 의사의 진단과 일치했다.

A. Choose the right answer for the underlined word.

1 Dogs also try to form a bond with humans.

개도 인간과의 유대를 형성하려고 노력한다.

(A) dissention   (B) site   (C) nature   (D) tie

2 The purpose of the humpback whale's song is still a mystery.

혹등고래가 노래하는 목적은 여전히 수수께끼이다.

(A) harmony   (B) start   (C) importance   (D) intention

3 But sometimes you will get caught in a conflict. (2001년 수능 예문 47~48번)

그러나 때때로 당신은 분쟁에 휘말리게 된다.

(A) security   (B) discord   (C) stain   (D) stress

4 Some people believe that quality is more important than cost or quantity of a product. 어떤 사람들은 상품의 가격이나 양보다는 질이 더 중요하다고 믿는다.

(A) kind   (B) amount   (C) profession   (D) steadiness

5 He moved up from second spot to become president of the firm.

그는 두 번째 위치에서 그 회사의 사장으로 승진했다.

(A) place   (B) mission   (C) connection   (D) struggle

6 With the advent of mass media, we are no longer limited by geographical boundaries. 대중매체의 출현으로 우리는 더 이상 지리적 경계에 제한을 받지 않는다.

(A) aim   (B) category   (C) dawn   (D) category

7 The educational systems, in these countries, reflect these values and do not put all of its emphasis on memorizing information.

이 나라들에서의 교육 제도들은 이러한 가치들을 반영하며 정보를 암기하는 데만 중점을 두지 않는다.

(A) goal   (B) reliability   (C) work   (D) significance

8 Smokers and non-smokers need to find some sort of middle ground, so that both groups can get along with each other.

흡연자와 비흡연자는 일종의 합의점을 찾아 양측 모두가 서로 사이좋게 지낼 수 있도록 해야 한다.

(A) kind   (B) number   (C) location   (D) objective

Answers   **A** 1. D   2. D   3. B   4. B   5. A   6. C   7. D   8. A

B. Fill in the blanks.

> quantity   purpose   spot   sort   occupation
> bond   conflict   advent   emphasis   consistency

1 Morality was the _____ of his speech.
도덕성이 그의 연설의 강조점이었다.

2 The _____ of new drug raised hope for the cure.
신약의 출현이 치료에 대한 희망을 높여 주었다.

3 The _____ may grow to unmanageable proportions.
갈등이 감당할 수 없을 정도로 커질 수 있다.

4 We have found an office that will serve our _____.
우리는 목적에 맞는 사무실을 찾았다.

5 There are two _____ of books required for basic bookkeeping.
기본 부기에 필요한 두 종류의 장부가 있다.

C. Choose the right answer.

1 The long-tailed animal was _____.
꼬리가 긴 동물이 발견되었다.

(A) bonded   (B) conflicted   (C) spotted   (D) sorted

2 World War II began with Germany's _____ of Poland.
제2차 세계 대전은 독일의 폴란드 점령으로 시작되었다.

(A) purpose   (B) advent   (C) emphasis   (D) occupation

3 Home economists recommend buying basic food items in large
_____. 가정학자들은 기본 식품을 대량으로 구입할 것을 권장한다.

(A) quantities   (B) occupations   (C) purposes   (D) consistencies

4 The _____ of sugar-rich foods appears to be the biggest reason for
tooth decay. 지속적인 고당분 음식 섭취가 충치의 가장 큰 원인인 것으로 보인다.

(A) consistency   (B) emphasis   (C) quantity   (D) advent

B 1. emphasis   2. advent   3. conflict   4. purpose   5. sorts
C 1. C   2. D   3. A   4. A

281

We *agree* on the problem but differ on how to solve it.
우리는 그 문제에는 의견이 일치하지만 해결 방법은 다르다.

differ   ⑧ 다르다 contradict, contrast, vary, stand apart
[dífər]   의견이 다르다 disagree, dispute, dissent

282

The idea revolutionized the industry and *completely changed* how people do business.
그 아이디어는 업계에 혁명을 일으켜 사람들이 사업하는 방식을 완전히 바꾸어 놓았다.

revolutionize   ⑧ 혁명[대변혁]을 일으키다 transform, reform, refashion
[rèvəlú:ʃənàiz]   - revolution ⑲ 혁명 revolt, rebellion, insurrection
   대변혁, 개혁 transformation, reform

283

Snakes do not possess legs, but many lizards do *have* legs.
뱀은 다리를 가지고 있지 않지만 많은 도마뱀들은 분명히 다리를 가지고 있다.

possess   ⑧ 소유하다, 지니다 have, own, hold
[pəzés]   (생각이) 사로잡다, (악령이) 씌다 control, obsess
   - possession ⑲ 소유, 소유물

284

You don't have to rush because I'm not in a *hurry* to leave.
나는 급하게 떠나지 않을 거니까 서두르지 않아도 돼.

rush   ⑧ 돌진하다, 급히 가다 advance, charge, dash
[rʌʃ]   급히 하다, 서두르다 hurry
   ⑲ 쇄도 surge, flood
   혼잡, 러시 bustle
   ⑱ 쇄도하는, 바쁜 busy

285

The show's *surprising* ending amazed the viewers.
그 극의 깜짝 결말은 시청자들을 놀라게 했다.

amaze   ⑧ 놀라게 하다, 경악시키다 astonish, surprise, shock, astound
[əméiz]

286

He reinforced the door to make it _stronger_ for the storm.
그는 태풍에 더 잘 견디도록 문을 보강했다.

reinforce   동 보강하다 support, strengthen, fortify
[rìːinfɔ́ːrs]   증강하다, 강화하다 increase, beef up, augment

287

We still need to _clean_ the house and polish these silverwares.
우리는 아직도 집을 청소하고 이 은제 식기들을 닦아야 한다.

polish   동 닦다, ~의 윤을 내다 gloss, shine, varnish
[pɑ́liʃ]   다듬다, 세련되게 하다 improve, refine, cultivate
   윤[광택]이 나다
   명 광택

288

Greg defied his parents, but later regretted that he _didn't listen_ to them.
Greg는 부모에게 반항했지만 나중에 그들의 말을 듣지 않은 것을 후회했다.

defy   동 반항하다, 도전하다 resist, challenge, confront, disobey
[difái]   피하다, 빠져나가다 escape, elude
   견뎌내다 withstand

289

The investors _expect_ and anticipate more economic growth.
투자자들은 더 많은 경제 성장을 예상하고 기대했다.

anticipate   동 예상하다 expect, predict, forecast, foresee
[æntísəpèit]   기대하다 expect, await, look forward to

290

He decided to incorporate her idea by _including_ it in his new book. 그는 자신의 새 책에 그녀의 아이디어를 포함시켜 집어넣기로 결정했다.

incorporate   동 포함하다, 함유하다 include, contain
[inkɔ́ːrpəreit]   집어넣다, 통합시키다 combine, consolidate, integrate

281 But ideas about how to punish children differ from culture to culture and family to family. (1999년 수능 예문 26번)

(어휘) punish 처벌하다
그러나 아이들에게 벌을 주는 방법에 대한 생각들은 문화마다 그리고 가정마다 다르다.

282 It is in the leisure or sports clothes that the greatest revolution has taken place. (1994년 1차 수능 예문 37번)

(어휘) leisure 여가, 레저   take place 발생하다
가장 큰 변혁이 일어난 것은 레저 또는 스포츠 의류에서이다.

283 A job, however unpleasant or poorly paid, was a man's most precious possession. (1998년 수능 예문 41번)

(어휘) unpleasant 불쾌한, 싫은   precious 귀중한
아무리 싫고 보수가 적어도 일자리는 남자의 가장 귀중한 소유물이었다.

284 I do my shopping in September to avoid the Christmas rush.

(어휘) avoid 피하다
나는 크리스마스 때의 혼잡을 피하기 위해 9월에 쇼핑을 한다.

285 What did amaze me about the small rock that fell from Mars was that it had traveled millions of miles across space to land here.

(어휘) Mars 화성   space 우주
화성에서 떨어진 그 작은 암석에 대해 내가 놀란 것은 그것이 우주를 가로질러 수백만 마일을 이동해 여기에 도착했다는 점이었다.

286 Monkeys constantly groom one another, thus reinforcing the social bonds necessary to their survival.

어휘 groom 다듬다, 손질하다   bond 유대, 결속   survival 생존
원숭이들은 끊임없이 서로의 털을 다듬어 주어 자신들의 생존에 필요한 사회적 유대를 강화한다.

287 Boxwood is close-grained, hard, and polishes nicely when waxed.

어휘 boxwood 회양목   close-grained 나뭇결이 고운[촘촘한]
회양목은 나뭇결이 촘촘하고 딱딱하며 왁스를 칠하면 윤이 잘 난다.

288 The experiment showed that most people are unable to defy a person in a position of authority and are capable of committing terrible acts that directly contradict their professed values.

어휘 experiment 실험   authority 권위   commit 저지르다   contradict 모순되다
그 실험은 대부분의 사람들이 권위가 있는 지위에 있는 사람에게는 반항할 수 없으며 자신이 공언하는 가치관에 직접적으로 모순되는 끔찍한 행동도 저지를 수 있다는 것을 보여 주었다.

289 Many modern inventions were anticipated by Leonardo da Vinci.

어휘 invention 발명(품)
현대의 많은 발명품들은 레오나르도 다빈치가 예상한 것들이었다.

290 Even though the Apple computers incorporated the use of this device, it was Microsoft's Windows that made the use of this device popular.

어휘 device 장치   use 용도, 기능
비록 애플의 컴퓨터들이 이 장치의 기능을 집어넣었지만 이 장치의 기능을 대중화시킨 것은 바로 마이크로소프트의 윈도였다.

A. Choose the right answer for the underlined word.

1 No one <u>anticipated</u> that Mr. Manning would get fired.

아무도 Manning 씨가 해고당하리라는 것을 예측하지 못했다.

(A) foresaw   (B) held   (C) charged   (D) surprised

2 The researcher's new finding seems to <u>defy</u> the laws of physics.

그 연구자의 새로운 발견은 물리학의 법칙에 어긋나는 듯하다.

(A) revitalize   (B) contain   (C) escape   (D) augment

3 You'll need to <u>polish</u> your English before you go off to the United States.

미국으로 떠나기 전에 영어 실력을 가다듬을 필요가 있다.

(A) contrast   (B) refine   (C) dash   (D) refashion

4 Tom never ceases to <u>amaze</u> us.

Tom은 끊임없이 우리를 놀라게 만든다.

(A) expect   (B) oppose   (C) astonish   (D) obsess

5 The invention of the computer <u>revolutionized</u> business procedures.

컴퓨터의 발명은 비즈니스 절차에 혁명을 일으켰다.

(A) withstood   (B) transformed   (C) glossed   (D) predicted

6 An ideal leader should <u>possess</u> the qualities of honesty, integrity, and decisiveness. 이상적인 지도자는 정직, 도덕성, 결단력이라는 자질들을 지니고 있어야 한다.

(A) have   (B) dispute   (C) combine   (D) awes

7 I often just grab a cheeseburger and <u>rush</u> back to the office and work.

나는 그냥 치즈버거로 간단히 끼니를 때우고 사무실로 돌아가 일할 때가 많다.

(A) hurry   (B) invigorate   (C) varnish   (D) rebel

8 The study's main impact will probably be to <u>reinforce</u> the beliefs that people already have.

그 연구의 가장 큰 영향은 아마도 사람들이 이미 가지고 있는 믿음을 강화해 주는 것일 것이다.

(A) advance   (B) own   (C) confront   (D) strengthen

Answers   A   1. A   2. C   3. B   4. C   5. B   6. A   7. A   8. D

B. Fill in the blanks.

| differ revolutionize possess rush amaze |
| reinforce polish defy anticipate incorporate |

1 They _____ the work to make the deadline.
그들은 마감 기한에 맞추려고 서둘러 일했다.

2 The idea of time is _____ in all languages of the world.
시간 개념은 세계의 모든 언어 속에 포함되어 있다.

3 Your 1-year-old's abilities will _____ you.
당신의 한 살짜리 아이의 능력이 당신을 깜짝 놀라게 할 것이다.

4 His invention single-handedly _____ the entire world.
그의 발명품은 단독으로 전 세계를 확 바꾸어 놓았다.

5 Rob's strange behavior _____ comprehension.
Rob의 이상한 행동은 이해할 수가 없다.

C. Choose the right answer.

1 I don't know what _____ me to agree to work Sundays.
내가 무엇에 씌어 일요일마다 일하겠다고 응하는지 모르겠다.

(A) possesses   (B) defies   (C) incorporates   (D) amazes

2 Radishes _____ in shape, size, and color according to the type.
무는 종류에 따라 형태, 크기, 색깔이 다르다.

(A) differ   (B) revolutionize   (C) rush   (D) defy

3 The visitors were well-dressed wearing _____ shoes.
손님들은 잘 차려입었고 광이 나는 구두를 신고 있었다.

(A) reinforced   (B) amazed   (C) differed   (D) polished

4 The fans are eagerly _____ the start of new season.
팬들은 새 시즌의 시작을 간절히 고대하고 있다.

(A) revolutionizing   (B) anticipating
(C) defying   (D) incorporating

B 1. rushed   2. incorporated   3. amaze   4. revolutionized   5. defies
C 1.A   2.A   3.D   4.B

291

Mickey was a tremendous help; he really played a *big* role.

Mickey가 굉장한 도움이 되었다. 그는 정말 큰 역할을 했다.

tremendous   휑 엄청나게 큰, 굉장한 huge, great, enormous, formidable
[triméndəs]   - tremendously 児 엄청나게

292

He is a very comic actor, but he is very *serious* in real life.

그는 아주 코믹한 배우지만 실생활에서는 아주 진지하다.

comic   휑 희극의, 희극적인
[kámik]   웃기는, 재미있는 funny, humorous, amusing
     명 희극 배우 comedian
     만화책 comic book

293

He had an extraordinary talent, but didn't want to show his *special* gift.

그는 비범한 재능이 있었지만 자신의 특별한 능력을 보여 주고 싶어 하지 않았다.

extraordinary   휑 놀라운 surprising, amazing, astonishing
[ikstrɔ́ːrdənèri]   비범한, 대단한 unusual, remarkable, exceptional

294

The earliest history was oral, passed down by *word of mouth*. 가장 초기의 역사는 구전이었는데 입에서 입으로 전해져 내려왔다.

oral   휑 구두의, 구전의, 구술의 spoken, vocal, verbal
[ɔ́(ː)rəl]   입의
     명 구술 시험

295

There will be intense rain and *strong* winds tomorrow.

내일은 폭우가 내리고 강한 바람이 불 것이다.

intense   휑 강렬한, 극심한 extreme, severe
[inténs]   치열한 fierce
     열심인, 열정적인 passionate, enthusiastic

296

His design was crude and *rough.*
그의 디자인은 조잡하고 거칠었다.

crude   (형) 대충의, 투박한, 거친 rough, makeshift
[kru:d]   단순한, 기초적인 simple, basic, primitive
               막된, 버릇없는 rude, vulgar
               천연 그대로의, 가공하지 않은 unrefined, raw, unprocessed

297

Vicky's family moved to this area because of its *rich* hills with fertile soil.
Vicky의 가족은 비옥한 토양이 있는 언덕들 때문에 이 지역으로 이사 왔다.

fertile   (형) 기름진, 비옥한 rich, productive, lush, fruitful
[fə́:rtəl]

298

The chair is *strong* and sturdy because it is made of steel.
그 의자는 강철로 만들어져 있어 강하고 견고하다.

sturdy   (형) 튼튼한, 견고한 strong, secure, solid, durable
[stə́:rdi]

299

The mother became desperate and *worried* when her son didn't come home.
그 어머니는 아들이 집에 돌아오지 않자 절망적이 되어 근심했다.

desperate   (형) 절망적인, 가망이 없는 hopeless, despairing
[déspərit]   필사적인, 절박한 urgent

300

Tina's eyes were moist with *tears.*
Tina의 눈이 눈물로 젖어 있었다.

moist   (형) 습한, 축축한, 젖은 damp, wet, humid, soggy
[mɔist]   눈물 어린 tearful
        - moisture (명) 습기, 수분 dampness, wetness, humidity

291   Katy Payne is a wonderful writer with a tremendous talent for integrating life with her research.

[어휘] integrate 통합하다
Katy Payne은 삶을 자신의 연구와 통합하는 데에 굉장한 재능을 가진 훌륭한 작가이다.

292   His ultimate goal in life is to become a successful comic.

[어휘] ultimate 궁극적인   goal 목표
그의 삶의 궁극적인 목표는 성공적인 희극 배우가 되는 것이다.

293   One of the extraordinary natural phenomena that disappeared as the size of American forests decreased was the occasional mass emigration of the gray squirrel.

[어휘] phenomena 현상들   disappear 사라지다   mass emigration 집단 이주
미국의 산림 면적이 줄어들면서 사라진 특이한 자연 현상들 중의 하나는 회색다람쥐의 간헐적인 집단 이주였다.

294   Sequoya, a Native American who was born about 1770, formed an alphabet of eighty-six letters that enabled him to put the oral Cherokee language into writing.

[어휘] enable 가능하게 하다
1770년경에 태어난 아메리카 원주민 Sequoya는 86자의 알파벳을 만들어 Cherokee 구어를 글자로 적을 수 있었다.

295   The intense competition for admission to the nation's top universities has had the effect of making admission to second-tier schools much more competitive as well.

[어휘] competition 경쟁   admission 입학   second-tier 이류의
전국의 일류 대학교에 입학하기 위한 치열한 경쟁은 이류 대학교의 입학 역시 더욱 경쟁적으로 만드는 효과를 가져왔다.

296 Ironmaking remained a crude process until 1832 when the first high-quality crucible steel was made.

(어휘) ironmaking 제강   crucible 도가니
1832년에 최초의 고급 도가니강이 만들어지기까지 제강은 초보적인 단계에 있었다.

297 Because the Nile helped irrigate crops and its overflows brought in fertile soil, the ancient Egyptians monitored the fluctuation of the Nile very closely.

(어휘) irrigate ~에 물을 대다   overflow 범람, 홍수   fluctuation 변동
나일 강이 농작물에 물을 대 주고 강의 범람이 비옥한 토양을 가져다주었기 때문에 고대 이집트인들은 나일 강의 변동을 아주 면밀하게 관찰했다.

298 Many large bridges were built with strong foundations, but unforeseen increased traffic load everywhere has caused some of the bridges to be less sturdy.

(어휘) foundation 기초   unforeseen 예상하지 못한
많은 큰 다리들은 튼튼한 기초 위에 세워졌지만 미처 예상하지 못했던 모든 곳의 교통량 증가로 일부 다리들이 덜 견고하게 되었다.

299 Many of the families in our community have relatives there and the situation there is utterly desperate with winter approaching and the threat of disease.

(어휘) community 지역 사회   utterly 완전히, 아주   threat 위협
우리 지역 사회의 많은 가정이 그곳에 친척들이 있으며 그곳의 상황은 겨울이 다가오는 데다 질병의 위협으로 완전히 절망적이다.

300 Then they fall down into warmer air, where another icy coat is made because of the moisture there. [1998년 수능 예문 20번]

(어휘) icy 얼음의
그 다음에 그것은 더 따뜻한 공기 속으로 떨어지는데, 그곳의 습기 때문에 또 다른 얼음 막이 만들어진다.

A. *Choose the right answer for the underlined word.*

1 Special construction materials were used to make the building especially <u>sturdy</u>. 특수한 건설 자재가 사용되어 그 빌딩을 특별히 견고하게 만들었다.

(A) fierce   (B) durable   (C) simple   (D) great

2 The volcanic soil in the valleys and lowlands is very <u>fertile</u>.
계곡과 저지의 화산 토양은 매우 비옥하다.

(A) productive   (B) humid   (C) tough   (D) amusing

3 He had to go through an <u>intense</u> training to become a pilot.
그는 비행사가 되기 위해 강도 높은 훈련을 거쳐야 했다.

(A) despairing   (B) astonishing   (C) enormous   (D) severe

4 He offended everyone at the party with his <u>crude</u> behavior.
그는 막된 행동으로 파티에 참석한 사람들을 불쾌하게 했다.

(A) lush   (B) rude   (C) strong   (D) remarkable

5 Clay is a material that has the fundamental characteristic of becoming plastic when <u>moist</u>. 찰흙은 축축하면 가소성이 좋아지는 기본 특성이 있는 물질이다.

(A) unprocessed   (B) hopeless   (C) damp   (D) rich

6 America is in <u>desperate</u> need of specific measures to help displaced workers. 미국은 해고 노동자들을 도울 구체적인 대책이 시급히 필요하다.

(A) incredible   (B) urgent   (C) rough   (D) solid

7 Talking and listening are kinds of auditory and <u>oral</u> communication.
말하기와 듣기는 청각 및 구두 의사소통의 종류들이다.

(A) primitive   (B) verbal   (C) surprising   (D) wet

8 Cheetahs prey on smaller mammals and birds, and their running speed is a <u>tremendous</u> asset for them.
치타는 더 작은 포유류와 새를 먹이로 삼으며 치타의 달리는 속도는 엄청난 자산이다.

(A) huge   (B) passionate   (C) secure   (D) fruitful

Answers   A   1. B   2. A   3. D   4. B   5. C   6. B   7. B   8. A

B. Fill in the blanks.

> tremendous   comic   extraordinary   oral   intense
> crude   fertile   sturdy   desperate   moist

1 Now she is just _____ to get any kind of job.
이제 그녀는 어떤 종류의 직업이라도 얻기 위해 필사적이다.

2 The _____ heat made everyone weak.
극심한 열기는 모두를 허약하게 만들었다.

3 The Middle East crisis is causing the price of _____ oil to go up.
중동 위기는 원유 가격을 상승시키는 원인이 되고 있다.

4 The country experienced a(n) _____ economic boom for the past three years. 그 나라는 지난 3년 동안 놀라운 경제 호황을 누렸다.

5 Food must be _____ in order to have a taste.
음식이 맛을 지니기 위해서는 수분이 있어야만 한다.

C. Choose the right answer.

1 The trade agreement will help our country _____.
그 무역 협정은 우리나라에 엄청난 도움이 될 것이다.

(A) desperately   (B) crudely   (C) tremendously (D) moistly

2 The table is reasonably solid and _____ even though it's made of plastic. 그 테이블은 플라스틱으로 만들어졌지만 꽤 단단하고 견고하다.

(A) intense   (B) extraordinary (C) fertile   (D) sturdy

3 The next time you visit a friend in the hospital, bring a funny movie or _____ book. 다음에 입원한 친구를 방문할 때는 재미있는 영화나 만화책을 가져와.

(A) tremendous   (B) desperate   (C) oral   (D) comic

4 The building of the canal has transformed the area from desert into _____ farmland. 그 운하가 건설되자 그 지역은 사막에서 비옥한 농지로 변모했다.

(A) intense   (B) fertile   (C) crude   (D) extraordinary

B 1. desperate   2. intense   3. crude   4. extraordinary   5. moist
C 1. C   2. D   3. D   4. B

301

Your symptom can be a *sign* of a serious illness.
당신의 증상은 중병의 징조일 수도 있어요.

symptom   몡 전조, 징후   sign, omen, mark
[símptəm]   증상   condition

302

It is very important to maintain your *customs* and traditions.
관습과 전통을 유지하는 것은 매우 중요하다.

tradition   몡 전통, 관습   practice, custom, convention, heritage
[trədíʃən]   전승   folklore
    - **traditional** 혱 전통적인, 전승의   conventional, customary

303

The theme of the movie was the *subject* that affects everyone.
그 영화의 테마는 모든 사람들에게 영향을 줄 수 있는 주제였다.

theme   몡 주제, 논제, 화제   subject, topic, point
[θiːm]   (작품의) 주제, 테마   motif

304

New York is not only the financial *center* but also the fashion capital of the world. 뉴욕은 금융 중심지일 뿐만 아니라 세계의 패션 수도이다.

capital   몡 수도, 중심지   center
[kǽpitəl]   자본, 자산, 원금   money, funds, asset
     혱 주요한, 으뜸가는   chief, main, superb
     자본의, 자산의

305

The sight was one of the most beautiful *scenes* I had ever seen. 그 광경은 내가 지금까지 본 가장 아름다운 장면 중의 하나였다.

sight   몡 시야, 시력   eyesight, vision
[sait]   광경, 경치   spectacle, scene
     시각   view
     동 보다, 발견하다   see, spot, view, observe

306 **We need to build a reservoir to *store* extra oil.**
우리는 여분의 기름을 보관하기 위한 저장 탱크를 만들어야 한다.

reservoir   명 저수지
[rézərvwà:r]   저장소 storage, tank, container
   저장, 축적, 비축 reserve, storage, supply

307 **There is an invisible boundary *dividing* the rich and the poor.** 부유한 사람들과 가난한 사람들을 나누는 보이지 않는 경계가 있다.

boundary   명 경계, 한계, 범위 border, limits, bounds, barrier
[báundəri]

308 **_Cut_ the cucumber into 2-inch segments.**
그 오이를 2인치 길이 조각들로 잘라라.

segment   명 단편, 조각 piece, slice, fragment
[ségmənt]   부분, 부문 section, part, portion
   동 나누다, 분할하다 divide (up)

309 **The team has the *ability* to score very quickly, which is an impressive capability.**
그 팀은 아주 빨리 득점하는 수완이 있는데, 그것은 인상적인 능력이다.

capability   명 능력, 재능, 역량 ability, capacity, competence
[kèipəbíləti]

310 **Mr. Knox is a man of consequence because of his *great success*.** Knox 씨는 크게 성공했기 때문에 중요한 인물이다.

consequence   명 결과, 영향 result, effect
[kánsəkwèns]   중요성, 중대함 importance, significance

301

An expert found that workers whose offices faced a natural setting had fewer symptoms of ill health and felt less pressured than those whose offices overlooked a parking lot.

어휘 feel pressured 압박감을 느끼다   overlook 내려다보다
한 전문가는 자연환경을 마주보는 사무실에서 일하는 직원들이 주차장이 내려다보이는 사무실에서 일하는 직원들보다 건강 이상의 증상이 더 적으며 스트레스를 덜 느낀다는 것을 발견했다.

302

Volunteerism is a tradition in the United States, but how many people realize that up to fifty-two percent of the adult population is engaged in some kind of volunteer service?

어휘 realize 깨닫다   adult 성인   be engaged in ~에 종사하다   service 봉사
자원봉사는 미국에서의 전통이다. 그러나 성인 인구의 최대 52퍼센트가 어떤 종류의 자원봉사에 참여하고 있다는 사실을 깨닫는 사람이 얼마나 될까?

303

Enjoy six theme areas complete with exciting rides, live shows and attractions from California and the West.

어휘 area 영역, 범위   attraction 매력, 볼거리
신나는 놀이 기구, 라이브쇼, 캘리포니아 주와 서부의 볼거리들이 완비된 여섯 개의 테마 구역에서 즐거운 시간을 보내세요.

304

Capital punishment has been a successful deterrent to crime since early biblical times.

어휘 capital punishment 극형, 사형   deterrent 억지 수단   biblical 성경의
사형은 성경 시대 초기부터 성공적인 범죄 억지 수단이 되어 왔다.

305

A body of a missing soldier was sighted 11 kilometers north of Poari.

어휘 missing 실종된
실종된 한 병사의 시신이 Poari 북쪽 11킬로미터 지점에서 발견되었다.

306 The main reservoir of mathematical talent in any society is thus possessed by children who are about two years old, children who have just learned to speak fluently.

[어휘] mathematical 수학적인   talent 재능   fluently 유창하게
어느 사회에서나 수학적인 재능의 주요 저장고는 이와 같이 말을 유창하게 하는 법을 막 배운 2살 정도 아이들이 소유하고 있다.

307 The people of the United States felt it was their mission to extend the "boundaries of freedom" to others by imparting their idealism and belief in democratic institutions.

[어휘] mission 임무   extend 확장하다   impart 전하다   idealism 이상주의
미국 국민들은 자신들의 이상주의와 민주 제도에 대한 믿음을 전하여 '자유의 경계'를 확대하는 것이 사명이라고 생각했다.

308 The community college is the most rapidly growing segment of higher education in the United States.

[어휘] community college 커뮤니티 칼리지(지역 주민 대상 전문 대학)   rapidly 빨리, 급속히
커뮤니티 칼리지는 미국 고등 교육 중에서 가장 빨리 성장하는 부문이다.

309 In fact, our newest model functions so well that its capability has been certified by the Consumer Association of America.

[어휘] function 기능하다   certify 인정하다
실제로 우리 새 모델은 기능이 아주 좋기 때문에 미국 소비자 협회로부터 그 성능을 인정받았다.

310 As the consequence of living in dry areas, the people realized the importance of conserving water.

[어휘] conserve 절약하다
건조한 지역에 사는 결과로 그 사람들은 물을 절약하는 것의 중요성을 깨달았다.

A. Choose the right answer for the underlined word.

1 The consequence of human-made pollution can be found in oceans, lakes, and rivers. 인간이 만든 오염의 결과물은 바다, 호수, 강에서 발견할 수 있다.

(A) practice   (B) focus   (C) competence   (D) result

2 His indefatigable drive is his greatest capital.
지칠 줄 모르는 추진력이 그의 가장 큰 자산이다.

(A) omen   (B) asset   (C) barrier   (D) slice

3 The rebellious students wanted to break with tradition.
그 반항적인 학생들은 전통과의 관계를 끊기를 원했다.

(A) section   (B) prospect   (C) convention   (D) spectacle

4 The symptoms of influenza are fever, headache, and muscular pain.
독감의 증상은 발열, 두통과 근육통이다.

(A) significances   (B) folklores   (C) means   (D) conditions

5 Underground reservoirs are important in the conservation of natural gas.
지하 저장 탱크는 천연가스의 보존에 중요하다.

(A) storages   (B) funds   (C) portions   (D) bounds

6 The medieval legend of Dr. Faust has been a recurrent theme in Western literature. 파우스트 박사에 대한 중세의 전설은 서양 문학에서 되풀이되어 온 주제이다.

(A) subject   (B) margin   (C) importance   (D) sign

7 The construction of the second factory would have a huge impact on manufacturing capability. 제2공장의 건설은 제조 역량에 막대한 영향을 줄 것이다.

(A) center   (B) capacity   (C) store   (D) custom

8 When light crosses the boundary from one transparent material to another, its direction generally changes.
빛이 한 투명한 물질에서 다른 물질로 경계를 넘어갈 때 일반적으로 그 방향이 바뀐다.

(A) point   (B) border   (C) reserve   (D) vision

Answers   A 1. D   2. B   3. C   4. D   5. A   6. A   7. B   8. B

B. Fill in the blanks.

symptom	tradition	theme	capital	sight	
reservoir	boundary	segment	capability	consequence	

1 After three weeks of endless sea, land is in _____.
망망대해에서 3주가 지나자 육지가 시야에 들어온다.

2 Now we realize that wealth is intellectual _____.
이제 우리는 부가 지적 자산이라는 것을 깨닫는다.

3 The _____ of matchmaking in Korea has been around for a very long time. 한국에서의 중매 풍습은 무척 오래되었다.

4 They live within the Saudi Arabia _____.
그들은 사우디아라비아 경계 내에 살고 있다.

5 The director, with the help of other volunteers, decides on a _____ for the show. 그 감독은 다른 자원봉사자들의 도움을 받아 그 영화의 테마를 결정한다.

C. Choose the right answer.

1 Extreme stress can mimic the _____ of a heart attack.
극도의 스트레스는 심장 마비 증상과 흡사하다.

(A) boundaries (B) capabilities (C) symptoms (D) traditions

2 The _____ are only at fifty-percent capacity because of the recent drought. 최근의 가뭄으로 인해 저수지들은 용량이 50%밖에 되지 않는다.

(A) themes (B) capitals (C) reservoirs (D) segments

3 The new supervisor has an excellent managerial _____.
새 감독관은 훌륭한 관리 능력이 있다.

(A) symptom (B) theme (C) tradition (D) capability

4 With a living tree, a hollow boring instrument can extract a small _____ from the bark to the core.
구멍 내는 도구는 살아 있는 나무의 껍질에서 중심까지 작은 조각을 추출해 낼 수 있다.

(A) reservoir (B) segment (C) sight (D) consequence

B 1. sight 2. capital 3. tradition 4. boundary 5. theme
C 1. C 2. C 3. D 4. B

311

Do not *walk* or wander around the park at night because it is dangerous. 위험하니까 밤에 공원에서 걷거나 돌아다니지 마라.

wander   동 떠돌다, 헤매다 roam, drift, stroll
[wándər]   벗어나다, 길을 잃다, 빗나가다 stray, digress, deviate

312

The police tried to capture the robber, but he was never *caught*. 경찰은 그 강도를 잡으려고 애썼지만 절대 잡히지 않았다.

capture   동 붙잡다, 체포하다 catch, arrest, detain
[kǽptʃər]   포착하다, 표현하다 depict, portray
           명 생포, 구금 arrest, imprisonment, detention

313

The bank was willing to extend my loan, *giving me extra time* to pay it off.
은행은 내 대출을 기꺼이 연장해 주어 내게 갚을 시간을 더 주려고 했다.

extend   동 뻗다 stretch (out)
[iksténd]   ~에 이르다 reach
           넓히다, 늘이다, 확장하다 widen, expand, enlarge
           늘리다, 연장하다 lengthen, prolong, elongate

314

Mark's answer doesn't indicate or *show* his intention.
Mark의 대답은 그의 의도를 암시하거나 보여 주지 않는다.

indicate   동 표시하다, 보여 주다 show, display
[índəkèit]   넌지시 나타내다, 암시하다 imply, suggest
           가리키다, 지적하다 point to, designate

315

A female mantis does not hesitate to consume her own mate if she is *hungry*.
암컷 사마귀는 배가 고프면 자신의 짝도 서슴없이 잡아먹는다.

consume   동 소모하다, 소비하다 use (up), spend
[kənsúːm]   먹어 치우다 eat, swallow, devour
           소멸하다, 파괴하다 destroy, devastate

316

I had to drag the bag because it was *too heavy to carry*.
가방이 너무 무거워서 질질 끌어야 했다.

drag	통 끌다, 질질 끌고 가다 pull, haul
[dræg]	(화제에) 끌어들이다 introduce, mention
	오래 끌다 delay, lag
	명 장애물, 짐 obstacle, burden

317

No one ever undertook such a dangerous *attempt*.
아무도 그렇게 위험한 시도를 감행한 적이 없다.

undertake	통 맡다, 책임지다 take on, assume
[ʌndərtéik]	~에 착수하다, 시도하다 start, set about, attempt

318

No one can't access or *get near* the scene of the accident.
아무도 사고 현장에 접근할 수 없다.

access	통 ~에 접속하다 get into, log on
[ǽksès]	~에 접근하다 get near
	명 진입, 입장 admission, entry
	입구, 통로 entrance

319

He claims to be reformed, but I don't notice any *change* in him. 그는 확 바뀌었다고 주장하지만 나는 그에게서 어떤 변화도 알아차릴 수 없다.

reform	통 개혁하다, 혁신하다 improve, better, renovate
[rifɔ́ːrm]	명 개혁, 혁신 improvement, renovation

320

The bullet lodged itself in his brain which was very difficult to *take out*. 총알이 그의 머릿속에 박혀 있어 꺼내기가 무척 어려웠다.

lodge	통 제기하다, 제출하다 raise, bring up, file
[lɑʤ]	숙박하다, 숙박시키다 accommodate
	박히다, 박다 stick, embed
	명 오두막, 산장 hut, cabin

311 **During the storm, the ship wandered from its course.**

폭풍우가 부는 동안 그 배는 항로에서 이탈했다.

312 **One-word titles or other short ones do not capture the interest of the readers.**

한 단어짜리 제목이나 다른 짧은 제목들은 독자들의 흥미를 끌지 못한다.

313 **How many of us would be willing to give up some minor convenience in the hope that this is might extend the life of man on earth by a hundred years?** (1996년 수능 예문 48번)

[어휘] minor 대수롭지 않은   convenience 편리, 편의

우리 중의 몇 명이나 이것이 지구상의 인간 수명을 100년 연장해 줄지도 모른다는 희망 속에서 사소한 편의를 기꺼이 포기하려고 할 것인가?

314 **Studies indicate that children who were formerly neglected as babies will improve significantly when they are given loving attention and care.**

[어휘] formerly 이전에   neglect 무시하다   significantly 크게, 의미심장하게

연구들은 이전에 아기였을 때 무시당했던 아이들이 애정 어린 관심과 보살핌을 받을 때 크게 개선될 수 있음을 보여 준다.

315 **If we look at the typical American diet, we can see that Americans consume too much meat and not enough grains, raw fruits, and fresh vegetables.**

[어휘] grain 곡물   raw 익히지 않은, 날것의

전형적인 미국인 식단을 살펴보면 미국인들은 고기는 너무 많이 먹고 곡물, 생과일, 신선한 채소는 충분히 먹지 않는 것을 볼 수 있다.

316 Staying cooped up in a college dorm room all winter this year was a real drag.

[어휘] coop up 가두어 넣다   dorm 기숙사
금년 겨울 내내 대학 기숙사 방에 갇혀 지내는 것은 정말 고역이었다.

317 During her husband's presidency, Jacqueline Kennedy undertook the coordination of the White House restoration.

[어휘] coordination 조정   restoration 복구, 복원
남편의 대통령 재임 기간 동안 Jacqueline Kennedy는 백악관을 복원하는 데 조정 역할을 맡았다.

318 However, many residents feel overburdened with the fact that a number of outsiders seem to overrun the area, depriving locals of access to their homeland.

[어휘] resident 거주자   overburden 과중한 부담을 지우다   deprive 박탈하다
그러나 많은 주민들은 그 지역에 외지인들이 넘쳐 나서 지역민들이 고향 땅으로의 통로를 빼앗기는 듯하다는 사실에 과중한 부담을 느낀다.

319 During the 1840s, Dorothea Dix was a leader in the movement for the reform of prison conditions.

[어휘] leader 지도자   movement 운동   prison 감옥   condition 상태
1840년대에 Dorothea Dix는 교도소 환경 개혁 운동의 지도자였다.

320 If a foreign object becomes lodged in the eye, medical help is necessary.

[어휘] foreign 이질적인   object 물체
이물질이 눈에 박히게 될 경우에는 의사의 도움이 필요하다.

A. Choose the right answer for the underlined word.

1 We wanted to <u>lodge</u> a complaint about the company's poor customer service. 우리는 그 회사의 형편없는 고객 서비스에 대해 불만을 제기하고 싶었다.

(A) bring up　　(B) get into　　(C) restructure　　(D) get near

2 He <u>wandered</u> into the wrong part of town.
그는 길을 잃고 동네의 엉뚱한 곳으로 갔다.

(A) absorbed　　(B) strayed　　(C) prolonged　　(D) pulled

3 The project is not something that I want to <u>undertake</u>.
그 프로젝트는 내가 착수하고 싶은 것이 아니다.

(A) raise　　(B) portray　　(C) devour　　(D) attempt

4 He <u>drags</u> his honorary degree into every discussion.
그는 토론할 때마다 자신의 명예 학위를 들먹인다.

(A) mentions　　(B) betters　　(C) suggests　　(D) preoccupies

5 Existing clients can <u>access</u> account information over the phone.
기존 고객은 전화로 계좌 정보를 이용할 수 있다.

(A) point to　　(B) set about　　(C) log on　　(D) take on

6 Each bus has a number displayed on the front of the bus to <u>indicate</u> its route. 각 버스에는 그것의 운행 노선을 나타내는 번호가 앞에 표시되어 있다.

(A) stretch　　(B) show　　(C) accommodate　(D) spend

7 From your viewpoint, how did the United States justify its efforts to <u>extend</u> its domains? 당신의 견해로는 미국이 영토를 확장하려는 자국의 노력을 어떻게 정당화했습니까?

(A) widen　　(B) depict　　(C) roam　　(D) embed

8 After months of a massive manhunt, the police were able to <u>capture</u> three escaped prisoners. 여러 달 동안의 대대적인 수색 끝에 경찰은 탈옥수 3명을 체포할 수 있었다.

(A) elongate　　(B) arrest　　(C) migrate　　(D) deviate

Answers   A 1.A   2.B   3.D   4.A   5.C   6.B   7.A   8.B

B. Fill in the blanks.

wander	capture	extend	indicate	consume
drag	undertake	access	reform	lodge

1 Users no longer had to go through the government's network to _____ the Internet.

사용자들은 인터넷에 접속하기 위해 더 이상 정부 네트워크를 통할 필요가 없었다.

2 The last such investigation was _____ in July 2011.

최근의 그러한 조사는 2011년 7월에 실시되었다.

3 The artist _____ the girl's personality in his photograph.

그 예술가는 자기 사진 속에 그 소녀의 성격을 담아냈다.

4 Doug doesn't like to _____ too much caffeine.

Doug는 카페인을 너무 많이 섭취하는 것을 좋아하지 않는다.

5 When Adelie penguins walk, their long, stiff tails _____ along the ground. 아델리펭귄이 걸을 때는 길고 뻣뻣한 꼬리가 땅에 질질 끌린다.

C. Choose the right answer.

1 We need to book a room at the Sky _____ .

우리는 스카이 로지에 방 하나를 예약해야 한다.

(A) Drag   (B) Access   (C) Reform   (D) Lodge

2 Biomedical research may soon discover a way to _____ human life.

생물의학 연구는 머지않아 인간 수명을 연장하는 길을 발견하게 될 것이다.

(A) indicate   (B) capture   (C) extend   (D) wander

3 A high belly is supposed to _____ a girl, while a lower belly signifies a boy. 배 위쪽이 불룩하면 여자아이를 나타내고 반면에 배 아래쪽이 불룩하면 남자아이를 의미한다.

(A) capture   (B) consume   (C) indicate   (D) undertake

4 The government is trying to fundamentally _____ its tax system.

정부는 세금 제도를 근본적으로 개혁하기 위해 노력 중이다.

(A) access   (B) reform   (C) lodge   (D) drag

B 1. access   2. undertaken   3. captured   4. consume   5. drag

C 1. D   2. C   3. C   4. B

321

After winning a lottery, he bought an enormous house much *too big* for his family.

복권에 당첨되고 나서 그는 거대한 집을 샀는데, 그의 가족에게는 너무 컸다.

enormous
[inɔ́ːrməs]
- 형 거대한, 엄청난, 대단한 huge, gigantic, tremendous, immense, vast
- enormously 부 거대하게, 엄청나게

322

The meeting is mandatory, so attendance is *required*.

그 모임은 의무적이어서 출석이 필수이다.

mandatory
[mǽndətɔ̀ːri]
- 형 강제적인, 의무적인 compulsory, binding, obligatory

323

His action was deliberate and *intentional*.

그의 행동은 신중하고 의도적이었다.

deliberate
[delíbərit]
- 형 계획적인, 의도적인 intentional, planned, calculated
- 신중한, 사려 깊은 careful, cautious, prudent
- 동 숙고하다 consider, think, reflect

324

Although he had abundant chances, he wasted *all* of them.

그는 기회가 아주 많았음에도 불구하고 그것들을 모두 놓쳤다.

abundant
[əbʌ́ndənt]
- 형 풍부한, 넘쳐 나는 plentiful, rich, ample
- abundance 명 넘칠 정도로 많음, 풍부함 wealth, affluence

325

We have to prevent these endangered animals from *dying out*. 우리는 멸종 위기에 처한 동물들이 맥이 끊기는 것을 막아야 한다.

endangered
[indéindʒərd]
- 형 멸종 위기에 처해 있는 threatened, exposed, defenseless

326

You can *catch cold easily* because it is very contagious.
감기는 전염성이 매우 강하므로 쉽게 걸릴 수 있다.

contagious   ⑱ 전염성의, 전염되기 쉬운 catching, transmissible, communicable,
[kəntéidʒəs]   infectious

327

Service at this hotel is always *quick* and prompt.
이 호텔의 서비스는 항상 빠르고 신속하다.

prompt   ⑱ 즉각적인, 즉석의 immediate, instant, timely
[prɑmpt]   신속한, 기민한 quick, rapid, swift
           ⑧ 자극하다, 고무하다, 유발하다 cause, inspire, stimulate

328

A radical candidate called for a series of *drastic changes*.
급진적인 한 후보자는 일련의 급격한 변화를 요구했다.

radical   ⑱ 근본적인, 기초적인 fundamental, basic
[rǽdikəl]   철저한, 극단적인, 급진적인 drastic, extreme, complete
     - radically ⑲ 근본적으로

329

He presented coherent ideas which were *sound* and *convincing.* 그는 심오하고 설득력 있는 논리 정연한 아이디어를 제시했다.

coherent   ⑱ 일관성 있는, 논리 정연한 logical, rational, sound, reasoned
[kouhí(:)ərənt]

330

He felt acute and *sharp* pain in his neck.
그는 목에 격심한 통증을 느꼈다.

acute   ⑱ 날카로운, 예리한 sharp, keen
[əkjúːt]   심한, 격렬한 sharp, violent, severe
          심각한 critical, crucial
          급성인 sudden

321 There is so much to be won and lost for fans on both sides that one can sense an enormous tension. (2002년 수능 예문 47~48번)

어휘 tension 긴장
양쪽의 팬들에게는 이기고 지는 것이 워낙 중요해 엄청난 긴장을 느낄 수 있다.

322 It is mandatory for most new vehicles to have a driver's side air bag while a passenger side air bag is optional.

어휘 vehicle 차량 passenger 승객 optional 선택적인
대부분의 새 차량은 운전석에 에어백 설치가 의무인 반면, 조수석의 에어백은 선택적이다.

323 Brown bears have three types of gaits: an even, deliberate one, a quick shuffle, and a fast gallop.

어휘 gait 걸음걸이 even 차분한 shuffle 발을 질질 끌며 걷기 gallop 전력 질주
불곰에게는 세 종류의 걸음걸이가 있다. 차분하고 신중한 걸음걸이, 빠르게 발을 끄는 걸음걸이, 전력 질주이다.

324 Lack of human contacts led to the variety and abundance of wildlife in the Demilitarized Zone (DMZ).

어휘 contact 접촉 variety 다양(성) wildlife 야생 생물
사람의 접촉이 없어 비무장지대(DMZ)에 다양하고 풍부한 야생 생물이 살게 되었다.

325 Some zoos now help the saving of endangered species, using their resources to nurture injured animals, and aid threatened species to breed.

어휘 species 종(種) resource 자원 nurture 키우다 breed 품종, 혈통
일부 동물원은 이제 자체의 자원을 이용해 다친 동물들을 키우고 위협받는 종의 번식을 도움으로써 멸종 위기종 구조를 돕는다.

326 Influenza is an acute viral disease of the respiratory tract that is extremely contagious and often reaches epidemic proportions.

[어휘] acute 급성의   viral 바이러스(성)의   respiratory tract 호흡기
독감은 전염성이 극도로 강하고 흔히 전염병 수준에 이르는 급성 바이러스성 호흡기 질환이다.

327 After reading Philip Morrison's paper, a fellow physicist was prompted to ask, "Wouldn't using gamma-rays be a good way to communicate across the galaxy?"

[어휘] fellow 동료   physicist 물리학자   gamma-ray 감마선
Philip Morrison의 논문을 읽고 난 한 동료 물리학자는 "감마선 이용이 은하계에서 훌륭한 통신 방법이 되지 않을까요?"라고 묻고 싶어졌다.

328 Because of the radical difference between a 15-passenger van and a standard passenger vehicle, it is essential that anyone who operates a 15-passenger van be properly trained.

[어휘] standard 표준적인   essential 필수적인   properly 적절하게
15인승 승합차와 일반 승용차 간의 현격한 차이 때문에 15인승 승합차를 운행하는 사람은 누구나 적절한 훈련을 받는 것이 필수이다.

329 We found the professor's talk on nuclear reactors quite coherent.

[어휘] nuclear reactor 원자로
우리는 원자로에 대한 그 교수의 이야기가 꽤 논리 정연하다고 느꼈다.

330 One of California's most acute problems is an inadequate water supply.

[어휘] inadequate 불충분한   water supply 급수 시설, 상수도
캘리포니아 주의 가장 심각한 문제들 중의 하나는 불충분한 급수 시설이다.

A. Choose the right answer for the underlined word.

1 The food shortage is <u>acute</u> in the northern part of the country.
그 나라의 북부에서 식량 부족이 극심하다.

(A) exposed　　(B) critical　　(C) binding　　(D) slow

2 The lawyer provided <u>coherent</u> and consistent argument based on evidence. 그 변호사는 증거를 토대로 논리 정연하고 일관된 주장을 제시했다.

(A) sound　　(B) drastic　　(C) catching　　(D) timely

3 Center for Disease Control tracks down <u>contagious</u> illnesses throughout the world. 질병통제센터는 전 세계의 전염성 질병을 찾아낸다.

(A) crucial　　(B) transmissible　　(C) gigantic　　(D) vast

4 The crash had more the appearance of a <u>deliberate</u> attempt than of an accident. 그 충돌은 사고라기보다는 계획적인 시도의 모습이 더 역력하다.

(A) rapid　　(B) defenseless　　(C) rational　　(D) intentional

5 In a formal paper it is <u>mandatory</u> to use footnotes each time a source is quoted. 공식 논문에는 출처가 인용될 때마다 각주를 사용하는 것이 필수이다.

(A) tremendous　　(B) plentiful　　(C) compulsory　　(D) communicable

6 Crops are <u>endangered</u>, as rice and wheat are susceptible to increasing amounts of ultra-violet radiation.
쌀과 밀은 증가하는 자외선 양에 민감하기 때문에 곡물 수확이 위기에 처해 있다.

(A) reasoned　　(B) threatened　　(C) insightful　　(D) calculated

7 Even though water may seem to be one of Earth's most <u>abundant</u> resources, it is important to realize that water is not as plentiful as it seems.
물이 지구에서 가장 풍부한 자원 중의 하나로 보일 수도 있겠지만 보이는 것만큼 풍부하지 않다는 것을 깨닫는 것이 중요하다.

(A) infectious　　(B) ample　　(C) sharp　　(D) obligatory

8 As photographic techniques have become more sophisticated, the scope of their application has expanded <u>enormously</u>.
사진 촬영 기술이 갈수록 정교해지면서 그 적용 범위가 대폭 확대되어 왔다.

(A) immensely　　(B) cautiously　　(C) extremely　　(D) suddenly

Answers　　**A** 1. B　2. A　3. B　4. D　5. C　6. B　7. B　8. A

B. Fill in the blanks.

enormous	mandatory	deliberate	abundant	endangered
contagious	prompt	radical	coherent	acute

1 This course is _____ for all undergraduate students.
이 과정은 모든 학부 학생들에게는 필수이다.

2 She is a(n) _____ observer of political matters.
그녀는 정치 문제에 대한 예리한 관찰자이다.

3 We'll greatly appreciate your _____ attention to this matter.
이 문제에 신속히 주의를 기울여 주시면 대단히 감사하겠습니다.

4 It has made animals, such as the giant panda, become _____.
그것은 자이언트판다와 같은 동물들을 멸종 위기에 처하게 만들어 왔다.

5 These _____ populations will mostly live in cities that do not have strong economies. 이 거대한 인구는 대부분 경제가 튼튼하지 않은 도시들에서 살게 될 것이다.

C. Choose the right answer.

1 The professor spoke in a slow and _____ way.
그 교수는 천천히 그리고 신중하게 말했다.

(A) endangered　(B) enormous　(C) mandatory　(D) deliberate

2 Have you ever noticed that yawning seems to be _____?
하품에 전염성이 있다는 것 알고 있었니?

(A) deliberate　(B) prompt　(C) contagious　(D) enormous

3 There was no _____ approach to solve with the problem.
그 문제를 해결한 논리 정연한 접근법이 없었다.

(A) mandatory　(B) endangered　(C) coherent　(D) acute

4 If there are civilizations on other planets, they are likely to be _____ different from ours. 다른 행성들에 문명이 있다면 그것들은 우리 문명과는 근본적으로 다를 가능성이 높다.

(A) radically　(B) contagiously　(C) promptly　(D) abundantly

B　1. mandatory　2. acute　3. prompt　4. endangered　5. enormous
C　1. D　2. C　3. C　4. A

331

Tom was *coming toward* Helen, but she didn't see him approaching her.
Tom이 Helen 쪽으로 오고 있었지만 그녀는 그가 다가오는 것을 보지 못했다.

approach 　⑧ 다가가다 move toward, come near
[əpróutʃ] 　　접촉하다 contact
　　　　　접근하다 address
　　　⑲ 접근법 method, style

332

If you can operate this machine, you can *use* any machine here. 네가 이 기계를 작동할 수 있다면 이곳의 어떤 기계이든 사용할 수 있다.

operate 　⑧ 움직이다, 작동하다 function, work, run
[ápərèit] 　　조종하다, 운전하다 control, drive
　　　　　운영하다 manage, run, direct
　　　　　수술하다

333

Bob tried his best to aid and cooperate with the police.
Bob은 최선을 다해 경찰을 돕고 협조했다.

cooperate 　⑧ 협력하다, 협동하다 work together, collaborate
[kouápərèit] 　서로 돕다, 협조하다 help, aid, assist

334

He is old enough to *know* and distinguish right from wrong. 그는 옳고 그른 것을 알고 구분할 정도로 나이가 들었다.

distinguish 　⑧ 구별하다 tell apart, differentiate
[distíŋgwiʃ] 　　식별하다, 알아차리다 make out, recognize, discern

335

No major war is going to *start*, but a minor one can erupt anytime. 대규모 전쟁은 일어나지 않겠지만 소규모 전쟁은 언제든 일어날 수 있다.

erupt 　⑧ 분출하다 burst
[irʌ́pt] 　　폭발하다 explode, discharge

336

They were astounded to hear the *shocking* news.
그들은 그 충격적인 소식을 듣고 깜짝 놀랐다.

astound   동 깜짝 놀라게 하다 surprise, amaze, shock, astonish
[əstáund]   - astounding 형 놀라운

337

The mayor *harmed* his reputation because he abused his power. 시장은 권력을 남용했기 때문에 자신의 명성을 훼손했다.

abuse   동 남용하다, 악용하다 misuse
[əbjú:z]   학대하다 mistreat, harm
[əbjú:s] 명   명 남용, 오용 misuse
           학대, 혹사 mistreatment, wrong

338

We wanted to convert the garage into a gym, but mother didn't like the *change*.
우리는 차고를 운동실로 개조하고 싶었지만 어머니는 그렇게 바꾸는 것을 좋아하지 않았다.

convert   동 전환하다 change, transform, alter
[kənvə́:rt]   개조하다 modify

339

The bullet barely grazed his arm leaving a just *scratch*.
총알은 그의 팔을 가까스로 스쳐 지나가면서 찰과상만을 남겼다.

graze   동 (가축이) 풀을 뜯어먹다 feed, forage
[greiz]   가볍게 스쳐 지나가다 brush, touch, glance
         명 찰과상 scratch, scrape

340

It's *green*, now, so proceed.
이제 녹색 불이니까 지나가자.

proceed   동 진행하다 continue, go on, keep on
[prəsí:d]   나가다, 이동하다 move, advance
         - proceeds 명 수익금 profits

Words in Reading

331 **As the waves approach the land without warning, they can look like a particularly violent tide rushing to the shore.**

[어휘] violent 사나운   tide 조수, 물결   rush 덤벼들다
예고 없이 파도가 육지로 다가올 때 그것은 해안으로 몰려오는 아주 사나운 물결처럼 보일 수 있다.

332 **Propeller planes can operate more efficiently than jet planes at airports where the air density is low.**

[어휘] propeller 프로펠러   efficiently 효과적으로   density 밀도
공기 밀도가 낮은 공항에서는 프로펠러기가 제트기보다 더 효율적으로 기동할 수 있다.

333 **Moreover, the weather will not cooperate with your traveling plans because the road conditions will be terrible.**

게다가 도로 사정이 나쁠 것이기 때문에 날씨가 당신의 여행 계획에 도움이 되지 않을 것입니다.

334 **Students attempt to distinguish themselves from the pack by going on humanitarian missions to far-flung and exotic places all over the world.**

[어휘] pack 무리, 떼   humanitarian 인도주의적인   far-flung 멀리 떨어진
학생들은 전 세계의 멀리 떨어진 이국적인 곳들로 인도주의 미션을 수행하러 감으로써 자신을 무리에서 돋보이게 하려고 시도한다.

335 **Lew Archer is more fascinated by the past patterns of relationships that erupt into the present than by the immediacies of violence and personal confrontation.**

[어휘] relationship 관계   immediacy 즉시성, 직접성   confrontation 대립, 대결
Lew Archer는 폭력과 개인적인 대립의 즉시성보다는 현재로 분출하는 과거의 관계 양상에 더 매료되어 있다.

336 **The brief Alaskan summer is accompanied by an astounding change in the flora and fauna of the tundra.**

(어휘) brief 짧은, 잠시 동안의　flora and fauna 동식물상　tundra 툰드라, 동토대
알래스카의 짧은 여름은 툰드라의 동식물상에 일어나는 놀라운 변화를 동반한다.

337 **The Grange, an agrarian organization founded in 1867, sought to correct economic abuses through cooperative enterprise.**

(어휘) cooperative 협동하는　enterprise 사업
1867년에 설립된 농업 기구인 농민 공제 조합은 협동 사업을 통해 경제 남용을 바로잡으려고 노력했다.

338 **Originally, the Pantheon was used as a temple where animal sacrifices were made to the Roman gods, but it was converted to a church in the 7th century.**

(어휘) originally 원래　temple 사원　sacrifice 제물
원래 판테온은 로마의 신들에게 동물 제물을 바치던 사원으로 이용되었지만 7세기에 교회로 개조되었다.

339 **Only with great difficulty, can the giraffe bend down to graze on the ground.** [1994년 2차 수능 예문 34번]

(어휘) bend down 몸을 구부리다
기린은 아주 힘을 들여야만 몸을 구부려 땅 위의 풀을 뜯어 먹을 수 있다.

340 **Some television watchers just turn on the TV and proceed to another activity, such as cooking, cleaning, etc.**

(어휘) activity 활동
일부 TV 시청자들은 그냥 TV를 켜고 요리, 청소 등과 같은 다른 활동을 계속한다.

A. Choose the right answer for the underlined word.

1   Alcohol is still the most commonly <u>abused</u> drug among American
   teenagers. 알코올은 미국 10대들 사이에서 아직도 제일 흔하게 남용되는 약물이다.

   (A) misused   (B) forage   (C) altered   (D) burst

2   Cattle <u>graze</u> on the dry uplands of the island of Hawaii.
   소들은 하와이 섬의 건조한 고지에서 풀을 뜯고 있다.

   (A) work   (B) continue   (C) harm   (D) feed

3   The function of ears in hearing is to <u>convert</u> the sound waves to nerve
   impulses. 청취에서의 귀의 기능은 음파를 신경 자극으로 전환시키는 것이다.

   (A) amaze   (B) change   (C) collaborate   (D) astonish

4   My client will <u>cooperate</u> fully with the police in this investigation.
   내 의뢰인은 이번 조사와 관련해 경찰에 적극적으로 협조할 것이다.

   (A) make out   (B) work together (C) keep on   (D) carry out

5   Mount St. Helens <u>erupted</u> in March 1980 after one hundred twenty-three
   years of silence. St. Helens 산은 123년 동안 침묵하고 나서 1980년 3월에 분화했다.

   (A) exploded   (B) transformed   (C) surprised   (D) mistreated

6   The discovery <u>astounded</u> the scientists who believed that the Arctic ice
   cap would not melt completely for at least 60 years.
   그 발견은 북극 만년설이 최소 60년 동안은 절대 녹지 않을 것으로 생각했던 과학자들을 깜짝 놀라게 했다.

   (A) aided   (B) discerned   (C) shocked   (D) modified

7   Now <u>proceed</u> onward to the immigration desk and have your passport
   ready. 이제 입국 창구로 가셔서 여권을 준비해 주십시오.

   (A) direct   (B) discharge   (C) advance   (D) brush

8   In written language, on the other hand, the same word is always spelt in
   the same way, so different words are easy to <u>distinguish</u> in print.

   〔1996년 수능 예문 35번〕

   반면에 문어에서는 같은 단어는 항상 같은 방식으로 철자가 표기되므로 다른 단어들은 활자화되었을 때 구별하기 쉽다.

   (A) move toward   (B) come near   (C) tell apart   (D) go on

B. Fill in the blanks.

| approach | operate | cooperate | distinguish | erupt |
| astound | abuse | convert | graze | proceed |

1 There will be an investigation of those who _____ their power.
권력을 남용한 사람들에 대한 조사가 있을 것이다.

2 The crowd _____ with cheers when the team scored in the bottom of ninth inning. 9회 말에 팀이 득점을 하자 관중들의 환호가 쏟아졌다.

3 The plan depends largely on his willingness to _____.
그 계획의 성패는 그의 협력하려는 의향에 크게 좌우된다.

4 Solar energy can be _____ for our use immediately.
태양 에너지는 우리들이 즉시 사용할 수 있도록 전환될 수 있다.

5 As the baby boomers _____ their 50s and 60s, many are demanding more products to help them retain their youth.
베이비붐 세대가 50, 60대가 되면서 많은 이들이 젊음을 유지하는 데 도움이 되는 상품들을 더 많이 요구하고 있다.

C. Choose the right answer.

1 There is something about Mary that _____ her from her peers.
Mary는 그녀의 친구들과 구별되는 무언가가 있다.

  (A) approaches   (B) grazes   (C) abuses   (D) distinguishes

2 The veterinarian had to _____ on Banji's leg.
수의사는 Banji의 다리를 수술해야만 했다.

  (A) operate   (B) convert   (C) erupt   (D) proceed

3 He _____ his elbow when he slipped and fell on the concrete floor.
그는 미끄러져 콘크리트 바닥에 넘어졌을 때 팔꿈치에 찰과상을 입었다.

  (A) abused   (B) operated   (C) grazed   (D) converted

4 All _____ will be donated to the care and well being of this wonderful animal shelter. 모든 수익은 이렇게 훌륭한 동물 수용소의 복지와 유지를 위해 기부될 것이다.

  (A) erupts   (B) astounds   (C) proceeds   (D) cooperates

B 1. abused   2. erupted   3. cooperate   4. converted   5. approach
C 1. D   2. A   3. C   4. C

341   **The patient was *awake* and conscious when the doctor left the room.** 의사가 방에서 나갔을 때 그 환자는 깨어 있었고 의식이 있었다.

conscious (형) 의식하는, 지각하는 aware
[kánʃəs] 의식이 있는 awake, alert
의식적인, 의도적인 deliberate, intentional
- consciously (부) 의식적으로

342   **The mistake was apparent to Sam who *noticed it quickly*.**
그 실수는 그것을 얼른 알아차린 Sam에게 명백했다.

apparent (형) 눈에 보이는, 분명한, 명백한 obvious, clear, evident, noticeable
[əpǽrənt] 외관상의, 겉보기의 seeming
- apparently (부) 보기에, 분명히

343   **Dr. Martin is the most *experienced* and competent doctor in this town.** Martin 박사는 이 도시에서 가장 경험 많고 유능한 의사이다.

competent (형) 유능한, 역량 있는 able, skilled, capable, experienced
[kámpitənt] 충분한, 만족할 만한 adequate, sufficient

344   **The result was so remarkable that everyone was *shocked*.**
그 결과가 아주 두드러져 모두가 충격을 받았다.

remarkable (형) 주목할 만한, 두드러진 notable, outstanding, conspicuous
[rimáːrkəbl] 놀랄 만한, 비범한 extraordinary, surprising, incredible

345   **The milk tasted sour because it went *bad*.**
우유가 상해서 신맛이 났다.

sour (형) 시큼한, 신 acid
[sauər] 시어진, 상한 spoiled, bad
언짢은, 싫은, 불쾌한 disagreeable, unpleasant
(동) 상하다, 상하게 하다 spoil, ruin, taint

346

The *beautiful* dress made Ellen even more striking.

그 아름다운 드레스가 Ellen을 더욱더 눈에 띄게 만들었다.

striking
[stráikiŋ]
형 두드러진, 주목할 만한 notable, outstanding
눈에 띄는, 인상적인 impressive, conspicuous, stunning
- strikingly 부 두드러지게

347

The report is very *detailed* and exhaustive.

그 보고서는 매우 상세하고 철저하다.

exhaustive
[igzɔ́:stiv]
형 철저한, 총망라한 thorough, complete, comprehensive

348

There was *nothing unusual* about his conventional speech.

그의 평범한 연설에서는 특별한 것이 전혀 없었다.

conventional
[kənvénʃənəl]
형 전통적인, 관습적인 traditional, customary
평범한 ordinary, plain
재래식의, 통상적인 standard, normal

349

An alternative school is for students who want *different* experiences.

대안 학교는 다른 경험을 원하는 학생들을 위한 학교이다.

alternative
[ɔ:ltə́:rnətiv]
형 대체하는, 대안의 substitute, other
전위의, 획기적인 unusual, different, unconventional
명 선택 가능한 것, 대안 choice, option

350

My grandfather's death was so abrupt and *sudden*.

할아버지의 죽음은 정말 돌연하고 갑작스러웠다.

abrupt
[əbrʌ́pt]
형 갑작스러운, 돌연한, 뜻밖의 sudden, unexpected, unanticipated
퉁명스러운, 무뚝뚝한, 거친 curt, blunt, short
- abruptly 부 갑자기; 퉁명스럽게

341 **Habits can be consciously strengthened, just as a student of the violin practices and memorizes different fingerings.**

어휘 habit 습관   practice 연습   memorize 외우다   fingering 운지법
습관은 바이올린을 배우는 사람이 다른 운지법을 연습해 암기하는 것과 똑같이 의식적으로 강화될 수 있다.

342 **The apparently homogeneous Dakota grasslands are actually a botanical garden of more than 400 types of grasses.**

어휘 homogeneous 동종의, 단일한   grassland 초원   botanical garden 식물원
겉보기에는 단일한 종류인 듯한 다코타 초원은 실제로는 400종이 넘는 풀로 이루어진 식물원이다.

343 **There are many job openings at present for competent graduates who combine business skills with an understanding of technology.**

비즈니스 능력과 과학기술 지식을 겸비한 유능한 졸업생들에게는 현재 일자리가 많다.

344 **The controversy generated by *Roots* was to be expected, but Alex Haley's work in turning his family history into a movie was a remarkable effort.**

어휘 controversy 논쟁   effort 노력
'뿌리'로 생겨난 논쟁은 예상된 것이었지만 Alex Haley가 자기 가족의 역사를 영화로 바꾼 일은 대단한 노력이었다.

345 **Generally, a material with a sour taste, such as vinegar or lemon juice, contains an acid.**

어휘 material 물질, 재료   vinegar 식초   contain 함유하다   acid 산, 산성 물질
일반적으로 식초나 레몬 주스와 같이 신맛이 나는 물질은 산을 함유하고 있다.

346 The wind chill factor, the combination of low temperature and wind speed, strikingly increases the degree of cold felt by a person who is outdoors.

(어휘) wind chill factor 풍속 냉각 지수   combination 결합   degree 정도
낮은 온도와 풍속의 결합물인 풍속 냉각 지수는 실외에 있는 사람이 느끼는 추위 정도에 따라 뚜렷이 증가한다.

347 Although the more exhaustive work needs to be done, efforts have been made to collect the songs and ballads of the American Revolution.

(어휘) collect 수집하다   revolution 혁명
더 철저한 작업이 이루어져야 하겠지만 미국 독립 혁명 당시의 노래와 민요를 수집하려는 노력이 있어 왔다.

348 Some countries are already using satellites for domestic communications in place of conventional telephone lines on land.

(어휘) domestic 국내의
일부 나라들은 이미 국내 통신망에 기존의 지상 전화선 대신 인공위성을 이용하고 있다.

349 For example, suppose that you have $25 to spend and have narrowed your alternatives to a textbook or a date.

(1994년 1차 수능 예문 47번)

(어휘) suppose 가정하다   narrow 좁히다
예를 들어 당신이 25달러를 쓸 수 있는데, 교과서나 데이트 비용으로 선택의 폭을 좁혔다고 가정해 보자.

350 A New Yorker might eye you suspiciously at first and after deciding it is safe to talk to you, might give you a rather abrupt explanation.

(어휘) eye 바라보다   suspiciously 수상하다는 듯이
뉴욕 사람은 처음에는 당신에게 수상하다는 듯이 바라볼 것이고 당신과 대화하는 것이 안전하다고 판단한 후에는 당신에게 다소 퉁명스럽게 설명해 줄 것이다.

A. Choose the right answer for the underlined word.

1 He always thought of himself as a competent writer.
그는 항상 자신을 유능한 작가로 여겼다.

(A) comprehensive　　(B) ordinary　　(C) short　　(D) skilled

2 These thoughts include not just conscious one. (1996년 수능 예문 22번)
이 생각들이 의식적인 것만 포함하는 것은 아니다.

(A) noticeable　　(B) awake　　(C) unpleasant　　(D) unanticipated

3 The researcher's sources for his findings were exhaustive.
그 연구자의 연구 결과에 대한 근거 자료는 철저했다.

(A) experienced　　(B) plain　　(C) unconventional　　(D) thorough

4 The lecture came to an abrupt end because someone yelled fire.
누군가가 불이 났다고 소리치는 바람에 그 강의는 갑자기 중단되었다.

(A) spoiled　　(B) intentional　　(C) sudden　　(D) conspicuous

5 We need to find several sources of alternative energy before all the current resources are used up. 우리는 현재의 모든 자원이 고갈되기 전에 몇 가지 대체 에너지원들을 찾아야 한다.

(A) complete　　(B) traditional　　(C) conspicuous　　(D) substitute

6 The Internet is truly a remarkable creation, because of how easily it allows people to communicate!
사람들이 정말 쉽게 의사소통을 할 수 있게 만들어 주므로 인터넷은 정말 대단한 창조물이다.

(A) extraordinary　(B) bad　　(C) seeming　　(D) capable

7 The bulk of our electricity is produced by conventional energy converters that are based on mechanical, indirect conversion of energy.
우리가 사용하는 전기의 대부분은 기계적이고 간접적인 에너지 전환을 기반으로 하는 재래식 에너지 전환기에 의해 생산된다.

(A) standard　　(B) impulsive　　(C) incredible　　(D) able

8 When these things are considered, it becomes apparent that the short story might be an especially good source of dramatic material.
이러한 것들을 고려할 때 단편 소설은 드라마 소재로 특히 좋은 자료가 될 수도 있다는 것이 명백해진다.

(A) notable　　(B) obvious　　(C) different　　(D) aware

B. Fill in the blanks.

conscious	apparent	competent	remarkable	sour
striking	exhaustive	conventional	alternative	abrupt

1 The new method is not meant to replace _____ means of testing.
새 방식이 기존 시험 수단을 대체한다는 의미는 아니다.

2 Patricia bears _____ resemblance to her mother.
Patricia는 엄마를 쏙 빼닮았다.

3 We also teach others without _____ effort.
우리 역시 의식적인 노력 없이 다른 사람들을 가르친다.

4 News of an accident struck a(n) _____ note in the victory celebration party. 그 사고 소식은 승리를 축하하는 파티에 찬물을 끼얹었다.

5 We have witnessed a(n) _____ turnaround in the company's economy.
우리는 그 회사의 경기가 뚜렷이 호전되는 것을 목격해 왔다.

C. Choose the right answer.

1 Unlike the common cold, flu tends to start _____.
일반 감기와 달리 독감은 갑자기 시작되는 경향이 있다.

(A) exhaustively　(B) striking　　(C) conscious　　(D) abruptly

2 The police did a(n) _____ search of the house checking every single corner. 경찰은 그 집을 구석구석 확인하면서 철저히 조사했다.

(A) sour　　　(B) exhaustive　(C) abrupt　　(D) alternative

3 The movie is _____, and some of the scenes are quite funny.
그 영화는 만족스러우며 일부 장면들은 무척 재미있다.

(A) competent　(B) conscious　(C) apparent　(D) striking

4 Works of science fiction fascinate readers by presenting _____ realities or glimpses of the future.
공상과학소설은 대체 현실을 제시하고 미래를 엿볼 수 있게 하여 독자들을 매료시킨다.

(A) remarkable　(B) conventional　(C) alternative　(D) sour

B 1. conventional　2. striking　3. conscious　4. sour　5. remarkable
C 1. D　2. B　3. A　4. C

351 **Voters elected Johnson as the next mayor.**
유권자들은 Johnson을 다음 시장으로 선출했다.

elect   동 선출하다 vote for
[ilékt]   선택하다, 결정하다 select, choose, decide (on)
         형 당선된, 선출된 selected, chosen
         - election 명 선거; 당선

352 **Everyone's eyes were drawn to the attractive woman.**
모든 사람들의 눈길이 그 매력적인 여성에게로 끌렸다.

draw   동 끌어당기다 pull, haul
[drɔ:]   (주의를) 끌다, 매혹하다 attract, entice
         (선으로) 그리다, 스케치하다 sketch
         (결론 · 정보를) 끌어내다, 도출하다 derive
         명 무승부 / 추첨

353 **He was able to improve his grades with a better effort.**
더 나은 노력으로 그는 성적을 향상시킬 수 있었다.

improve   동 개선하다, 향상시키다 enhance, better, reform, advance
[imprú:v]   나아지다, 개선되다 get better, pick up

354 **It was cheaper to lease a car than to buy it.**
차를 한 대 사는 것보다 임대하는 편이 더 싸다.

lease   동 임대하다 rent, let, charter
[li:s]   임차하다 rent, hire
         명 임대차 계약 rental contract[agreement]

355 **Evil can easily influence and infect innocent children.**
악은 순진한 아이들에게 쉽게 영향을 미쳐 물들게 한다.

infect   동 오염시키다, 감염시키다 contaminate, pollute
[infékt]   악에 물들게 하다, 타락시키다 corrupt, taint
         - infectious 형 전염성의, 퍼지기 쉬운
         - infection 명 감염, 전염

356 **I wanted to confront the manager, but he refused to *meet*.**
나는 매니저와 대면하고 싶었지만 그는 만나기를 거부했다.

confront   통 직면하다, 맞서다 face, meet, deal with
[kənfrʌnt]   (문제가) ~에 닥치다 face, challenge
                (증거를) ~에게 들이대다 present

357 **I'll participate and *be a part of* this worthy event.**
나는 참가해 의미 있는 행사의 일원이 될 것이다.

participate   통 참여하다, 함께하다 take part, join, share
[pɑːrtísəpèit]

358 **Although he likes to draft his own speeches, the last was *written* for him.**
그는 자신의 연설을 직접 작성하기를 좋아하지만 지난번 연설은 다른 사람이 작성해 준 것이다.

draft   통 (초안을) 작성하다 draw up, write, compose
[dræft]   징집하다 enlist
          명 초고, 초안 outline, rough copy

359 **These cases have been *set aside* to be allocated to experienced workers.** 이 일은 숙련공들에게 배당하기 위해 따로 떼어 두었다.

allocate   통 할당하다, 배분하다 set aside, assign, distribute, allot
[ǽləkèit]   배치하다 locate, designate

360 **It will accelerate the growth of crops, thus *speeding up* the harvest.** 그것은 작물의 성장을 촉진해 수확 시기를 앞당겨 줄 것이다.

accelerate   통 촉진하다, 빠르게 하다 hasten, quicken, expedite
[əksélərèit]   속도를 높이다, 가속하다 speed up

351 The president elect became busier after the election because of the worsening economic condition.

어휘 election 선거　worsen 악화되다　economic 경제의
대통령 당선자는 악화되는 경제 상황 때문에 선거 후에 더 바빠졌다.

352 Some proposed solutions to making megacities livable include the creation of new economic development zones to draw population away from large cities.

어휘 solution 해결책　megacity (인구 1천만 이상의) 거대 도시　livable 살기 좋은
거대 도시를 살기 좋은 도시로 만들기 위해 제안된 일부 해결책에는 큰 도시에서 인구를 끌어내기 위한 새 경제 개발 구역의 조성이 포함되어 있다.

353 Although originally a German innovation, kindergarten got its real start in the United States as a movement to provide an improved learning environment for children.

어휘 innovation 혁신, 새 제도　kindergarten 유치원　environment 환경
유치원은 원래 독일에서 고안된 새 제도였지만 어린이들에게 개선된 학습 환경을 제공하려는 운동으로서 미국에서 실제로 시작되었다.

354 I need to remind you that your lease is up next month because you haven't said anything about it.

어휘 remind 상기시키다
당신이 임대에 대해 아무 말도 하지 않으셨기 때문에 다음 달에 임대 기간이 끝난다는 것을 상기시켜 드려야겠습니다.

355 Infectious diseases may be spread by viruses and bacteria.

어휘 spread 퍼뜨리다, 확산시키다
전염성 질환은 바이러스와 박테리아에 의해 확산될 수 있다.

356 **Each candidate was thoughtful and careful in confronting the serious issue of racism.**

어휘 candidate 후보   thoughtful 사려 깊은   racism 인종 차별
각 후보는 인종 차별이라는 심각한 쟁점을 대할 때는 사려 깊고 신중했다.

357 **However, because Bell had decided to participate in the exhibition at the last minute, he had to set up his booth in a remote corner of the convention center.**

어휘 exhibition 박람회   remote 외딴
그러나 Bell이 마지막 순간에 박람회에 참가하기로 결정했기 때문에 그는 컨벤션 센터의 외진 구석에 부스를 설치해야 했다.

358 **It has been months since he started writing his thesis, but he is still working on his first draft.**

어휘 thesis 논문
그는 논문을 쓰기 시작한 지 여러 달이 되었지만 아직도 1차 초안을 작성하고 있다.

359 **During the Second World War, all important resources in the United States were allocated by the federal government.**

어휘 federal 연방의
2차 세계 대전 중에 미국 내의 모든 중요한 자원은 연방 정부에 의해 분배되었다.

360 **Current demographic trends, such as the fall in the birth rate, should favor accelerating economic growth in the long run.**

어휘 current 현재의   demographic 인구 통계의   trend 추세   favor ~에 유리하다
출생률 하락 같은 현재의 인구 통계 추세는 결국 가속화되는 경제 성장에 유리하게 작용할 것이다.

A. Choose the right answer for the underlined word.

1   The scientist's main goal was to <u>accelerate</u> the growth process.
    과학자들의 주요 목표는 성장 과정을 촉진하는 것이었다.

    (A) take part   (B) set aside   (C) speed up   (D) draw up

2   This is the problem that <u>confronts</u> every level of government.
    이것은 모든 수준의 정부에 닥치는 문제이다.

    (A) distributes   (B) pulls   (C) faces   (D) decides on

3   You have to clean your wound carefully, otherwise, it would be <u>infected</u>.
    상처를 주의해 닦아 내야 한다. 그렇지 않으면 감염될 것이다.

    (A) contaminated (B) quickened   (C) reformed   (D) enticed

4   The government will <u>allocate</u> more public funds to rural areas through
    reform and development. 정부는 더 많은 공적 자금을 개혁과 개발을 통해 농촌 지역에 분배할 것이다.

    (A) challenge   (B) assign   (C) expedite   (D) pollute

5   If you do not have any blank paper, <u>draft</u> the outline in any other empty
    space of the examination itself. 백지가 없으면 시험지의 빈 공간에 개요를 작성하세요.

    (A) compose   (B) sketch   (C) select   (D) corrupt

6   Immigrants were <u>drawn</u> to the United States by the growing cities and
    industries. 이민자들은 성장하는 도시와 산업 때문에 미국에 끌렸다.

    (A) advanced   (B) attracted   (C) hastened   (D) designated

7   <u>Participate</u> in your community's recycling program by recycling your
    paper, glass and plastic containers, and your aluminum cans.
    종이, 유리 및 플라스틱 용기, 알루미늄 캔을 재활용해 지역 재활용 프로그램에 참여하세요.

    (A) Charter   (B) Join   (C) Write   (D) Reform

8   The search team <u>elected</u> to suspend the rescue operation for the night.
    수색팀은 야간에 구조 활동을 일시 중단하기로 결정했다.

    (A) derived   (B) chose   (C) shared   (D) threatened

B. Fill in the blanks.

elect	draw	improve	lease	infect
confront	participate	draft	allocate	accelerate

1 He decided to _____ in a play.

그는 연극에 참가하기로 결정했다.

2 My laptop is _____ by computer viruses.

내 노트북은 컴퓨터 바이러스에 감염되어 있다.

3 They _____ him with evidence of his crime.

그들은 그의 범행 증거를 그에게 들이댔다.

4 We need to _____ more funds to the project.

우리는 그 프로젝트에 더 많은 자금을 배당해야 한다.

5 In order to _____ interest of another person, you need to be interested in what the other person is saying to you.

다른 사람의 관심을 끌기 위해서는 다른 사람이 당신에게 하는 말에 관심을 가져야 한다.

C. Choose the right answer.

1 You need to read the _____ carefully before you sign it.

서명하기 전에 임대차 계약서를 주의 깊게 읽어 봐야 한다.

(A) election　　(B) draw　　(C) draft　　(D) lease

2 Newer models of roller coasters _____ from zero to 50 MPH in only 15 seconds! 더 새로운 모델의 롤러코스터는 단 15초 만에 시속 0에서 50마일까지 속도가 붙는다!

(A) accelerate　　(B) infect　　(C) allocate　　(D) participate

3 The shop steward, the first-level officer in a labor union, is _____ by its members. 노조의 최고위 간부인 노조 대표는 조합원들에 의해 선출된다.

(A) elected　　(B) allocated　　(C) leased　　(D) confronted

4 He began waking up early every morning to go jogging, and he started to _____ his diet. 그는 매일 아침 일찍 일어나 조깅하기 시작했고 식단을 개선하기 시작했다.

(A) draw　　(B) improve　　(C) participate　　(D) accelerate

B 1. participate　2. infected　3. confronted　4. allocate　5. draw
C 1. D　2. A　3. A　4. B

361

He has adequate skills but not *enough* experiences to get a good job. 그는 충분한 기술이 있지만 좋은 직장을 얻기에는 경력이 모자란다.

adequate   ⑱ 충분한 enough, sufficient, ample
[ǽdəkwit]   적당한 moderate, tolerable

362

It is very *hard to satisfy* Mrs. Picky because she is very particular about everything.
Picky 씨는 모든 것에 아주 까다롭기 때문에 그녀를 만족시키기가 무척 어렵다.

particular   ⑱ 특별한, 특정한 specific, special, peculiar
[pərtíkjulər]   꼼꼼한, 까다로운 fussy, picky

363

It was a magnificent game between two *outstanding* teams.
그것은 탁월한 두 팀 간의 훌륭한 경기였다.

magnificent   ⑱ 장엄한, 웅장한, 당당한 grand, splendid, impressive, stately
[mægnífisənt]   훌륭한, 굉장히 멋진 excellent, superb

364

The communal *common* room is available for all students.
공동 휴게실은 모든 학생들이 사용할 수 있다.

communal   ⑱ 공동의, 공공의 public, shared, common, mutual
[kəmjúːnəl]   집단들이 관련된 collective

365

It was a mammoth challenge which took a *great* effort to overcome. 그것은 극복하기에 아주 큰 노력이 필요한 거대한 도전이었다.

mammoth   ⑲ 매머드, 거대한 것
[mǽməθ]   ⑱ 거대한 gigantic, huge, vast, enormous, immense

366

His story sounded so *real* and authentic.
그의 이야기는 아주 사실적이고 진짜처럼 들렸다.

authentic   형 믿을 만한, 확실한 reliable, trustworthy
[ɔ:θéntik]   진짜인, 진품인 real, actual, genuine
     - authentically 부 확실히

367

He is the leading scientist in this *important* research.
그는 이 중요한 연구의 대표적인 과학자이다.

leading   형 대표적인, 선두의 most important, foremost, chief, primary
[lí:diŋ]

368

**You apply for a *second* or subsequent visa three months
later.** 세 달 후에 2차 즉 후속 비자를 신청해라.

subsequent   형 그 뒤의, 차후의 following, later, succeeding
[sʌ́bsìkwənt]   다음의 next
     - subsequently 부 그 뒤에, 나중에

369

Hot summer days make people feel lazy and sluggish.
더운 여름날은 사람들을 나른하고 둔하게 만든다.

sluggish   형 게으른 lazy
[slʌ́giʃ]   느린 slow
     부진한 poor, weak

370

The coach had a stern and *serious* look after we lost the game.
우리가 경기에서 패한 후에 코치는 엄하고 심각한 표정을 지었다.

stern   형 엄격한, 가혹한 firm, strict, severe
[stə:rn]   심각한 serious, grave

361

One of California's greatest problems is providing adequate water to meet the needs of its expanding populations.

[어휘] provide 공급하다   meet 충족시키다   needs 수요   expand 팽창하다
캘리포니아 주의 최대 문제들 중의 하나는 팽창하는 인구의 수요를 충족시키기에 충분한 양의 물을 공급하는 것이다.

362

To make their predictions, they study the previous pattern of earthquake activities in a particular area.

[어휘] prediction 예측, 예언   previous 이전의   earthquake 지진
그들은 지진을 예측하기 위해 특정 지역의 예전 지진 활동 패턴을 연구한다.

363

The Empire State Building is reputed to be one of the most magnificent buildings constructed in the Twentieth Century.

[어휘] reputed 유명한   construct 건설하다
Empire State 빌딩은 20세기에 건설된 가장 웅장한 빌딩 중의 하나로 유명하다.

364

The house has only one communal room, where her family eats, sleeps, and works.

그 집에는 공동으로 사용하는 방 하나만 있어서 그곳에서 그녀의 가족은 먹고 자고 일한다.

365

The construction of mammoth shopping malls has contributed to the decline of small stores in neighboring towns.

[어휘] construction 건설   mall 쇼핑몰   contribute 기여하다   decline 몰락, 퇴조
초대형 쇼핑몰들의 건설이 이웃 도시들에 있는 작은 상점들의 몰락에 일조해 왔다.

366   The stories of Sarah Orne Jewett are considered by many to be more authentically regional than those of Bret Harte.

(어휘) regional 지역적인

Sarah Orne Jewett의 이야기는 Bret Harte의 이야기보다 확실히 더 지역적이다.

367   Despite these drawbacks, wind energy is a leading alternative to the use of fossil fuels, and the use of wind energy continues to grow rapidly.

(어휘) drawback 결점, 단점   alternative 대안   fossil fuel 화석 연료   rapidly 급속히

이런 단점들에도 불구하고 풍력은 화석 연료 사용의 가장 유력한 대안이어서 풍력 사용이 계속 급증하고 있다.

368   Vice President Lyndon Johnson became President of the United States following the death of John F. Kennedy and was subsequently elected to a full-term in 1964.

(어휘) following ~ 후에   full-term 임기를 다 채우는

부통령 Lyndon Johnson은 John F. Kennedy 대통령의 사망 후에 미국 대통령이 되었으며 1964년에 정식 대통령으로 선출되었다.

369   Housing construction, however, remained sluggish, mainly because the cost of new homes has risen much faster than average incomes.

(어휘) average 평균의   income 소득

그러나 주로 평균 소득보다 새 집 가격이 더 빨리 상승했기 때문에 주택 건설이 계속 부진했다.

370   Psychologists have found that stern disciplinary measures do not always make a child more well-behaved.

(어휘) disciplinary measures 징계 조치, 처벌   well-behaved 품행이 바른, 예의 바른

심리학자들은 가혹한 처벌이 아이를 항상 더 예의 바르게 만들지는 않는다는 것을 발견했다.

A. Choose the right answer for the underlined word.

1   The lizard called the Gila monster is ordinarily sluggish and clumsy.
    Gila monster라는 도마뱀은 대개 행동이 느리고 서투르다.

    (A) following   (B) slow   (C) mutual   (D) trustworthy

2   Insect pests are among the leading causes of crop failure.
    병충해는 흉작의 대표적인 원인 중의 하나이다.

    (A) chief   (B) immense   (C) splendid   (D) special

3   The painting looked so real that many experts believed it was authentic.
    그 그림은 너무나 진짜 같아서 많은 전문가들이 그것을 진품이라고 믿었다.

    (A) stately   (B) common   (C) tolerable   (D) genuine

4   You've never had a real amusement park experience if you haven't ridden
    on a mammoth roller coaster.
    당신이 초대형 롤러코스터를 타 보지 않았다면 진짜 놀이공원을 한 번도 경험해 본 적이 없는 것이다.

    (A) primary   (B) succeeding   (C) enormous   (D) lazy

5   It is very difficult for him to eat out because he is very particular about
    food. 그는 음식에 대해 무척 까다롭기 때문에 외식하기가 무척 어렵다.

    (A) superb   (B) serious   (C) foremost   (D) fussy

6   Cheetah capturing and subsequent breeding projects in zoos worldwide
    has been successful. 전 세계적으로 치타를 포획한 후에 동물원에서 번식시키는 프로젝트가 성공하고 있다.

    (A) weak   (B) grave   (C) later   (D) collective

7   The teacher gave his student a stern warning not to be late again.
    그 교사는 학생에게 다시 늦지 말라고 엄중히 경고했다.

    (A) real   (B) firm   (C) important   (D) next

8   And in forty-two countries, available supplies of food were not adequate
    to supply the caloric requirements of their populations.
    그리고 42개국에서는 이용할 수 있는 식량 공급량이 국민들의 필요 열량을 공급하기에 충분하지 않았다.

    (A) huge   (B) picky   (C) sufficient   (D) poor

Answers   A 1. B   2. A   3. D   4. C   5. D   6. C   7. B   8. C

B. Fill in the blanks.

adequate	particular	magnificent	communal	mammoth
authentic	leading	subsequent	sluggish	stern

1 So far, he is the _____ candidate in the election.

지금까지 그는 선거에서 가장 유력한 후보이다.

2 I found a restaurant that serves _____ South American food.

진짜 남미 음식을 제공하는 레스토랑을 발견했다.

3 The manufacturer stopped making that _____ model last month.

그 제조업체는 지난달에 그 특정한 모델을 만드는 것을 중단했다.

4 With a(n) _____ look on his face, the father said "no."

아버지는 얼굴에 엄한 표정을 지으며 "안 돼."라고 말했다.

5 A(n) _____ action has to be taken in order to completely solve the problem. 그 문제를 완전히 해결하기 위해서는 다음 조치를 취해야 한다.

C. Choose the right answer.

1 The view from Mark's house was truly _____.

Mark의 집에서 보이는 경치는 정말 장관이었다.

(A) leading   (B) mammoth   (C) magnificent   (D) authentic

2 A little better, but I still feel _____.

조금 나아졌지만 여전히 기운이 없다.

(A) stern   (B) adequate   (C) sluggish   (D) particular

3 Bees cannot live alone because they are fitted for _____ life.

벌은 공동체 생활에 적합하게 되어 있기 때문에 혼자서 살 수 없다.

(A) communal   (B) stern   (C) subsequent   (D) magnificent

4 It was a(n) _____ task to clean the house after the party.

파티가 끝난 후에 집 안을 청소하는 것은 엄청난 큰일이었다.

(A) mammoth   (B) leading   (C) authentic   (D) sluggish

B 1. leading   2. authentic   3. particular   4. stern   5. subsequent

C 1. C   2. C   3. A   4. A

371 **You can *change* or substitute any color you like.**
네가 좋아하는 어떤 색깔로든 바꾸거나 교체할 수 있다.

substitute 동 대체하다, 대리하다 replace, exchange, switch, supplant
[sʌ́bstitjùːt] 명 대리자, 대체물 replacement
　　　　　　　형 대체의, 대리의 backup, alternative

372 **He tried to *represent* and mirror the teachings of his mentor.**
그는 멘토의 가르침을 보여 주고 반영하려고 노력했다.

mirror 동 비추다, 반영하다 reflect, represent, echo
[mírər] 명 거울

373 **Mark emerged as our team leader when he *came out* and played his best game.**
Mark가 나와 최고의 경기를 펼치자 그는 우리 팀의 리더로 떠올랐다.

emerge 동 나오다, 나타나다, 떠오르다 arise, appear, come up
[imə́ːrdʒ] 분명해지다, 알려지다 become apparent, become known

374 **I can't *make* a hamburger, but I can fix a sandwich for you.**
너한테 햄버거는 만들어 줄 수 없지만 샌드위치는 해 줄 수 있어.

fix 동 고정하다, 달다 fasten, secure
[fiks] 고치다, 바로잡다 repair, mend
　　　　(음식을) 준비하다 prepare, make
　　- fixed 형 고정된, 일정한 set, unchanging

375 **David didn't utter a word at first, and then he *spoke* for one hour.** David는 처음에는 한마디도 말하지 않더니 그 후에 1시간 동안 말했다.

utter 동 말하다, 발언하다, 이야기하다 say, speak, express, articulate
[ʌ́tər] 형 전적인, 완전한 absolute, complete, total
　　- utterly 부 전적으로, 완전히

376

The *spokesperson* issued a statement.
대변인이 성명을 발표했다.

issue   동 발표하다, 공포하다 announce / 발행하다 publish
[íʃuː]   지급하다, 발급하다 give out, hand out
          나오다, 발하다 come forth, emit
          명 발행물 publication
          주제, 쟁점 topic, matter, subject / 문제 problem, concern

377

Tom tries to mimic his elder brother and *copy* what he does.
Tom은 형을 흉내 내어 그가 하는 행동을 모방하려고 노력한다.

mimic   동 흉내 내다 imitate, copy, impersonate
[mímik]

378

Allen swayed his sister's mind and *influenced* her decision.
Allen은 여동생의 마음을 움직여 그녀의 결정에 영향을 주었다.

sway   동 흔들다, 동요시키다 swing, fluctuate
[swei]   (마음을) 움직이다, ~에 영향을 주다 influence, persuade, affect

379

He *kept* the information himself, withholding it from the police. 그는 경찰에 그 정보를 알리지 않고 혼자 간직하고 있었다.

withhold   동 주지 않다, 보류하다 keep (back), retain, suppress
[wiðhóuld]   말리다, 억제하다 hold back, check, restrain

380

He *cut off* all ties and isolated himself in a remote cabin.
그는 모든 관계를 끊고 외딴 오두막에서 따로 떨어져 지냈다.

isolate   동 떼어 놓다, 고립시키다, 분리하다 separate, set apart, cut off,
[áisəleit]   segregate
          격리하다 quarantine

Words in Reading

371 People buy insurance in order to substitute a small, certain, tolerable loss for a large, uncertain, catastrophic one.

[어휘] tolerable 견딜 만한   uncertain 불확실한   catastrophic 파멸적인, 최악의
사람들은 크고 불확실하고 파국적인 손실을 작고 확실하고 견딜 만한 손실로 대체하기 위해 보험에 가입한다.

372 Anthropology holds up a great mirror to humanity and lets us look at ourselves in our infinite diversity.

[어휘] anthropology 인류학   humanity 인간(성)   infinite 무한한   diversity 다양성
인류학은 인류에 커다란 거울을 들이대어 우리로 하여금 무한한 다양성 속에서 우리 자신을 바라보게 해 준다.

373 The abstract expressionist movement emerged in New York City in the 1940s.

[어휘] abstract expressionist 추상적 표현주의   movement 운동
추상적 표현주의 운동은 1940년대 뉴욕 시에서 생겨났다.

374 The aged live with enforced leisure, on fixed income, subject to many continual illnesses. (1995년 수능 예문 26번)

[어휘] enforced 강요된, 강제적인   continual 끊임없는, 거듭되는
노인들은 강요된 여가를 보내며 고정된 소득으로 생활하며 거듭되는 여러 질병에 시달린다.

375 Many doctors and nurses were utterly convinced of the medicine's strength.

[어휘] convinced 확신하는   medicine 약   strength 효력, 효능
많은 의사와 간호사들은 그 약의 효능을 전적으로 확신했다.

376 **Thus, the most important issue facing these countries is understanding the differences among cultures.**

어휘 face ~에 닥치다   culture 문화
그러므로 이 나라들에 닥치고 있는 가장 중요한 문제는 문화들 사이의 차이를 이해하는 것이다.

377 **Researchers have discovered that dolphins are able to mimic human speech.**

어휘 discover 발견하다   speech 말, 언어
연구자들은 돌고래가 인간 언어를 흉내 낼 수 있다는 것을 발견해 왔다.

378 **Salesmanship is the ability to sway people to willingly buy products or support new ideas.**

어휘 salesmanship 판매 기술   ability 능력, 수완   willingly 기꺼이
판매 기술은 사람들의 마음을 움직여 기꺼이 상품을 사거나 새 아이디어를 지지하게 하는 능력이다.

379 **He was found guilty of withholding information about the terrorist offences from the authority.**

어휘 be found guilty 유죄 판결을 받다   terrorist offence 테러 범죄   authority 당국
그는 그 테러 범죄들에 대한 정보를 당국에 신고하지 않은 죄목으로 유죄 판결을 받았다.

380 **She was working as a civilian nurse in Cuba, where army Majors William Gorgas and Walter Reed were conducting experiments to isolate the cause of the disease.**

어휘 civilian 민간인   major 소령   conduct 실시하다   experiment 실험
그녀는 쿠바에서 민간인 간호사로 일하고 있었는데, 그곳에서 육군 소령 William Gorgas와 Walter Reed가 그 질병의 원인을 분리하기 위한 실험을 진행하고 있었다.

A. Choose the right answer for the underlined word.

1 The trees were <u>swaying</u> gently in the wind.

나무들이 바람에 부드럽게 흔들리고 있었다.

(A) representing　(B) expressing　(C) appearing　(D) swinging

2 You can <u>substitute</u> honey for sugar.

설탕을 꿀로 대체할 수 있다.

(A) imitate　(B) publish　(C) secure　(D) switch

3 The project was an <u>utter</u> disaster.

그 프로젝트는 완전히 엉망이었다.

(A) unchanging　(B) alternate　(C) remote　(D) complete

4 The politician <u>emerged</u> from the scandal with his reputation intact.

그 정치인은 자신의 명성에 타격을 입지 않고 스캔들에서 벗어났다.

(A) arose　(B) retained　(C) articulated　(D) persuaded

5 A portion of an employee's wages is <u>withheld</u> by the employer for income taxes. 직원 급여의 일부는 고용주에 의해 소득세로 공제된다.

(A) kept　(B) fluctuated　(C) reflected　(D) separated

6 There are numerous manuals available with instructions on how to <u>fix</u> a bicycle. 자전거를 고치는 법이 수록된 수많은 설명서를 구할 수 있다.

(A) repair　(B) hold　(C) affect　(D) replace

7 His political stands <u>isolated</u> him from his peers.

그의 정치적 입장이 그를 동료들로부터 고립시켰다.

(A) handed out　(B) held back　(C) cut off　(D) came forth

8 When high voltage is applied to the electrodes of a vacuum tube, a stream of electrons <u>issues</u> from the negative electrode.

진공관의 전극에 고압 전류를 흐르게 하면 음극에서 전자들이 나온다.

(A) supplant　(B) quarantines　(C) emits　(D) prepares

B. Fill in the blanks.

substitute	mirror	emerge	fix	utter
issue	mimic	sway	withhold	isolate

1 The train _____ from the dust of clouds.
   기차가 자욱한 흙먼지에서 빠져나왔다.

2 I will go right now and _____ the problem.
   내가 지금 당장 가서 그 문제를 바로잡겠다.

3 The lottery winner's name was _____ by request.
   복권 당첨자의 이름은 요청에 의해 공개되지 않았다.

4 Kids often _____ their parents.
   아이들은 자주 부모를 흉내 낸다.

5 The art and literature _____ the philosophies and ideas of the changing era. 예술과 문학은 변화하는 시대의 철학과 사상을 반영한다.

C. Choose the right answer.

1 The _____ teacher had a difficult time handling rowdy students.
   그 대체 교사는 말썽 많은 학생들을 다루느라 어려움을 겪었다.

   (A) isolated   (B) utter   (C) fixed   (D) substitute

2 During the 10th century, the Chinese government _____ heavy iron coins. 10세기에 중국 정부는 무거운 철 주화를 발행했다.

   (A) swayed   (B) emerged   (C) issued   (D) mimicked

3 It's very hard to _____ "sorry" especially to your loved ones.
   특히 당신이 사랑하는 사람들에게 "미안하다"라고 말하기가 무척 힘들다.

   (A) withholding   (B) substitute   (C) utter   (D) emerge

4 I tried to _____ his opinion in favor of the new antismoking law.
   나는 그의 의견에 영향을 주어 새 금연법에 찬성하게 만들려고 노력했다.

   (A) mimic   (B) sway   (C) mirror   (D) issue

B 1. emerged   2. fix   3. withheld   4. mimic   5. mirror
C 1. D   2. C   3. C   4. B

381   **Peter is an *essential* and indispensable member of our group.** Peter는 우리 그룹에서 없어서는 안 될 필수적인 구성원이다.

indispensable   형 필수의, 빼놓을 수 없는 essential, central, critical, vital
[ìndispénsəbl]

382   **It is very *important* to deal with the major causes of climate change.** 기후 변화의 주요 원인을 다루는 것이 매우 중요하다.

major   형 주요한, 중대한 important, significant, main, principal
[méidʒər]   매우 큰 large, sizable
               명 전공 specialty
               동 전공하다 specialize

383   **The ending was sensational and *shocking*.**
그 결말은 놀랍고 충격적이었다.

sensational   형 세상을 깜짝 놀라게 하는, 선풍적인 amazing, startling, exciting
[senséiʃənəl]   선정적인, 충격적인 shocking
               훌륭한, 멋진 excellent, superb, impressive

384   **His answer was vague because he wasn't sure what to say.**
무슨 말을 해야 할지 잘 몰라서 그의 대답은 애매모호했다.

vague   형 막연한, 애매한, 부정확한 imprecise, ambiguous
[veig]   불확실한, 불분명한 unclear, obscure
            (형체가) 희미한, 흐릿한 indistinct, blurred, faint

385   **The shy boy stayed *quiet* during the meeting.**
그 수줍은 소년은 모임이 진행되는 동안 조용히 있었다.

shy   형 부끄럼 타는, 소심한 timid, bashful, reserved
[ʃai]   조심성 있는, 의심 많은 cautious, wary, suspicious
    - shyness 명 수줍음

386   *Constant* and incessant **noise drove Mark crazy.**

지속적이고 끊임없는 소음이 Mark를 미치게 만들었다.

incessant	혱 끊임없는 endless, uninterrupted, ceaseless, constant
[insésənt]	- incessantly 閈 끊임없이

387   **It was a** painstaking **task, requiring everyone to work** *carefully*.

그것은 모든 사람이 주의해 일할 필요가 있는 힘든 과제였다.

painstaking	혱 공들이는 careful, meticulous
[péinstèikiŋ]	힘든 exacting, demanding
	- painstakingly 閈 공들여; 힘들여

388   **These two models are** equivalent **in speed, but aren't** *equal* **in price.** 이 두 모델은 속도 면에서는 동등하지만 가격 면에서는 똑같지 않다.

equivalent	혱 동등한, 대등한 equal, same, comparable, parallel
[ikwívələnt]	몡 동등한 것, 등가물

389   **He likes** contemporary **music, but doesn't like** *modern* **art.**

그는 요즘 음악은 좋아하지만 현대 미술은 좋아하지 않는다.

contemporary	혱 현대의 modern, current, present
[kəntémpərèri]	동시대의 coexisting

390   **The teacher made** drastic **changes which students thought were** *too much*. 그 교사는 학생들이 지나치다고 생각할 정도로 급격한 변화를 일으켰다.

drastic	혱 격렬한, 강렬한 violent, severe
[drǽstik]	과감한, 급격한 radical, extreme

381

In the Navajo household, grandparents and other relatives play indispensable roles in raising children.

어휘 relative 친척   role 역할   raise 키우다
Navajo 족 가정에서는 조부모와 다른 친척들이 아이를 키우는 데 긴요한 역할을 한다.

382

When Garfield interviewed top people in major industries, however, he found that they knew how to relax and could leave their work at the office.

어휘 industry 산업   relax 편히 쉬다
그러나 Garfield가 주요 산업계의 최고위층 인물들을 인터뷰했을 때 그들이 휴식을 취하는 법을 알고 있으며 일거리를 사무실에 두고 갈 수 있다는 것을 발견했다.

383

Most important in the spread of the modern movements in the United States was the sensational Armory Show of 1913 held in New York.

어휘 spread 확산   Armory Show 1913년 뉴욕에서 열린 미국 최초의 국제 현대 미술전
미국에서 현대적인 흐름의 확산에 가장 중요했던 것은 뉴욕에서 열려 선풍적인 인기를 끈 1913년의 Armory Show였다.

384

These criteria, however, was so vague that candidates had little choice but to detect the literary preferences of the examiner. (1997년 수능 예문 47번)

어휘 criterion 기준, 척도   detect 탐지하다   preference 기호, 취향   examiner 시험관
그러나 이런 기준들은 무척 애매해서 응시자들이 시험관의 문학 취향을 탐지하는 것 이외에는 별다른 도리가 없었다.

385

Shyness then retreats, because, instead of worrying about how you will live your life, you forget yourself as you become absorbed in the living of it.

어휘 retreat 물러가다   worry 걱정하다   absorbed 몰두한
그러면 수줍음은 물러가는데, 왜냐하면 당신이 삶을 어떻게 살 것인지에 대해 걱정하는 대신에 그 삶을 사는 데 몰두하며 자신을 잊게 되기 때문입니다.

386 **It has been suggested that people who watch television incessantly may become overly passive.**

(어휘) overly 지나치게   passive 수동적인
TV를 끊임없이 보는 사람들은 지나치게 수동적이 될 수 있다는 설이 제기되어 왔다.

387 **In order to validate their findings, paleontologists painstakingly examine all of the fossils they dig up.**

(어휘) validate 입증하다   paleontologist 고생물학자   fossil 화석   dig up 파내다
자신의 발견물의 유효성을 입증하기 위해 고생물학자들은 자신들이 발굴하는 모든 화석을 공들여 조사한다.

388 **The conclusions of that initial test showed you drank the equivalent of three bottles of wine, and therefore were well over the legal limit for driving while intoxicated.**

(어휘) conclusion 결론   initial 최초의   legal limit 법정 한도   intoxicated 술 취한
그 1차 테스트의 결과는 당신이 와인 3병에 상당하는 양의 술을 마셨고 따라서 음주 운전의 법정 한도를 훨씬 초과한 것으로 나타났습니다.

389 **Contemporary hearing aids can be so tiny that they fit within the frame of a pair of eyeglasses.**

(어휘) hearing aids 보청기   tiny 아주 작은   frame 틀, 테
요즘 보청기는 아주 작아서 안경테 안에 들어갈 수도 있다.

390 **He requested cities and provinces take drastic measures to prevent the pandemic.**

(어휘) request 요청하다   province 도(道)   measure 조치   pandemic 대유행병
그는 대유행병을 예방하기 위한 과감한 조치를 취할 것을 각 시도에 요청했다.

A. Choose the right answer for the underlined word.

1   Scientists performed a <u>painstaking</u> experiment.
과학자들은 힘든 실험을 진행했다.

   (A) coexisting   (B) demanding   (C) vital   (D) sizeable

2   The mother finally got tired of her son's <u>incessant</u> complaining.
어머니는 마침내 아들의 끊임없는 불평에 신물이 났다.

   (A) dramatic   (B) critical   (C) constant   (D) cautious

3   In terms of precipitation, ten inches of snow is <u>equivalent</u> to an inch of
rain. 강수량 면에서 10인치의 눈은 1인치의 비와 동일하다.

   (A) comparable   (B) unclear   (C) significant   (D) extreme

4   Bats are extremely <u>shy</u> creatures and avoid humans if at all possible.
박쥐는 극히 조심성이 많은 동물이어서 가능하면 사람들을 피한다.

   (A) uninterrupted (B) wary   (C) radical   (D) blurred

5   Global warming would have <u>drastic</u> changes for the planet.
세계적인 온난화는 지구에 극심한 변화를 가져올 것이다.

   (A) severe   (B) meticulous   (C) ceaseless   (D) reserved

6   The Constitution's <u>vague</u> nature has given it the flexibility to be adapted
when circumstances change. 헌법의 모호한 특성은 상황이 변할 때 변용될 수 있는 융통성을 부여해 왔다.

   (A) present   (B) imprecise   (C) central   (D) main

7   Mathematicians find computers <u>indispensable</u> for solving difficult
equations that would otherwise take days to calculate.
수학자들은 다른 방법으로는 계산하는 데 며칠이 걸릴 어려운 방정식을 푸는 데 컴퓨터가 필수라고 생각한다.

   (A) essential   (B) exciting   (C) startling   (D) endless

8   An earthquake that is less than 2 on the Richter Scale can hardly be felt
by anyone, but anything that is measured around 6 is considered a <u>major</u>
earthquake. 진도 2 이하의 지진은 누구든 거의 느낄 수 없지만 6 정도로 측정되는 것은 대규모 지진으로 여겨진다.

   (A) quite   (B) current   (C) large   (D) timid

B. Fill in the blanks.

indispensable	major	sensational	vague	shy
incessant	painstaking	equivalent	contemporary	drastic

1 Goethe was _____ with Beethoven.
Goethe는 Beethoven과 동시대 사람이었다.

2 The project required a(n) _____ labor.
그 프로젝트는 고된 노동을 필요로 했다.

3 You shouldn't give _____ answers during a job interview.
구직 면접에서는 불분명한 답변을 해서는 안 된다.

4 I couldn't stand the _____ noise from outside.
밖에서 나는 끊임없는 소음을 견딜 수가 없었다.

5 Car manufacturing is considered to be the _____ industry in the
United States. 자동차 제조업은 미국에서 주요 산업으로 여겨진다.

C. Choose the right answer.

1 Money is _____ to our daily lives.
돈은 우리의 일상생활에 반드시 필요하다.
(A) indispensable (B) shy   (C) painstaking   (D) incessant

2 Mary was praised for doing a(n) _____ job on her report.
Mary는 보고서를 훌륭히 작성했기 때문에 칭찬을 받았다.
(A) equivalent   (B) contemporary (C) sensational   (D) vague

3 Jessica was quiet and _____ when Mr. Lander first met her.
Jessica는 Lander 씨가 그녀를 처음 만났을 때 조용하고 수줍어했다.
(A) major   (B) sensational   (C) shy   (D) drastic

4 Losing a job or a court case is _____ to losing a painful battle.
실직하거나 소송에서 지는 것은 고통스러운 전투에서 지는 것과 같다.
(A) contemporary (B) indispensable (C) major   (D) equivalent

B 1. contemporary   2. painstaking   3. vague   4. incessant   5. major
C 1. A   2. C   3. C   4. D

391

The process is too complicated, so I prefer a simpler *way*.
그 과정이 너무 복잡해서 나는 더 간단한 방법을 선호한다.

process
[práses]

(명) 처리 방법, 공정 way, method, means
과정, 절차, 진행 procedure, course, operation
(동) 처리하다 deal with, handle, manage

392

There are too many restrictions and *limitations*.
너무 많은 제약과 제한이 있다.

restriction
[ristríkʃən]

(명) 제한, 규제, 제약 regulation, restraint, constraint, limitation

393

The restaurant offers a *wide* variety of food choices.
그 레스토랑에서는 매우 다양한 메뉴를 제공한다.

variety
[vəráiəti]

(명) 다양성 diversity, multiplicity
여러 가지, 가지각색 assortment, mix, collection, array

394

**The outcome of the game wasn't decided until the very
end.** 그 경기의 결과는 최후까지 판가름 나지 않았다.

outcome
[áutkʌm]

(명) 결과, 결론 result, ending, conclusion, consequence

395

**Tom is my favorite colleague. I really enjoy *working with
him*.** Tom은 내가 가장 좋아하는 동료이다. 그와 함께 일하는 것은 정말 즐겁다.

colleague
[káliːg]

(명) 동료 coworker, associate, collaborator

396

There is a big change in people's *view* and perception about crime. 범죄에 대한 사람들의 시각과 인식에 큰 변화가 있다.

perception   명 지각, 인식 awareness, sense, notion
[pərsépʃən]   이해, 직관 understanding, insight, observation

397

Listen to the counsel of your parents, they'll always give you good *advices*. 부모님의 조언을 들어라. 그분들은 항상 좋은 충고를 해 줄 것이다.

counsel   명 권고, 조언, 충고 advice, suggestion, guidance
[káunsəl]   변호사, 법률 고문 legal advisor, lawyer
     동 ~에게 조언하다, 권고하다 advise, recommend, suggest

398

Mr. Ponder's *amazing* weight lost has done marvels for him. Ponder 씨의 놀라운 체중 감량은 그에게 놀라운 결과를 가져왔다.

marvel   명 놀라움, 경이, 경이적인 결과 astonishment, sensation, spectacle
[má:rvəl]   동 놀라다, 감탄하다 wonder, be amazed

399

The scandal caused outrage in Korea, *angering* many people. 그 스캔들은 한국에서 격노를 일으켜 많은 사람들을 화나게 만들었다.

outrage   명 격분, 격노 anger, fury, rage
[áutreidʒ]   동 격분하게 하다 upset, infuriate

400

Fishing is one of the most popular *leisure* pursuits. 낚시는 가장 인기 있는 여가 활동 중의 하나이다.

pursuit   명 추구, 탐구 quest, seeking
[pərsú:t]   추적, 추격 pursuing, hunt, chase
     취미 hobby, pastime, leisure activity

391 Using samples from the 217 miles below the earth's surface, these geologists are studying the natural processes which have affected the canyon over its 4-billion-year history.

(어휘) surface 표면　geologist 지질학자　affect 영향을 미치다　canyon 협곡
이 지질학자들은 지표면에서 217마일 아래 지점의 표본을 이용해 40억 년 역사에 걸쳐 그 협곡에 영향을 미쳐 온 자연의 진행 과정을 연구하고 있다.

392 China is under pressure from the United States and other countries to reduce its trade surplus, increase its interest rates, or release restrictions on its currency.

(어휘) pressure 압력　trade surplus 무역 수지 흑자　currency 통화
중국은 미국과 다른 나라들로부터 무역 수지 흑자를 줄이고 금리를 인상하거나 통화 규제를 풀라는 압력을 받고 있다.

393 Granville T. Woods appears to have surpassed nearly every other Black inventor of his time in the quantity and variety of his inventions.

(어휘) surpass ~보다 낫다, 초월하다
Granville T. Woods는 발명품의 양과 다양성에서 동시대의 거의 모든 다른 흑인 발명가를 능가했던 것처럼 보인다.

394 A superstition is the belief that the outcome of an event can be influenced by an unrelated object, behavior, or circumstance.

(어휘) superstition 미신　belief 믿음　influence ~에 영향을 주다　circumstance 환경
미신은 한 사건의 결과가 관련 없는 물체나 행동 또는 환경에 의해 영향을 받을 수 있다는 믿음이다.

395 I was having trouble thinking up new ideas for my client's marketing plan, so I brought some colleagues together for a quick brainstorming session.

(어휘) brainstorming session 브레인스토밍 회의 (창의적 아이디어를 생각해 내는 회의)
나는 고객의 마케팅 계획에 대한 새 아이디어를 생각해 내기가 힘들어 번쩍 아이디어 회의를 하려고 동료 몇 명을 불러 모았다.

396 The scientists argued that babies at that age could not possibly have learned societal standards of beauty, and thus, perceptions of beauty must be innate.

어휘 argue 주장하다　societal 사회의　standard 기준　innate 타고난, 선천적인
과학자들은 그 나이의 아기들이 미에 대한 사회의 기준을 배웠을 리 없으므로 미에 대한 인식은 선천적이라고 주장했다.

397 Many large companies have begun to organize wellness programs that counsel employees and offer them physical fitness classes.

어휘 wellness 건강　physical fitness 신체 건강, 체력
여러 대기업들이 직원들에게 조언해 주고 체력 단련 수업을 제공해 주는 건강 프로그램을 마련하기 시작했다.

398 He marvels at the jobs that nature did in inventing so many and such different plants.

어휘 nature 자연　plant 식물
그는 자연이 그렇게 많고 그토록 다양한 식물들을 만들어 낸 일들에 경탄한다.

399 I was surprised and outraged to see that she had gone ahead with her plans without consulting us first.

어휘 go ahead with 추진하다　plan 계획　consult ~에게 상의하다
나는 그녀가 먼저 우리와 상의하지 않고 그녀의 계획을 추진한 것에 놀랐고 격분했다.

400 Americans are supposed to have certain inalienable rights, including "Life, Liberty and the Pursuit of Happiness."

어휘 inalienable 양도할 수 없는, 빼앗을 수 없는　right 권리　liberty 자유
미국인들은 '생명, 자유, 행복 추구'의 권리를 포함하는 특정한 양도할 수 없는 권리들을 가져야 한다.

A. Choose the right answer for the underlined word.

1 Later, however, <u>restrictions</u> were lifted. [2002년 수능 예문 18번]
그러나 나중에 규제가 철폐되었다.

(A) constraints   (B) rages   (C) conclusions   (D) observations

2 Perhaps money should not be an all-consuming <u>pursuit</u> in one's life.
삶에서 돈이 온통 마음을 사로잡는 추구 대상이 되어서는 안 될 것이다.

(A) quest   (B) ending   (C) coworker   (D) hobby

3 He believed drinking heavily was the only way to express his <u>outrage</u>.
그는 술을 많이 마시는 것이 분노를 표출하는 유일한 방법이라고 믿었다.

(A) assortment   (B) fury   (C) limitation   (D) astonishment

4 It took a long time to devise a <u>process</u> for homogenizing milk.
우유를 균질화하는 공정을 고안하는 데 긴 시간이 걸렸다.

(A) pastime   (B) method   (C) result   (D) suggestion

5 The repetition of punishment by the parents does not lead to a positive <u>outcome</u>. 부모에 의한 처벌의 반복은 긍정적인 결과를 내지 않는다.

(A) operation   (B) consequence   (C) regulation   (D) anger

6 When the Erie Canal was built in the 1820s, it was the engineering <u>marvel</u> of its time. 1820년대 Erie 운하가 건설되었을 때 그것은 당시 공학 기술의 경이였다.

(A) multiplicity   (B) pursuing   (C) spectacle   (D) way

7 For instance, a mother's good <u>counsel</u> cannot work on her son and fathers often side with their sons. [1997년 수능 예문 46번]
예를 들자면 엄마의 훌륭한 조언은 아들에게 효과를 발휘하지 못하고 아버지는 자주 아들을 두둔한다.

(A) restraint   (B) collaborator   (C) advice   (D) opinion

8 People who make friends with many different types of people seem to have a greater <u>variety</u> of friends during their adult life.
여러 다른 유형의 사람들과 사귀는 사람들은 성인기에 더 다양한 친구가 있는 듯하다.

(A) diversity   (B) guidance   (C) activity   (D) chase

Answers   A 1. A   2. A   3. B   4. B   5. B   6. C   7. C   8. A

B. Fill in the blanks.

process	restriction	variety	outcome	colleague
perception	counsel	marvel	outrage	pursuit

1 The mayor's scandal caused public _____.
시장의 스캔들은 대중의 분노를 일으켰다.

2 The police are in _____ of the suspect.
경찰이 용의자를 추적하고 있다.

3 The agreement led to the loosening of travel _____ to the country.
그 협정은 그 나라에 대한 여행 규제 완화로 이어졌다.

4 It is interesting that our _____ change according to what we do for
a living. 우리의 인식이 우리의 직업이 무엇인가에 따라 변하는 것이 흥미롭다.

5 The restaurant served food which was hardly edible, and with little
_____ on the menu. 그 레스토랑은 거의 먹을 수 없는 음식을 제공했고 메뉴가 다양하지 않았다.

C. Choose the right answer.

1 We _____ at the sight of the great big waterfall.
우리는 그 어마어마하게 큰 폭포를 보고 감탄했다.

(A) outraged (B) marveled (C) counseled (D) restricted

2 At that time, I had many close _____ and friends.
그 당시에 나는 절친한 동료와 친구가 많았다.

(A) colleagues (B) processes (C) pursuits (D) perceptions

3 The army _____ all personnel entering or leaving the service.
군대는 입대하거나 제대하는 모든 병력을 처리한다.

(A) marvels (B) restricts (C) outrages (D) processes

4 She was the best general _____ this company has ever had.
그녀는 이 회사에 근무했던 역대 최고의 법무 팀장이었다.

(A) perception (B) variety (C) outcome (D) counsel

B 1. outrage 2. pursuit 3. restrictions 4. perceptions 5. variety
C 1. B 2. A 3. D 4. D

333